ALEX PERRY
THE GOOD MOTHERS

THE TRUE STORY OF THE WOMEN WHO TOOK ON THE WORLD'S MOST POWERFUL MAFIA

WILLIAM
COLLINS

William Collins
An imprint of HarperCollins*Publishers*
1 London Bridge Street
London SE1 9GF

WilliamCollinsBooks.com

First published in Great Britain in 2018 by William Collins

1

A catalogue record for this book is
available from the British Library

ISBN 978-0-00-822210-9 (hardback)
ISBN 978-0-00-822211-6 (trade paperback)

Maps by Martin Brown

Printed and bound in Great Britain by
CPI Group (UK) Ltd, Croydon, CR0 4YY

MIX
Paper from
responsible sources
FSC
www.fsc.org   FSC™ C007454

THE GOOD MOTHERS

For the good daughters

and for Tess, always

Contents

Maps   ix
Author's Note   xi

ACT ONE: A VANISHING IN MILAN

I	3
II	15
III	24
IV	37
V	43
VI	59
VII	74
VIII	87

ACT TWO: REBELLION IN ROSARNO

IX	105
X	119
XI	128

XII	135
XIII	142
XIV	144
XV	155
XVI	165
XVII	178

ACT THREE: ITALY AWAKES

XVIII	195
XIX	200
XX	204
XXI	212
XXII	222
XXIII	233
XXIV	244
XXV	259
XXVI	267
Acknowledgements	279
Notes	285
Illustration Credits	299
Index	301

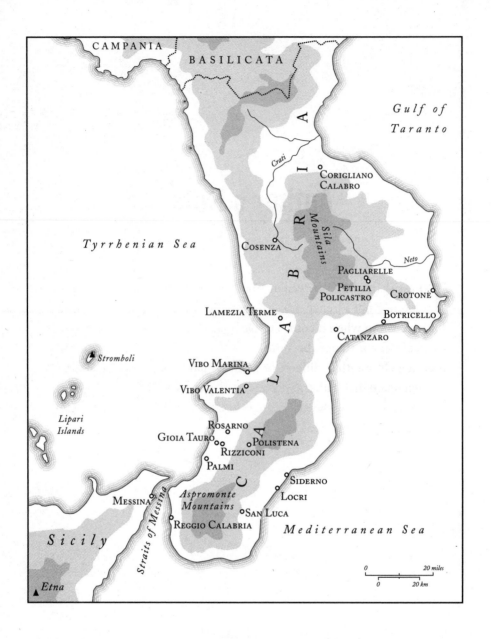

CAMPANIA

BASILICATA

*Gulf of
Taranto*

Crati

CORIGLIANO
CALABRO

B
R
I
A

Tyrrhenian Sea

*Sila
Mountains*

COSENZA

Neto

PAGLIARELLE

A
L
A

PETILIA
POLICASTRO

CROTONE

LAMEZIA TERME

BOTRICELLO

CATANZARO

Stromboli

VIBO MARINA

VIBO VALENTIA

C
A
L

*Lipari
Islands*

ROSARNO

GIOIA TAURO

POLISTENA

RIZZICONI

PALMI

C

SIDERNO

*Aspromonte
Mountains*

LOCRI

MESSINA

Straits of Messina

SAN LUCA

REGGIO CALABRIA

Mediterranean Sea

Sicily

▲ *Etna*

| 0 | | 20 miles |
| 0 | | 20 km |

Author's Note

To assist the English reader, I have used anglicised place names: Florence not Firenze, for example. By contrast, I have observed Italian custom when it comes to individuals' names. Maria Concetta Cacciola, for instance, becomes Concetta, or 'Cetta, at the second mention. In another difference from Anglo-Saxon custom, Italian women retain their father's surname after marriage. Thus Lea Garofalo kept her name after she married Carlo Cosco but the couple's daughter was called Denise Cosco.

ACT ONE

A VANISHING IN MILAN

I

The symbol of Milan is a giant serpent devouring a screaming child.[1] The first city of northern Italy has had other totems: a woolly boar, a golden Madonna and, more recently, the designer labels that make Milan the fashion capital of the world. But the eight-hundred-year-old image of a curled snake sinking its fangs into the writhing, blood-soaked body of an infant has remained its most popular emblem, adorning flags and bas reliefs on the city walls, the Alfa Romeo badge and the Inter Milan jersey. It's an oddly menacing standard for a people more normally associated with family and food, and a strangely crude one for a city whose artistry reaches the sublime heights of da Vinci's *The Last Supper* – and most Milanese generally profess ignorance of its meaning. In more candid moments, however, some will confess they suspect that the image owes its endurance to the way it illuminates a dark truth at the heart of their city: that the dynamism and accomplishment for which Milan is famous depends, among other things, on who you are prepared to destroy.

In the four days they spent in Milan in late November 2009 before her father killed her mother, then erased any trace of her from the world, Denise Cosco could almost believe her family had transcended its own special darkness. Denise was seventeen. Her mother was Lea Garofalo, a thirty-five-year-old *mafioso*'s daughter, and her father was Carlo Cosco, a thirty-nine-year-old cocaine smuggler. Lea had married Carlo at sixteen, had Denise at seventeen, witnessed Carlo and his brother kill a man in Milan at twenty-one and helped send Carlo to the city's San Vittore prison at twenty-two. Denise had grown up on the run. For six years, from 1996 to 2002, Lea had hidden herself and her daughter away in the narrow, winding alleys of the medieval town of Bergamo in the foothills of the Alps. Lea had made it a game – two southern girls hiding out in Italy's grey north – and in time the two had become each other's worlds. When they walked Bergamo's cobbled streets, an elfin pair holding hands and curling their dark hair behind their ears, people took them for sisters.

One night in 2000, Lea glanced out of their apartment to see her old Fiat on fire. In 2002, after a scooter was stolen and their front door set alight, Lea told Denise she had a new game for them – and walked hand-in-hand with her ten-year-old daughter into a *carabinieri* station where she announced to the startled desk officer that she would testify against the mafia in return for witness protection. From 2002 to 2008, mother and daughter had lived in government safe houses. For the past eight months, for reasons Denise understood only in part, they'd been on their own once more. Three times Carlo's men had caught up with them. Three times Lea and Denise had escaped. But by spring 2009, Lea was exhausted, out of money and telling Denise they were down to two last options. Either they somehow found the cash to flee to Australia, or Lea had to make peace with Carlo.

If neither was likely, reconciliation with Carlo at least seemed possible. The state had dropped its efforts to prosecute him using Lea's evidence, and while that infuriated her, it also meant she was no longer a threat to him. In April 2009, she sent her husband a message saying they should forgive and forget, and Carlo appeared to agree. The threats stopped and there were no more burned-out cars. Carlo began taking Denise on trips around the old country in Calabria. One

September night he even talked Lea into a date and they drove down to the coast, talking into the early hours about the summer they'd met, all those years before.

So when in November 2009 Carlo invited his wife and daughter to spend a few days with him in Milan, and Denise, her hand over the phone, looked expectantly at her mother, Lea shrugged and said OK, they'd make a short break of it. Lea's memories of Milan in winter were of a cold, dismal city, the trees like black lightning against the sky, the winds tumbling like avalanches through the streets, driving small monsoons of icy rain before them. But Denise would love Milan's shops, Lea and Carlo needed to talk about Denise's future and ever since the summer Lea had found herself wondering about Carlo again. Twenty years earlier, he had held her face in his gorilla hands and promised to take her away from the mafia and all the killing – and Lea had believed him chiefly because he seemed to believe himself. Lea still wore a gold bracelet and necklace Carlo had given her back then. There was also no doubt that Carlo loved Denise. Maybe Denise was right, thought Lea. Perhaps the three of them *could* start over. The idea that Carlo's new geniality was part of some elaborate plot to catch her off-guard was just too far-fetched. There were easier ways to kill someone.

Lea Garofalo had outclassed Carlo Cosco from the start. Carlo had earned his position with the clans but Lea was born a mafia princess, a Garofalo from Pagliarelle, daughter of east coast 'Ndrangheta aristocrats. Carlo was as broad and handsome as a bear but Lea was altogether finer, her natural elegance accentuated by high cheekbones, a slim frame and her long, thick curly dark hair. Carlo's stuttering grasp of Italian and his sullen, taciturn manner was never more noticeable than when he was with Lea, who spoke with the sophistication of a northerner and the passion of a southerner, laughing, arguing and crying all in the same five minutes. In any other world, it would have been the natural order of things for Lea to have walked out on Carlo a few years into their marriage and never looked back.

At least Carlo was making an effort not to gloat, thought Lea. He had a friend drop round 100 euros for the train tickets to Milan. When Lea and Denise pulled into the city's central station, Mussolini's opulent glass-and-marble monument to northern order and power, Carlo himself picked them up in a black Audi and took them to the Hotel Losanna, a cosy backstreet place a block from the Corso Sempione, Milan's Champs-Elysées, and a short walk from their old family apartment on Viale Montello. And for the next four days, Carlo refused even to discuss the past. He didn't mention the 'Ndrangheta or how Lea had broken *omertà* or the way she almost destroyed everything for which he and his brothers had worked. Instead, Denise said the three of them enjoyed a 'quiet and pleasant' mini-vacation, the kind of family holiday they'd never had. Milan's Ferrari show-rooms and Armani stores were a million miles from the goat pastures of Calabria, and Carlo seemed happy for his wife and daughter to enjoy it. With his coat tugged around his shoulders in the Milanese style, and Lea and Denise in jeans and thick down jackets, the three of them wandered the canals and the polished stone piazzas, eating pizza and *cannoli* and window-shopping in the nineteenth-century *galleria* across from Milan's flamboyant Gothic Duomo. Carlo paid for everything: clothes for Denise, dinners for the three of them, coffees and *gelatos*. Carlo even fixed it for the two women to get their eyebrows done at a beauty salon owned by his friend Massimo. Another time, when Lea was out of hash, Carlo summoned a cousin, Carmine Venturino, and made sure she didn't pay.

It wasn't perfect, of course. Denise was busy nurturing a teenage addiction to cigarettes and an aversion to heavy Italian food. Carlo, seeing his wife and daughter for only the second time in thirteen years and noticing how alike they were, couldn't help be transported back to the day, nineteen years earlier, when sixteen-year-old Lea had eloped with him to Milan. Meanwhile Lea was struggling to hold her nerve. She'd asked Carlo not to tell anyone she was in Milan but already he'd gone ahead and introduced her to Massimo and

Carmine, and Carmine, for one, seemed more than just a friend to Carlo. She also had the recurrent feeling that they were being followed.

Lea found herself turning to an old habit. Denise's mother had long needed a joint or two just to get to sleep at night and, as the butts Denise found in their room attested, she was now also smoking steadily through the day. Sleep and peace were good, of course, and a real rarity for Lea. But you had to wonder at the wisdom of getting stoned around Carlo, a *mafioso* who had spent the last thirteen years chasing her across Italy trying to kill her.

Still, the trip went better than Lea might have feared. Initially, she had asked Denise to stay with her when Carlo was around because, said Denise, 'if I was there, nothing was going to happen to her.' Soon, however, Lea felt safe enough to be left alone with her husband. On the night of 23 November, Denise went to bed early and Lea and Carlo ate out alone. If the years had tightened Lea's nerves, time seemed to have relaxed Carlo. He was now a barrel of a man, with thick ears, a close-shaven head and a boxer's nose, but his manner was gentle and attentive. When Lea mentioned Denise's plan to go to Milan University, Carlo offered to keep an eye on her. When Carlo volunteered that he'd set aside €200,000 for his daughter and Lea scolded him for the tens of thousands he'd spent trying to track them down – 'and for no reason, because you always arrived too late!' – Carlo, unusually, took the slight well. After he paid the bill, Carlo took Lea on a drive through the city, the pair of them gliding through the empty streets in silence, just taking in the sights and each other's company. So distracted was Carlo that he ran a red light, delighting Lea, who was treated to the sight of the big *mafioso* trying to wriggle out of a ticket.

Watching them together in those days – Lea smoking and laughing, Carlo rubbing his bruiser's neck and letting a smile soften his frown – Denise said you could see they had been in love once. You might even believe it would work out for the three of them. 'We actually ate together, all three of us, as a family,' Denise said later. Carlo 'was showing us how caring and kind he was'. And there was no denying Lea still had it. Even without a cent in her pocket, and despite everything that had happened, her mother was still a rare and beautiful thing, a Calabrian forest sprite with the same pure spirit that had marked her out from every other girl in Pagliarelle all those years ago. Carlo, Denise felt sure, had to be falling for Lea again. 'I had absolutely no bad thoughts about my father,' she said.

Lea and Denise's last day in Milan was 24 November 2009. The two women were planning to take the 11.30 p.m. sleeper back to Calabria. In their room at the Losanna, Lea and Denise packed. To help take the bags to the station, Carlo brought round a big grey Chrysler he had borrowed from a friend.

As he loaded their cases, Carlo asked Denise whether she'd like to eat that evening with her cousins: Uncle Giuseppe, Aunt Renata and their two boys, eighteen-year-old Domenico and Andrea, fifteen. Denise should grab the chance to spend time with her family, said Carlo. A night alone would also give her parents the chance to discuss a few last things.

Denise agreed. She and Lea then walked into town to do some final shopping. It was an overcast day, only just above freezing, and a dull chill echoed off the granite buildings. CCTV later showed Lea in a black jacket with its furry collar turned in and Denise in a thick white jacket with her hood up and a black backpack over the top. Mother and daughter wandered around the arcades, warming themselves in cafés and grabbing lunch at a McDonald's, just happy to be out together in the city and, for once, not looking over their shoulders.

An hour after dark, just before 6 p.m., Denise called Carlo. She and Lea were near the Arch of Peace in Sempione Park, not far from the hotel, she said. A few minutes later, Carlo arrived in the Chrysler, flicked on his hazard lights and reminded Denise through the driver's window that she was expected for dinner with her cousins. Lea didn't want to go: even if she was getting on better with Carlo, she wanted nothing to do with his family. Carlo suggested he drop off Denise, then return to take Lea out for a quiet dinner. After everyone had eaten, Carlo and Lea would pick Denise up again and all three of them would head over to the station. The women agreed. 'See you at the station, *mama*,' said Denise to Lea as she jumped into the car. 'Later,' replied Lea. 'I'm going to have a drink.'

Carlo drove Denise to No. 6 Viale Montello on the edge of Milan's Chinatown. A large, grubby six-storey walk-up of more than a hundred apartments arranged around a drab internal courtyard, No. 6 Viale Montello had once belonged to the Maggiore Ospedale, one of Europe's first public hospitals when it opened in 1456. But the place had fallen into disrepair and was later abandoned, and in the 1980s the 'Ndrangheta from Pagliarelle had taken it over as a live-in hub for their heroin and cocaine business. The ground floor was now filled with half a dozen cheap Chinese stores – groceries, laundries, *tabacs* – whose metal shutters were decorated with extravagant graffiti. Most of the apartments were home to immigrants from China, Romania, Albania, Poland, Eritrea and Nigeria, tenants whose own uncertain legal status ensured they were no friends of the law. The rest was given over to around a dozen mafia families. Carlo, Lea and Denise had lived in one apartment in the early 1990s. Carlo's elder brothers Vito and Giuseppe were still installed in others with their wives and children. It was to these rooms that tons of cocaine and heroin were transported every year before being repackaged and shipped north into Europe.

Carlo left Denise with her Aunt Renata at 6.30 p.m. at Bar Barbara, a Chinese-run café on Piazza Baiamonti at the end of Viale Montello, then drove off to fetch Lea. Denise ordered an espresso. Renata said dinner was minestrone and cold cuts. Denise told her aunt she wasn't all that hungry, so she and Renata went to an Asian supermarket a few doors down to buy her a small tray of sushi. Denise tried to pay but Renata wouldn't hear of it.

Looking back, Denise would say it was around then that the make-believe stopped. Back at her cousin's second-floor apartment in Viale Montello, Denise ate her sushi alone. Then she sat with Renata, Domenico and Andrea as they had their soup and meat in front of the TV. Far from the family get-together Carlo had described, her cousins were in and out all evening. Her Uncle Giuseppe wasn't even home, which was doubly strange as there was a big game that night, AC Milan away to Barcelona. There was something else, too. When Denise had spent time with Renata before, she remembered thinking that her aunt was a jealous wife, always calling Giuseppe to ask where he was, who he was with, what he was doing and when he was coming home. That night, Denise noticed, Renata didn't call Giuseppe once.

Denise, who after years on the run had developed a sixth sense for these things, began to feel something was off. Around 8 p.m. she called her mother. Lea's phone was unobtainable. That was odd too. Lea always made sure her phone was charged. Denise sent her mother a text. 'Something like "Where the hell are you?"' Denise said later in court.

The big game started at 8.40 p.m. Barcelona scored quickly. Denise texted Lea a couple more times. Still no answer. Renata told Denise not to worry about smoking in front of the family – no one would tell Carlo – and as the evening wore on, Denise found she was chain-smoking. Her cousins groaned as Barcelona scored a second goal just before half-time. Sometime after 9 p.m., just when Denise was beginning to feel truly unnerved, Giuseppe stuck his head around the door, registered the score and Denise's presence, then left again. A few minutes after that, Denise's phone rang. It was Carlo. He would be over in a few minutes to pick Denise up to take her to the station. She should wait for him downstairs at her Uncle Vito's first-floor apartment.

Denise kissed her cousins and her aunt goodbye, then took the stairs to Vito's. Carlo hadn't arrived so Vito's wife, Giuseppina, made coffee. It was after 9.30 p.m. now – more than three hours since Denise had last heard from her mother – and she was fighting a rising sense of panic. After a while, Vito appeared at the door. Behind him, down the corridor, Denise caught a glimpse of her father at the entrance to another apartment. She hadn't even known Carlo was in the building. Instead of fetching her, he was talking to his brother Giuseppe and two other men. Carlo glanced at his daughter, and called over that she should wait for him in the car. Denise went down to the street and found the Chrysler. Lea wasn't in it. By now, it was 10 p.m. When Carlo got in, Denise asked him immediately: 'Where's my mother?'

'I left her around the corner,' replied Carlo. 'She didn't want to come in and see everyone.'

Carlo drove in silence to a street behind Viale Montello. Denise regarded him. He looked upset, she thought. The way he was driving, barely focusing on the road. *'Scossato,'* she said later. Shaken.

When they turned the corner, Lea wasn't there. Denise was about to speak when Carlo cut her off. Lea wasn't waiting for them, said Carlo, because what had happened was that Lea had asked him for money and he had given her 200 euros but she had screamed at him that it wasn't enough, so he had given her another 200 but she'd stormed off anyway. They hadn't eaten dinner. Actually, said Carlo, he hadn't eaten at all.

Carlo fell silent. Denise said nothing.

You know what your mother's like, said Carlo. There's nothing anyone can do.

Carefully, Denise asked her father, 'Where is my mother now?'

'I've no idea,' replied Carlo.

Denise thought her father was a terrible liar. 'I didn't believe him for a nanosecond,' she said. 'Not one word.' All his kindness over the last few days, all the opening doors, fetching coats and driving them around – his whole Milanese *bella figura* act – all of it was gone. Carlo appeared to have regressed. He seemed raw, almost primal. He wouldn't even look at her. And suddenly Denise understood. The dinner with her cousins. The calls to Lea that wouldn't go through.

The endless hanging around. The urgent discussion between the men in the apartment opposite. Lea had been right all along. Denise, who had begged her mother to let them go to Milan, had been catastrophically wrong. 'I *knew*,' said Denise. 'I knew immediately.'

Denise understood two more things. First: it was already too late. Denise hadn't spoken to her mother for three and a half hours. Lea never turned off her phone for that long and certainly not before telling Denise. *It's done*, thought Denise. *He's already had time.*

Second: confronting her father would be suicide. If she was to survive, in that moment she had to accept Lea's fate and fix it in her mind not as possible or reversible but as certain and final. At the same time, she had to convince her father that she had no idea about what had happened, when in reality she had no doubt at all. 'I understood there was very little I could do for my mother now,' said Denise. 'But I couldn't let *him* understand *me*.' Inwardly, Denise forced her mind into a tight, past-tense dead end. 'They've done what they had to do,' she told herself. 'This was how it was always going to end. This was inevitable.' Outwardly, she played herself as she might have been a few minutes earlier: a worried daughter looking for her missing mother. The speed of events helped. It was absurd, even unreal, how in a moment Denise had lost her mother, her best friend and the only person who had ever truly known her. She didn't have to pretend to be struggling to catch up. She even had the feeling that if she willed it hard enough, she might bring Lea back to life.

It was in this state, with Carlo in a daze and Denise acting like there was still hope in the world, that father and daughter drove all over Milan. 'We went to all the places we had been,' said Denise. 'Where we'd had a drink, where we'd eaten pizza, the hotel where we had stayed, over to Sempione Park. We went to a local café, a shopping centre, the McDonald's where we had lunch and the train station, where my father bought two tickets for my mother and me. We went all over the city. I was phoning and texting my mother all the time. And of course, we found nothing and nobody.'

Around midnight, just after the train to Calabria had departed, Denise's phone rang. Denise was startled to read the word 'mama' on the screen. But the voice on the other end belonged to her Aunt Marisa, Lea's sister in Pagliarelle, and Denise remembered that she had borrowed her cousin's phone before leaving for Milan.

Gathering herself, Denise told Marisa that Lea was nowhere to be found and that they had just missed their train back to Calabria. 'Have you heard from her?' Denise asked her aunt. 'Did she call you?'

Aunt Marisa replied she had had a missed call from Lea sometime after 6.30 p.m. but hadn't been able to reach her since. Marisa was calling to check that everything was all right. Denise replied that Lea's phone had been dead all night.

'They made her disappear,' Marisa told Denise, just like that, with Carlo sitting right next to Denise in the car.

'She was so matter-of-fact,' Denise said. 'Like she assumed we all expected it. Like we all felt the same.'

Denise and Carlo kept driving around Milan until 1.30 a.m. Finally, Denise said there was nowhere else to look and they should file a report with the police. Carlo drove her to a *carabinieri* station. The officer told Denise she had to wait forty-eight hours to make out a missing person's report. With Carlo there, Denise couldn't tell the officer that she and Lea had hidden for years from the man standing next to her, so she thanked the officer and they returned to Renata's, where her aunt opened the door half-asleep in her dressing gown.

Renata was surprised to hear Lea was even in town. 'We came up here together,' Denise explained. 'We didn't tell you because we didn't want to cause any trouble.' The three of them stood in the doorway for a second. Denise found herself looking at her father's clothes. He'd had them on all evening. It had been in that jacket, thought Denise. That shirt. Those shoes.

Carlo broke the silence by saying he would keep looking for Lea a little while longer and headed back to his car. Renata said Denise could sleep in Andrea's room. To reach it, Denise had to walk through

Renata's and Giuseppe's bedroom. 'I could see Giuseppe wasn't there,' she said later. 'And I ignored it. I ignored everything *for a year*. I pretended nothing had happened. I ate with these people. I worked in their pizzeria. I went on holiday with them. I played with their children. Even when I knew what they had done. I had to be so careful with what I said. They were saying my mother was alive even after I hadn't seen her for more than a year. I just made out like I didn't know. But I knew. I knew right from that first moment.'

II

In Calabria, Lea Garofalo's disappearance needed no explanation. The mafia even had a term for people who, one day, just vanished: *lupara bianca* ('white shotgun'), a killing which left no corpse, seen by no one. In Pagliarelle, the remote mountain village on the arch of Italy's foot where Lea and Carlo were born, people knew never to speak Lea's name again.

They wouldn't be able to forget her entirely. Lea's modest first-floor studio, its shutters and drainpipes painted bubblegum pink, was only yards from the main piazza. But the four hundred villagers of Pagliarelle had learned long ago to live with their ghosts. In three decades, thirty-five men and women had been murdered in mafia vendettas in Pagliarelle and the nearby town of Petilia Policastro, including Lea's father Antonio, her uncle Giulio and her brother Floriano. In such a place, in such a family, Lea's disappearance could seem inevitable, even a kind of resolution. Years later, her sister Marisa would look up at Lea's first-floor window from the street below and say: 'Lea wanted freedom. She never bowed her head. But for people who follow the 'Ndrangheta, this choice is considered very eccentric. Very serious. You want to be free? You pay with your life.' Really, Marisa was saying, there was nothing anyone could do.[1]

Alessandra Cerreti knew many of her colleagues shared that view. When she arrived in Calabria from Milan seven months earlier as the province's newest anti-mafia prosecutor, she had been struck by how many Calabrians still accepted the 'Ndrangheta as an immutable fact of life. Outside southern Italy, the mafia was regarded as a movie or a novel, an entertaining, even glamorous legend that might once have held some historic truth but which, in a time of more sophisticated concerns such as financial crises or climate change or terrorism, felt like a fable from a bygone era. Not so in Calabria. Like their more famous cousins in Sicily and Naples, the 'Ndrangheta had been founded in the mid to late nineteenth century. But while the Sicilians, in particular, had seen their power steadily eroded by a state crackdown and popular resistance, the 'Ndrangheta had grown ever stronger. The organisation was still run by its original founders, 141 ancient shepherding and orange-farming families who ruled the isolated valleys and hill towns of Calabria. Its foot soldiers were also still quietly extorting billions of euros a year from Calabria's shopkeepers, restaurant owners and *gelato* makers – and murdering the occasional hard-headed *carabinieri* or judge or politician who stood in their way. What had transformed the 'Ndrangheta, however, was a new internationalism. It now smuggled 70 to 80 per cent of the cocaine and heroin in Europe. It plundered the Italian state and the European Union for tens of billions more. It brokered illegal arms deals to criminals, rebels and terrorists around the world, including all sides in the Syrian civil war. By the prosecutors' count, by 2009 the 'Ndrangheta's empire took in fifty countries, a quarter of the planet, from Albania to Togo, linking a mob war in Toronto to a lawyer's assassination in Melbourne, and the ownership of an entire Brussels neighbourhood to a cocaine-delivering pizzeria in Queens, New York, called Cucino a Modo Mio ('Cooking My Way'). By the dawn of the second decade of the new millennium, the 'Ndrangheta was, by almost any measure, the most powerful criminal syndicate on earth.

If ruthless violence was the fuel of this global empire, astounding wealth was its result. Every year, the organisation amassed revenues of $50–$100 billion,[2] equivalent to up to 4.5 per cent of Italian GDP, or twice the annual revenues of Fiat, Alfa Romeo, Lancia, Ferrari and Maserati combined. So much money was there that cleaning and hiding it required a whole second business. And so good had the Calabrians become at money laundering, pushing billions through restaurants and construction companies, small offshore banks and large financial institutions, even the Dutch flower market and the European chocolate trade, that Alessandra's fellow prosecutors were picking up indications that other organised crime groups – Eastern Europeans, Russians, Asians, Africans, Latin Americans – were paying the 'Ndrangheta to do the same with their fortunes. That meant the 'Ndrangheta was managing the flow of hundreds of billions or even trillions of illicit dollars around the world.

And it was this, the 'Ndrangheta's dispersal of global crime's money across the planet, that ensured the Calabrians were in everyone's lives. Billions of people lived in their buildings, worked in their companies, shopped in their stores, ate in their pizzerias, traded in their shares, did business with their banks and elected politicians and parties they funded. As rich as the biggest businesses or banks or governments, 'Ndrangheta-managed money moved markets and changed lives from New York to London to Tokyo to São Paolo to Johannesburg. In the first two decades of the new millennium, it was hard to imagine another human enterprise with such influence over so many lives. Most remarkable of all: almost no one had ever heard of it.

The 'Ndrangheta – pronounced *un-drung-get-a*, a word derived from the Greek *andraganthateai*, meaning society of men of honour and valour – was a mystery even to many Italians.[3] In truth, this ignorance was due as much to perception as deception. Many northern Italians had trouble even imagining wealth or achievement in the south. And the contrast *was* striking. The north had Florence and Venice, *prosciutto* and *parmigiana*, Barolo and balsamic, the Renaissance and the Enlightenment, AC Milan and Inter Milan, Lamborghini and Maserati, Gucci and Prada, Caravaggio, Michelangelo, Pavarotti, Puccini, Galileo, da Vinci, Dante, Machiavelli, Marco Polo, Christopher Columbus and the Pope. The south had lemons, mozzarella and winter sun.

This was, Alessandra knew, the great lie of a united Italy. Two thousand years earlier, the south had been a fount of European civilisation. But by the time the northern general Giuseppe Garibaldi amalgamated the Italian peninsula into a single nation in 1861, he was attempting to join the literate, the industrial and the cultured with the feudal, the unschooled and the unsewered. The contradiction had proved too great. The north prospered in trade and commerce. The south deteriorated and millions of southerners left, emigrating to northern Europe, the Americas or Australia.

In time, the provinces south of Rome had come to be known as the *Mezzogiorno*, the land where the midday sun blazed overhead, a dry, torpid expanse of peasant farmers and small-boat fishermen stretching from Abruzzo through Naples to the island of Lampedusa, 110 kilometres from North Africa. For much of the south, such a sweeping description was a clumsy stereotype. But for Calabria, the toe, it was accurate. The Romans had called it Bruttium and for 250 kilometres from north to south, Calabria was little more than thorn-bush scrub and bare rock mountains interspersed with groves of gnarled olives and fields of fine grey dust. It was eerily empty: more than a century of emigration had ensured there were four times as many Calabrians and their descendants outside Italy as in their homeland. When she drove out of Reggio and into the countryside, Alessandra passed a succession of empty towns, deserted villages and abandoned farms. It felt like the aftermath of a giant disaster – which, if you considered the centuries of grinding destitution, it was.

Still, there was a hard beauty to the place. High up in the mountains, wolves and wild boar roamed forests of beech, cedar and holly oak. Below the peaks, deep cracks in the rock opened up into precipitous ravines through which ice-cold rivers raged towards the sea. As the incline eased, woods gave way to vines and summer pastures, followed by estuary flats filled with lemon and orange orchards. In summer, the sun would scorch the earth, turning the soil to powder and the prickly thorn-grass to roasted gold. In winter, snow would cover the mountains and storms would batter the cliffs on the coast and drag away the beaches.

Alessandra wondered whether it was the violence of their land that bred such ferocity in Calabrians. They lived in ancient towns built on natural rock fortresses. In their fields, they grew burning chilli and intoxicating jasmine and raised big-horned cows and mountain goats which they roasted whole over hearths stoked with knotted vine wood. The men hunted boar with shotguns and swordfish with harpoons. The women spiced sardines with hot peppers and dried trout in the wind for months before turning the meat into a pungent brown stew. For Calabrians, there was also little divide between the holy and the profane. On saints' days, morning processions would be followed by afternoon street feasts at which the women would serve giant plates of *maccheroni* with *'nduja*, a hot, soft pepper sausage the colour of ground brick, washed down with a black wine that stained the lips and seared the throat. As the sun began to sink, the men would dance the *Tarantella*, named after the effects of the poisonous bite of the wolf spider. To the tune of a mandolin, the beat of a goat-skin tambourine and a song about thwarted love or a mother's love or the thrill of a hot spurt of blood from a stabbed traitor's heart, the men would compete for hours to see who could dance fastest and longest. 'The Greece of Italy', wrote the newspapers, though in reality that was an insult to Greece. Unlike its Ionian neighbour, southern Italy's legal economy hadn't grown since the millennium. Unemployment among the young, at more than one in two, was the worst in Europe.

*

The south had experienced one kind of development, however. Many southerners saw Garibaldi's creation of a northern-dominated Italian state as an act of colonisation. Already damned for who they were, they cared little for northern opinions of what they did. Across the *Mezzogiorno*, from the birth of the Republic, brigands ruled. Some organised themselves into family groups. In the century and a half since unification, a few hundred families in Naples, Sicily and Calabria had grown rich. And as criminal rebels secretly subverting an occupying state, they used the intimacy and loyalty of family and a violent code of honour and righteous resistance to draw a veil of *omertà* over their wealth. Even in 2009, Calabria's crime bosses still dressed like orange farmers. It was only in the last few years that the Italian government had begun to grasp that these brutish men, with their bird-faced women and tearaway sons, were among the world's great criminal masterminds.

There was, at least, no mystery to who ran the 'Ndrangheta. The south's lack of progress was social as much as material. Tradition held that each family was a miniature feudal kingdom in which men and boys reigned supreme. The men granted their women little authority or independence, nor even much of a life beyond an existence as vassals of family property and honour. Like medieval kings, fathers paired their girls off as teenagers to seal clan alliances. Beatings of daughters and wives were routine. To men, women were desirable but feckless, not to be trusted to stay faithful or direct their own lives but to be kept strictly in line for their own good. Women who were untrue, even to the memory of a husband dead for twenty years, were killed, and it would be their fathers, brothers, sons and husbands who did it. Only blood could wash clean the family honour, the men would say. Often they burned the bodies or dissolved them in acid to be sure of erasing the family shame.

Such a perversion of family would have been extraordinary in any time or place. It was especially so in Italy, where family was close to sacred.[4] The severity of the misogyny prompted some prosecutors to compare the 'Ndrangheta with Islamist militants. Like ISIS or Boko Haram, 'Ndranghetisti routinely terrorised their women and slaughtered their enemies in the service of an immutable code of honour and righteousness.

So, yes, Calabria's prosecutors would say, the life of an 'Ndrangheta woman like Lea Garofalo was tragic. And, yes, the 'Ndrangheta's inhuman sexism was one more reason to destroy it. But that didn't mean the women were much use in that fight. Almost from the day in April 2009 that Alessandra arrived from Milan, her colleagues told her the women in the mafia were just more of its victims. 'The women don't matter,' they said.[5] When they heard of Lea's disappearance, her colleagues conceded the news was heartbreaking, especially for those who had known Lea and Denise in witness protection. But Lea's death was merely a symptom of the problem, they insisted. It had no bearing on the cause.

Alessandra disagreed. She claimed no special insight into family dynamics. Alessandra was thirty-nine, married without children, and her appearance – slim, meticulously dressed, with short straight hair in a sharp, boyish parting – emphasised cool professionalism. When it came to The Family, however, Alessandra argued that it was only logical that women would have a substantial role in a criminal organisation structured around kin. Family was the lifeblood of the mafia. Like an unseen, uncut umbilical cord, family was how the mafia delivered nourishing, fortifying power to itself. And at the heart of any family was a mother. Besides, argued Alessandra, if the women really didn't matter, why would the men risk it all to kill them? The women *had* to be more than mere victims. As a Sicilian and a woman inside the Italian judiciary, Alessandra also knew something about patriarchies that belittled women even as they relied on them. Most of her colleagues missed the importance of 'Ndrangheta women, she said, because most of them were men. 'And Italian men underestimate all women,' she said. 'It's a real problem.'

At the time Lea Garofalo went missing, evidence to support Alessandra's views was on display in every Italian newspaper. For two years, the press had filled its pages with the lurid allegations and distinctly conservative attitudes of a state prosecutor in Perugia called Giuliano Mignini. Mignini had accused an American student, Amanda Knox – with the assistance of two men, one of whom was Knox's boyfriend of five days – of murdering her British flatmate, Meredith Kercher. Mignini alleged the two men were in thrall to Knox's satanic allure. Taking his lead from Mignini, a lawyer in the case described Knox as a 'she-devil … Lucifer-like, demonic … given over to lust'. Fifty-nine years old, a devout Catholic and father of four daughters, Mignini later told a documentary maker that though the forensic evidence against Knox was scant, her 'uninhibited' character and 'lack of morals' had convinced him. 'She would bring boys home,' he mused. 'Pleasure at any cost. This is at the heart of most crime.'[6]

In the end, Knox and her boyfriend were acquitted on appeal, twice, and the prosecutors castigated by Italy's Supreme Court for presenting a case with 'stunning flaws'. But at the time of Lea's disappearance, Knox was days from being found guilty for the first time and Mignini's version of events – that an unmarried American woman who had slept with seven men was just the kind of fiendish deviant to have sex slaves murder her roommate – was the accepted truth.

Alessandra didn't lecture her colleagues on female emancipation. In their own lives they were free to hold whatever views they wished and she wasn't about to let any of them think she was asking for special treatment. But when it came to cracking the *omertà* that cloaked Europe's biggest mafia, Alessandra argued that the state had pragmatic reasons to care about the prejudice of gangsters. The 'Ndrangheta was as near perfect a criminal organisation as any of them would ever encounter. It had been around for a century and a half, employed thousands around the world and made tens of billions a year. It was not only the single biggest obstacle standing in the way of Italy finally becoming a modern, united nation, but also a diabolical perversion of the Italian family, which was the heart and essence of the nation. And yet until a few years earlier, the Italian state had been barely aware of its existence. When she arrived in Reggio Calabria, no one at the Palace of Justice could give Alessandra more than rough estimates of how many men the 'Ndrangheta employed or where it operated or even, to the nearest $50 billion a year, how much money it made. The kind of free will and independence that Lea Garofalo represented, and the murderous chauvinism rained down on her as a result, represented one of the few times the 'Ndrangheta had ever broken cover. Lea's evidence against Carlo Cosco was also one of the prosecutors' first ever peeks inside the organisation. The 'Ndrangheta's violent bigotry wasn't just a tragedy, said Alessandra. It was a grand flaw. With the right kind of nurturing, it might become an existential crisis. 'Freeing their women,' said Alessandra, 'is the way to bring down the 'Ndrangheta.'

III

Alessandra Cerreti was born on 29 April 1970 in the eastern Sicilian port of Messina.[1] In twenty-two years away, she'd only rarely visited her home town. Now she was living in Reggio Calabria, Messina's sister city, three miles across the water, and rarely out of sight of it. She realised she'd never noticed how Messina changed through the day. At dawn, a pink light would lift its piazzas, boulevards and palm trees out of a purple gloom. At midday, the sun painted the scene in primary colours: blue sea, red roofs, yellow hills, and the white cone of Mount Etna to the south. Sunset was a languid affair, as the wind slackened and Messina sank back into the dusk under clouds edged with orange filigree. Night ushered in a Mediterranean glamour, a fathomless black set off by a necklace of white lights strung like pearls along the coast road.

It was a scene that had drawn artists and writers for generations. Those raised beside the Straits of Messina, however, have long understood that the truth of the place is in what lies beneath. The Straits are a narrow, plunging abyss formed when Africa and Europe collided fifty million years ago and Africa bent down towards the centre of the earth. In this underwater chasm, the rushing currents created when the Ionian and Tyrrhenian seas meet make for some of the most disturbed waters in all the oceans. Boiling whirlpools and sucking vortexes trap yachts and fishing boats. Slewing tides send ferries and freighters skidding sideways towards the rocks. Those peering into the depths can see startled bug-eyed fish, and even sharks and whales, shot to the surface from the sea floor 250 metres below. The swirling winds of the Straits reflect this turmoil, inverting the normal pattern of hot air over cold to create an optical illusion called the *Fata Morgana* in which boats and land on the horizon appear to float upside down in the sky.

On land, human history has mirrored this natural upheaval. Reggio and Messina were founded by Greek colonists whose king, Italos, eventually gave the country its name. But for three millennia, the Straits have been continuously conquered and appropriated, first by Syracusans in 387 BC, then by Campanians, Romans, Vandals, Lombards, Goths, Byzantines, Arabs, Normans, Hohenstaufen German kings, Angevins, Aragonese, Spanish Habsburgs (twice), Ottomans, Barbary pirates, reactionary French Bourbons and Bonapartists, before finally, in 1860 and 1861, Reggio and Messina were captured by Giuseppe Garibaldi in the war that unified Italy. The wealth of its occupiers had given Messina and Reggio their ancient, yellow-stone harbours, their Arabic street names and an early artistry that found exquisite expression in the Riacce Bronzes, two sculptures of naked, bearded warriors dating from 450 BC discovered by a snorkeller off the Calabrian coast in 1972. But this early globalism also had its costs. It was through the Straits' ports that the Black Death entered Europe from Asia in 1346, going on to wipe out two-thirds of the continent's population. In 1743, by which time humanity's numbers had barely recovered, plague returned a second time, killing 48,000 in Messina alone. Next to those disasters, the deadly earthquakes of 1783 and 1894 were largely forgotten, though not the quake and ensuing twelve-metre tsunami of 28 December 1908 which flattened both Reggio and Messina, killing 200,000 people. Rebuilt entirely, the twin cities were levelled again by Allied bombers in 1943.

Assailed by tempests, consumed by catastrophe, the people of the Straits could be forgiven for thinking they were cursed. Many used magic and folk wisdom to account for their suffering. In the *Odyssey*, Homer had written about two sea monsters which lived on opposing sides of the Straits. Surging out from Calabria, the six-headed Scylla would snatch sailors from the decks of their ships, while from Sicily Charybdis would suck entire boats under the waves with her insatiable thirst. People explained Etna's deadly eruptions by describing the mountain as the home of Vulcan, or sometimes of Cyclops, both of them angry, thundering types with low opinions of mortals. The tremors people felt under their feet were said to be the shifting grip of Colapesce, the son of a fisherman who took a deep dive one day, saw that Sicily was held up by a single, crumbling column and stayed in the depths to prevent its collapse. The floating islands which appeared over Reggio, meanwhile, were thought to be glimpses of Avalon, to which the fairy-witch Morgan le Fay (after whom the *Fata Morgana* was named) spirited a dying King Arthur. Up there too, it was said, was *The Flying Dutchman*, a ghost ship doomed to sail the oceans for ever.

Alessandra would carry the feel of the Straits with her all her life. It was there in the way a winter's chill would remind her of the morning breeze off the city docks or how the first days of summer would almost instantly change her forearms from alabaster to honey. It was there, too, in her distaste for the way people often seemed to prefer fiction over truth. While most children were delighted to find themselves growing up in a world of gods and castles in the sky, Alessandra was unmoved. Stories of monsters and fairies were entertaining, but to Alessandra they obscured the deadly reality of the Straits. Every summer, she watched as Messina's coastguards heaved a steady procession of dripping, blanketed stretchers onto the docks. It made no sense to her to imagine these regrettable, preventable deaths as part of some mystical grand plan. There was little logic, either, in the other spurious legends that Sicilians would spin to glorify their island.

In 1975, when Alessandra was five, a twenty-six-year-old from Messina called Giovanni Fiannacca swam to Calabria in 30 minutes and 50 seconds, a record that was to stand for forty years. Alessandra's neighbours proclaimed Fiannacca the greatest distance swimmer in Sicily, perhaps even of all time. The reality, as Alessandra knew – and knew her neighbours knew – was that he had timed his crossing to coincide with a particularly strong east–west tide which would have carried a rubber duck to Calabria.

In another life, in another land, Alessandra might have forgiven these illusions and the credulous adults who repeated them. But her home was the birthplace of Cosa Nostra. By the 1970s, the Sicilian mafia was operating all but unopposed on the island. It was a state-within-a-state, extracting taxes via extortion, dividing up public contracts among mafia companies, settling disputes, delivering punishments – and lying, cheating and murdering to preserve its position. Yet no one said a thing. To inquisitive outsiders, Sicilians would claim the mafia was a fable, a cliché or even a groundless slur. To themselves, they would characterise it in more mythic terms, as an ancient Sicilian brotherhood built on courage, honour and sacrifice. Never mind that it was the mafia itself which cooked up these romantic legends and embellished them with more recent folklore, such as their story about how *mafiosi* rode Allied tanks to liberate Sicily in the Second World War. Never mind that in their hearts most Sicilians knew they were being lied to. Just as the islanders found it hard to accept the indifference shown to their city by Nature and Man, so most preferred not to confront the truth that their fellow Sicilians had grown rich by robbing and killing them.

Alessandra lamented her neighbours' complicity in these deceptions, even as she understood it. Decades later, reading sensational newspaper accounts of mafia adventures, she would react the same way she had as a child. The facts about the tyranny and the killing were plain. Why dress them up as something else? What Alessandra truly detested, however, was the way outsiders assisted the mafia's myth-making. Two weeks before she was born, Mario Puzo, an American pulp magazine writer, sold the screenplay of his book, *The Godfather*, to Paramount for $100,000. A year later, Francis Ford Coppola was directing Al Pacino in the movie on location in Savoca, twenty-five miles south of Messina.

The film, one of the most successful of all time, contained elements of truth. The Corleone family *was* a crime syndicate from south of Palermo. There also *had* been a disagreement inside the mafia in the 1950s over whether to enter narcotics trafficking, a dispute which did lead to an internal war. What Alessandra found unforgivable was the way Hollywood used southern Italians' daily tragedy as a device to make its dramas more compelling. She shared none of Coppola's empathy for the men who murdered their wives and girlfriends. She could make no sense of the women either, passive, giddy creatures who allowed their men to lead them from love to betrayal to an early death. Nor did she recognise any of the film's sombre majesty or mournful grandiloquence in the blood that stained the gutters as she walked to school. When Alessandra was eight, two ambitious bosses, Salvatore Riina ('the butcher of Corleone') and Bernardo Provenzano ('the tractor', so-called because, in the words of one informer, 'he mows people down'), began what became an all-out mafia war by assassinating several Sicilian rivals.[2] The decade and a half that followed, spanning most of Alessandra's adolescence, became known as *la mattanza*, 'the slaughter'. More than 1,700 Sicilians died. *Mafiosi* were shot in their cars, in restaurants, as they walked down the street. In a single day in Palermo in November 1982, twelve *mafiosi* were killed in twelve separate assassinations. Yet through it all, foreign tourists would arrive in Messina asking for directions to The Godfather's village. No, thought Alessandra. This was a hideous, wilful delusion. It was a lie. It had to be corrected.

As the bodies piled up in the first few months of *la mattanza*, Alessandra's teacher asked her class of eight-year-olds to write an essay about what they wanted to be when they grew up. Let your minds wander, said the teacher. You can be anything at all, anywhere in the world. Excited by the chance to escape Messina's violence and fear, most of Alessandra's classmates wrote whimsies about becoming princesses or moving to America or flying a rocket to the moon. Alessandra said she would be staying put. *I want to be an anti-mafia prosecutor*, she wrote. *I want to put gangsters behind bars.*

It was to pursue her ambition that in 1987, at the age of seventeen, Alessandra took the train north to become a law student. Pulling into Milan's central station the next day, she found herself in a different nation. But Alessandra quickly assimilated. She graduated from Milan University in 1990, qualified as a magistrate in Rome in 1997 and joined the elite Anti-Mafia and Anti-Terrorism Directorate in Milan in 2005, at the age of thirty-four. Over the next four years, she investigated the 'Ndrangheta's expansion across northern Italy, uncovered billion-euro tax evasion in the art world, sat as a judge in a high-profile terrorist recruitment case and, on a quiet weekend, married a rising anti-mafia *carabinieri* officer, Paolo Blanca.[3]

No one was surprised that Alessandra married into the job. Few outsiders would tolerate the life of a mafia prosecutor's spouse. The wide autonomy Italy's anti-mafia prosecutors enjoyed in their investigations was about the only freedom they possessed. The constant threat to her life required Alessandra to exist in isolation behind a wall of steel – literally, in the case of her office door and her armour-plated car – and for her to be escorted by four bodyguards twenty-four hours a day. Spontaneity was out of the question; all her movements were planned a day in advance. A normal life – meeting friends and family, eating out, shopping – was impossible. 'We go nowhere with crowds because of the risk to others,' said Alessandra. For the same reason, she and Paolo had long ago decided against children. 'I would have to fear for them,' she said. 'As we are, I have no fear for me or my husband.'

Alessandra didn't relish the sacrifices the job demanded. But she had come to accept them as useful to developing the character she needed to face the mafia. Her response to the mafia's romanticism and glamour remained what it had been in Messina: an insistence on the facts. To some, Alessandra knew, she could seem cold and aloof, living a grey half-life ruled by procedure, discipline and evidence. She told herself she needed this distance – from *mafiosi*, from their victims, even from life – to preserve her perspective. Passion and blood and family and tragedy – that was the mafia, and the mafia was enemy. She had to be the opposite: intellectual, forensic and dispassionate.

By thirty-nine, what once had been girlish obstinacy had matured into poise, stoicism and self-possession. In her office in the Palace of Justice, Alessandra kept her desk clear and her office spartan. Besides a photograph of the legendary Sicilian prosecutors Giovanni Falcone and Paolo Borsellino, she hung only a graphite drawing of Lady Justice and a pastel of the Straits of Messina. Among her staff, the young female prosecutor's icy focus was a favourite topic of discussion. She wasn't scared or emotional, as some of the men had predicted. Rather, she was unwavering, scrupulous and unnervingly calm – *legale*, they said – her rebukes all the more crushing for their dispassion, her smiles all the more disarming for their unexpectedness.

Inside this narrow, monotone life, Alessandra permitted herself a few indulgences. Every August she and Paolo took off on a foreign holiday without their bodyguards, telling no one where they were going – 'the only time I can be free,' she said. On a shelf in her office, she kept a collection of fifty snow globes arranged in three neat rows, a comically gaudy record of a decade of dull international crime conferences. Alessandra also liked to dress well. To court, she wore slim dark suits over a plain white blouse. To the office, she wore woollen winter shawls with leather boots, or stretch jeans with a biker's jacket, or heels with a sleeveless summer dress, her toes and fingernails painted chocolate in winter and tangerine in summer. This was not about looking good to the world. Anti-mafia prosecutors were rarely seen by anyone. Rather, this was about freedom. To do her job and not be defined by it, to accept its restrictions and not be beaten by them, to face the threats of ten thousand *mafiosi* and respond with a woman's grace and elegance – that was true style and, in a world of male brutality, a display of adamant and unyielding femininity.

Throughout her time in the north, Alessandra had kept a close watch on the southern battle against the mafia. It had been a long and bloody fight. After the state intervened to try to stem *la mattanza* in the 1980s, judges, policemen, *carabinieri*, politicians and prosecutors became targets too. In Palermo alone, Cosa Nostra killed eleven judges and prosecutors. On 23 May 1992, the mafia detonated half a ton of explosives under an elevated highway outside the city on which Giovanni Falcone, Italy's most celebrated anti-mafia prosecutor, was driving with his wife and three police bodyguards. The explosion was so big it registered on Sicily's earthquake monitors. Hearing the news of Falcone's assassination, his co-prosecutor Paolo Borsellino, who had grown up in the same Palermo neighbourhood and had always been somewhat in Falcone's shadow, remarked, 'Giovanni beat me again.' Two months later, Borsellino and five policemen were killed by a car bomb outside the home of Borsellino's mother in Palermo. Six houses were levelled and fifty-one cars, vans and trucks set on fire.

Falcone's death was to Italians what President John F. Kennedy's was to Americans: everyone can remember where they were when they heard the news. To the tight group of Sicilians like Alessandra who had taken up the fight against Cosa Nostra, the loss of their two champions was deeply personal. At the time, Alessandra was a twenty-two-year-old law graduate in Rome who had just begun training to be a magistrate. Falcone's and Borsellino's sacrifice only made the two prosecutors seem more heroic. 'They were the inspiration for a generation,' she said. 'Their deaths made us stronger.' To this day, the two prosecutors remain the titans against whom all Italian prosecutors measure themselves. A picture of either Falcone or Borsellino, and generally both, hangs on the wall of every anti-mafia prosecutor's office in Italy, often accompanied by a famous Falcone one-liner. 'The mafia is a human phenomenon and, like all human phenomena, it had a beginning, an evolution and will also have an end,' was one favourite. 'He who doesn't fear death dies only once,' was another.

In time, even Cosa Nostra would acknowledge that the murders had been a miscalculation. They gave the prosecutors' political masters no choice but to abandon attempts to negotiate a peace with the mafia and try to crush it instead. Around 150,000 soldiers were dispatched to Sicily. The two prosecutors' deaths also prompted renewed appreciation of their achievements. The chief accomplishment of Falcone, Borsellino and their two fellow prosecutors, Giuseppe di Lello and Leonardo Guarnotta, was finally to disprove the grand Sicilian lie. After decades of denial, Cosa Nostra was exposed not as a myth or a movie but a global criminal organisation, headquartered in Sicily, with extensive links to business and politics in Italy and around the world. The climax of their investigations, the Maxi Trial, saw 475 *mafiosi* in court, accused of offences ranging from extortion to drug smuggling to 120 murders.

How had Falcone and Borsellino succeeded? Many of their accomplishments hinged on a new 1982 law, the crime of mafia association, which outlawed a mere relationship with the mafia, even without evidence of a criminal act. That effectively made it a crime just to be born into a mafia family and was aimed squarely at the *omertà* and close blood relations on which the mafia was built. The new legislation worked. First a handful, then scores, then hundreds of *mafiosi* turned *pentiti* (literally 'penitents'). A host of otherwise innocent family members did the same. From their evidence, Italy's prosecutors were able to construct a picture of Cosa Nostra's internal structure for the first time.

The Sicilians' other innovation was to abandon the mercurial autonomy traditionally enjoyed by individual prosecutors. Independence from political masters, who were often the target of anti-mafia investigations, remained essential. But prosecutors' habitual individualism had often found expression in less helpful fashion, such as fighting each other for position. By contrast, Palermo's anti-mafia prosecutors worked as an indivisible team, the 'anti-mafia pool', as they called themselves, which shared information, diffused responsibility and co-signed all warrants. In that way, they ensured their work was coordinated and efficient, and never depended on the continuing good health of any one of them.

So it was that in the months after the deaths of Falcone and Borsellino, other prosecutors – first Gian Carlo Caselli; then the Sicilians Piero Grasso, Giuseppe Pignatone and his deputy Michele Prestipino – picked up where their storied predecessors left off. And in a further decade and a half, the Palermo prosecutors and Palermo's elite flying squad largely finished what their predecessors had started. By the mid-2000s, nearly all Cosa Nostra's bosses were in jail, its links to senior politicians were exposed and its rackets, while they still existed, were a shadow of what they had once been. Capping the prosecutors' success, in April 2006 at a small, sparsely furnished cottage outside Corleone, Pignatone and Prestipino were present for the arrest of Cosa Nostra's remaining *capo tutti*, seventy-three-year-old Bernardo Provenzano, who had been on the run for forty-three years.

On visits back to Sicily, Alessandra saw the transformation in her homeland. In the streets of Palermo and Messina, a new popular movement called Addiopizzo ('Goodbye *Pizzo*', mafia slang for extortion) united shopkeepers, farmers and restaurateurs in a refusal to pay protection. Tens of thousands of anti-mafia protesters marched arm-in-arm through the streets. Cosa Nostra, in its weakened state, was unable to respond. When *mafiosi* firebombed an anti-mafia *trattoria* in Palermo, the city's residents found the owners new premises on a busy junction in the centre of town where they opened up again and quickly became one of the city's most celebrated destinations. In time, Palermo and Messina could boast city-centre shops run by an activist group called Libera ('Free'), which sold olive oil, sauces, wine and pasta made exclusively by farmers who refused to pay protection to Cosa Nostra.

But as the war on Cosa Nostra wound down, a fresh threat took its place. During *la mattanza*, across the water in Calabria the 'Ndrangheta had initially toyed with joining Cosa Nostra's war on the state, and even killed a couple of policemen for itself. But the Calabrians soon realised that with the Sicilians and the government so distracted, the strategic play was not to side with Cosa Nostra but to take its narco-business. The 'Ndrangheta paid the Sicilians' debts to the Colombian cocaine cartels, effectively buying them out as the Latin Americans' smuggling partners.

Carlo Cosco arrived in Milan in 1987, the same year as Alessandra. Carlo's intention was not to fit into northern Italy, however, but to conquer it – and his timing was perfect. The 'Ndrangheta was pushing its drug empire north across Europe. Milan was a key beachhead in that expansion. And there had never been a business like cocaine smuggling in Europe in the 1990s and 2000s. After saturating the US market, South American producers were looking to other territories for growth. Europe, with twice the population of North America and a similar standard of living but, in the 1980s, a quarter of its cocaine consumption, was the obvious opportunity. With the 'Ndrangheta's help, the cartels flooded the continent with cocaine. By 2010, the European cocaine market matched the American one at 350 tons a year, worth 22 billion euros. In Spain and Britain, the drug became as middle class as Volvos and weekend farmers' markets.

In the estimate of Italy's prosecutors, the 'Ndrangheta accounted for three-quarters of that. So rich, and so fast, did the 'Ndrangheta grow, it was hard to keep track. On wiretaps, *carabinieri* overheard 'Ndranghetisti talking about buried sacks of cash rotting in the hills, and writing off the loss of a few million here or there as inconsequential. At Gioia Tauro port on Calabria's west coast, officers were seizing hundreds of kilos of cocaine at a time from shipping containers but reckoned that they found less than 10 per cent of what was passing through. A glimpse of quite how big the 'Ndrangheta had grown came in the early hours of 15 August 2007 – the Ascension Day national holiday in Italy – when two 'Ndrangheta gunmen shot and killed four men and two boys aged eighteen and sixteen connected to a rival clan outside a pizzeria in Duisberg, in Germany's industrial heartland. Northern Europe was apparently now 'Ndrangheta territory.

Italy, and Europe, had a new mafia war to fight. And though its empire was now global, the 'Ndrangheta remained as attached to Calabria as Cosa Nostra had been to Sicily. In April 2008, two of the prosecutors who had humbled the Sicilian mafia, Giuseppe Pignatone, now sixty, and Michele Prestipino, fifty, had their requests for transfer to Calabria accepted. Their friend and ally in the Palermo flying squad, Renato Cortese, went with them. As the three cast around for a team who might do to the 'Ndrangheta what had been done to Cosa Nostra, they realised they faced a problem. Many Italian prosecutors baulked at the idea of an assignment to what was universally regarded as both a backwater and enemy territory. In 2008, only twelve of the eighteen prosecutor positions in Calabria were filled and the province had just five anti-mafia specialists. In Milan, however, Alessandra applied. She was ready to return to the south, she told her bosses. She understood the work would be 'riskier' and more 'difficult and compli- cated'. That just made it all the more urgent.[4]

In April 2009, Alessandra and Paolo packed up their apartment in Milan and flew south, following the sun down the west coast of Italy. As the plane started its descent, Alessandra saw the Aeolian Islands to the west, then Sicily and the snows of Etna to the south, then the streets of Messina below. As she passed over the broad blue of the Straits, she regarded the white foam trails of the rusty freighters as they rounded the tip of the Italian peninsula and turned north to Naples, Genoa, Marseilles and Barcelona. Not for the first time, it occurred to Alessandra that the lazy arc of this shore would, from a suitable distance, form the shape of a very large toe.

Alessandra's new security detail met her and Paolo at Reggio airport. They took the expressway into town as a two-car convoy. The road climbed high above the city, skirting the dusty terraces that led up into the Calabrian hinterland. Below were the cobbled streets and crumbling apartment blocks whose names were familiar to Alessandra from dozens of investigations into shootings and fire-bombings. Somewhere down there, too, were the bunkers, entire underground homes where 'Ndrangheta bosses would hide for years, surfacing through hidden doors and tunnels to order new killings and plan new business.

As they reached the northern end of Reggio, the two cars took an off-ramp and plunged down into the city, dropping through twisting hairpins, bumping over ruts and potholes, plunging ever lower through tumbling, narrow streets before bottoming out just behind the seafront. Once on the flat, the drivers accelerated and flashed through the streets, past abandoned hotels, boarded-up cinemas and empty villas before turning back up towards the hills and sweeping through the gates of a *carabinieri* barracks. In its 3,500 years of existence, Reggio had been a Mediterranean power, the birthplace of the kingdom of Italia, a Norman fortress and a Riviera resort. Now it was bandit country. Entire neighbourhoods were off-limits to *carabinieri* or prosecutors. For Alessandra and Paolo, home for the next five years would be a bare-walled officer's apartment jammed into the barracks roof with a view of the Straits of Messina.

IV

Denise slept for an hour and a half the night Lea disappeared.[1] The next morning, 25 November 2009, she ate breakfast with her Aunt Renata, walked with her to the kindergarten where she worked, then spent the morning silently smoking cigarettes with Andrea and Domenico in a nearby piazza. In the afternoon, Carlo phoned and told her to meet him at Bar Barbara. On the way there, Denise ran into a cousin from Lea's side of the family, Francesco Ceraudo, who lived in Genoa. She told Francesco that Lea was missing and asked him if he had seen her. Francesco blanched. 'Do you know anything?' Denise asked. 'Absolutely not,' he said, and walked on.

The entire Cosco clan were in Bar Barbara: Carlo, his brothers Vito and Giuseppe, and Aunt Renata. Giuseppe and Renata were playing video poker in the corner. Giuseppe won 50 euros and, clumsily, gave the winnings to Denise. After a while, the *carabinieri* called Denise on her mobile and said they needed to speak to her. During the call, a squad car pulled up outside. Vito asked what was happening. 'Lea's missing,' Carlo told him.

The Coscos weren't about to let one of their own go to the *carabinieri* alone. Vito dropped Carlo and Denise at the station around 8.30 p.m., and father and daughter entered together. Inside, however, *carabiniere* Marshal Christian Persurich told Carlo he had to talk to

Denise unaided. Persurich showed Denise to an interview room. He informed her that in Calabria her Aunt Marisa had reported Lea missing. Marisa had also told the *carabinieri* that Lea had testified against the 'Ndrangheta and that she and Denise had spent time in witness protection. Lea had now been missing for more than twenty-four hours. Persurich needed the whole story. Denise should take her time and leave nothing out. The interview would be strictly confidential.

Denise nodded. 'If my mother's missing,' she began, 'then it's probably because she's been killed by my father.'

Marshal Persurich interviewed Denise for five hours, finishing just before 2 a.m. Denise emerged to find Carlo pacing the waiting room, demanding that the officers let him read her statement. Seeing his daughter, Carlo confronted her. 'What did you tell these people?!'

'You asked us to Milan,' Denise replied blankly. 'We spent a few days together. You were meant to pick her up. But you couldn't find her. Then we looked for her all over.'

Carlo looked unconvinced. Five hours for that?

On the way back to her cousin's, Carlo and Denise stopped at a restaurant, the Green Dragon, named after the symbol of Milan. Inside was Carmine Venturino, the cousin who had given Lea some hash to smoke. Carmine had a babyish face and looked like a born truant, and Denise had liked him from the moment she met him at a wedding in Calabria the previous summer. But that night they had nothing to say to each other. After Carmine and Carlo had a brief, hushed discussion, Carlo walked his daughter back to Viale Montello. There, Denise slept in Andrea's room for a second night.

The next morning, Carlo, Denise and a friend of Carlo's, Rosario Curcio, saw a lawyer in town. Carlo told the lawyer he wanted to see Denise's statements. The lawyer asked Denise what she'd told the *carabinieri*. Denise repeated what she had told Carlo: that she and her mother had come up to Milan to spend a few days with her father and Lea had vanished on their last night. She began crying. The lawyer said he could arrange to have Lea's disappearance publicised on national television. There was a show, *Chi l'ha Visto?* (*Have You Seen Them?*), which appealed for information on missing people. 'Oh, for fuck's sake!' cried Carlo. The lawyer didn't get it at all. Carlo stood up and walked out, leaving Denise crying in the lawyer's office.

After Denise recovered, she, Carlo and Rosario drove to a beauty salon owned by Rosario's girlfriend, Elisa. Carlo took Rosario aside for another quiet talk. Elisa asked Denise what was going on. Denise burst into tears once more and told Elisa that her mother had gone missing two nights before. Elisa said that was strange because Rosario had vanished for a few hours the same evening. They'd had a date, said Elisa, but Rosario had cancelled, then switched off his phone. When she finally got through to him around 9 p.m., he'd told Elisa something about having to fix a car with Carmine. It didn't make sense. Why the sudden rush to fix a car? Why at night? Denise was about to say something when Carlo interrupted to say he was taking Denise back to Viale Montello. She slept in her cousin's room for a third night.

The next day, three days since Lea had disappeared, Denise detected an improvement in Carlo's mood. He announced that he and Denise would drive to Reggio Emilia, not far from Bologna, to stay the night with another cousin. They left in the early afternoon. While her father drove, Denise watched silently as the winter sun flashed through the poplar trees like a searchlight through the bars of a fence. How could her mother just vanish? How could anyone be there one minute, and there be no sign of her the next? How would she ever talk to her father again?

In Reggio Emilia, Denise went to bed early while Carlo and his cousin went out for dinner. The following morning, Carlo drove Denise back to Milan, changed cars to a blue BMW and announced that he and Denise were leaving immediately for Calabria with two other friends. As they were packing, Carmine arrived to say goodbye. Denise was struck by his expression. Stiff and formal, she thought. Something about the way he wouldn't look her in the eye.

From the back seat of the BMW, Denise watched as Milan's grand piazzas and chic boutiques gave way to the flat, grey farmland north of Florence, then the rust-coloured hills of Tuscany and Umbria and finally, as the sun sank into the sea to the west, the towering black volcanoes around Naples and Pompeii. It was dark by the time they crossed into Calabria. Denise felt the road change from smooth asphalt to worn, undulating waves. The car negotiated an almost endless succession of roadworks, then plunged into the steep valley of Cosenza, skimming the cliffs as it wound down into the abyss before hitting the valley floor.

Soon Denise felt the car turn left and accelerate back up into the hills. She registered the tighter turns and the sound of tyres scrabbling on loose stones. The cold of the window dried her tear tracks to a salty crust. As the car filled with the smell of pines, the conversation between the three men took on a giddy, jubilant tone. 'The only thing in my head was my mother,' she said. 'I was just sitting in the back, crying. But the others – they were so happy. Chatting and smiling and joking and laughing out loud.'

After an hour of climbing, the car crested a mountain pass and began to descend. At the edge of a forest, by the side of a stream, they came to a small village. They were heading to the one place where Carlo could be sure Denise would never speak out of turn again. Pagliarelle.

'Pagliarelle' comes from the word *pagliari*, meaning shelter. The name commemorated how for thousands of years, as the winter snows melted, Calabria's shepherds would lead their sheep and goats up a track into the mountains and find a stream on whose banks they would graze their animals for weeks at a time. Keeping one eye out for wolves and another on the sea on the horizon, the men would collect pinewood, barbecue goat meat, drink wine and sleep in a handful of open-sided shacks that they roofed with fir and clay. In the twentieth century, the track leading from the nearby town of Petilia Policastro was tarred, electricity arrived and the shepherds' rest grew into a modest settlement of grey-stone, red-tiled townhouses gathered around a small central square. The name survived, as did the stream, which was channelled into a fountain in the piazza where, as children, their mothers would send Lea and Carlo to fill buckets for the day.

It was here, high up in the frozen, granite mountains of eastern Calabria, that Denise found herself walking a tightrope of pretence in the weeks after Lea's disappearance. Lea hadn't just been Denise's mother. After so many years alone together, she had defined Denise's life. Now Denise found herself back in the place that her mother had tried to escape for so long, adrift among the people she was sure had killed her. It was impossible to know how to behave. With no body and no funeral, Denise couldn't mourn. Carlo was telling people that Lea had run off, maybe to Australia, and Denise found herself having to make believe that her murderous father hadn't really killed her courageous mother at all but that, rather, her fickle mother had abandoned her husband and only child and jetted off to a new life in the sun. Denise knew the way she looked so much like Lea – the same hair, the same cheekbones – made her an immediate object of suspicion. Worse, Carlo was making so much of Denise's return. After years of problems with his wife and daughter, the boss finally had both his women where they belonged – and he wanted everyone to know. Ten days after Lea's disappearance, Carlo organised an eighteenth birthday party for Denise, inviting hundreds of people from Pagliarelle and Petilia Policastro and even buying Denise a car. When Denise refused to go, Carlo went ahead with the party anyway.

Mostly, Denise spent her days trying to learn from her Aunt Marisa, with whom she was now living. Ever since Lea had first denounced the 'Ndrangheta in 1996, Marisa had been forced to pull off a daily performance in Pagliarelle. Convincing an entire village they needed to have no doubts about her had required Marisa not just to tell lies but to live them too. In her mind, Marisa suffocated any affection she had for Lea and focused instead on the resentment she felt towards her sister for the trouble she had caused. Denise realised she would have to learn to hate her mother, too. 'I knew my aunt and her family,' said Denise. 'I knew how they thought. My idea was to understand their mentality and see if I could also work out how to live there. I didn't want to end up like my mother. I wanted to keep living.'

V

D enise wasn't the only one living a lie in Pagliarelle. Watching Lea's daughter offered the *carabinieri* one of their best leads for finding out what had happened to Lea. But any reminder of the state's relationship with Lea, or any hint that it might continue with her daughter, would be enough to condemn Denise. The *carabinieri* decided the state's only visible presence in Pagliarelle should remain the lone village policeman. Unseen and unheard, however, scores of officers would watch Pagliarelle day and night.

Over the years, the challenge posed by the mafia had compelled Italy's security services to innovate. To pursue violent 'Ndranghetisti through mountain terrain had led the Calabrian *carabinieri* to form a unique Special Forces-style squad, the *cacciatori* ('hunters'), a unit made up of snipers, bomb disposal experts, heavy weapons operators, helicopter pilots and Alpinists. The sight of a *cacciatori* helicopter gunship flying low over the Aspromonte mountains was a corrective to anyone who doubted the state was fighting a war in southern Italy.

But even the *cacciatori*'s resources paled next to those commanded by Italy's covert intelligence units. Around the world, only a few specialised police units are permitted to eavesdrop on suspects' telephone calls or spy on them electronically. In Italy, a measure of the mafia threat was that all three police forces – the domestic police, the militaristic *carabinieri* and the Guardian di Finanza, which specialised in economic crime – had surveillance divisions that employed thousands. In 2009, the Italian state was tapping a total of 119,553 phones and listening to 11,119 bugs. Almost no type of reconnaissance was forbidden. To establish targets' whereabouts, plain-clothes officers followed them, filmed them through hidden mini cameras and larger zoom lenses set up at a distance – several miles across the valley, in the case of Pagliarelle – and tracked their phones' GPS signal. To find out what the subjects were saying, they hacked their text messages, phone calls, emails and social media chats.

In Reggio, almost an entire floor of the gracious building that served as the city's *carabinieri* headquarters had been transformed into a humming indoor field of electronic espionage. At the centre was a control room from which chases and operations were coordinated. Around it were twenty smaller offices, each dedicated to a different surveillance operation. Every room was packed with scores of screens, servers, modems and snaking thick black wires. Working without interruption in six-hour shifts that ran continuously, day and night, officers in Reggio and an identical team in Milan had been following bosses like Carlo for years. Chosen for their facility with dialects and their ability to inhabit the skin of their subjects, the operators knew their subjects so well they could decipher the meaning of their words from a euphemism or even an inflection in their voice. The Calabrian teams also had a particular skill with bugs. They planted devices in cars, homes and gardens. They bugged a basement laundry whose underground, signal-cutting location made it a favourite 'Ndrangheta meeting place. They bugged an orange orchard where a boss liked to hold meetings, and for the same reason bugged a forest. One time they even bugged a road where one boss took walks, ripping up the asphalt and re-laying it with tar embedded with listening devices.

Such entrepreneurialism brought results. In early 2008, the squad hunting 'Ndrangheta supremo Pasquale Condello, by then fifty-seven and on the run for eighteen years, observed that every two weeks, as though he were on a schedule, Condello's nephew would shake his surveillance in the centre of Reggio, swapping from the back of one motorbike to another in a series of choreographed changes. The *carabinieri* were convinced the manoeuvres were in preparation for meeting Condello. One day, an officer noticed that the nephew always wore the same crash helmet. A few nights later, a *carabinieri* officer punctured the silencer on a car, then drove it up and down outside the nephew's house to cover the sound of a second officer breaking in and switching the helmet with an identical one implanted with a tracer. When it was time for the next rendezvous, the *carabinieri* followed the nephew through his usual multi-ride acrobatics then, using the tracer, to a small pink house in a back alley on the south side of Reggio Calabria. Surrounded by more than a hundred *cacciatori*, Condello surrendered without a fight.

This was the front line on which Alessandra had imagined herself working when she transferred to Calabria. But a staffing shortfall meant that on arrival she was assigned to Reggio as a city judge. Her knowledge of Milan and Calabria and her interest in 'Ndrangheta women notwithstanding, she was forced to watch the Lea Garofalo case unfold from afar.

Still, there were advantages to such a gentle start. For one, the undemanding hours allowed plenty of time to learn the lay of the land. Alessandra kept pace with active investigations by chatting to officers at the *carabinieri*'s headquarters, a short walk from the Palace of Justice. At other moments, she researched the 'Ndrangheta's history. In her office, she assembled piles of case files, *carabinieri* surveillance transcripts, *pentiti* statements, academic papers, history books and even accounts of Calabrian folklore.

To a Sicilian like Alessandra, the origins of the 'Ndrangheta felt familiar. The organisation was at its strongest away from the big cities in the hundreds of small mountain hamlets like Pagliarelle nestling in the valleys that led away from the coast. As in Sicily, many of these settlements had been the cradle of some of Europe's first civilisations. Alessandra read how paintings of bulls dating from 12,000 BC had been found in Calabrian caves. By 530 BC, Pythagoras was teaching mathematics in Kroton (later Crotone) on the plain below Pagliarelle while the citizens of nearby Sybaris were drinking wine piped to their homes by vinoducts. Like Sicilians, Calabrians had their own archaic language, in this case Grecanico, a Greek dialect left over from the Middle Ages when Calabria had been part of the Byzantine Empire.

Something else that Calabria had in common with Sicily: from the beginning, it was a land apart. Many of the valleys were accessible only from the sea, naturally isolated behind steep mountainsides, thick pine forests and, in winter, snows that could cut off villages for months. For thousands of years, there had been no one to defend the families who lived in these valleys. They tended olive trees, fished the ocean and scanned the horizon as invading armies sailed by from Rome, Germany, Arabia, Spain, France, Italy and America. They were poor, resilient and resolutely autonomous, and as Italy's north steadily eclipsed the south, their estrangement from the rest of the Italian peninsula only grew. When in 1861 a group of northerners began to send bureaucrats, teachers and *carabinieri* into the valleys to proclaim the rule of a newly united Italy, it was the families who repudiated, thwarted and occasionally killed the colonisers.

At first, the families had no connection to the mafia. The phenomenon of organised crime first emerged in Italy in the 1820s with the Camorra in Naples and then in the 1840s and 1850s with what became Cosa Nostra in Sicily. In both cases, ordinary criminals found themselves in jail with educated, bourgeois revolutionaries who were fighting foreign domination and feudalism, and who often organised themselves in masonic sects. As patriots, the rebels taught the future *mafiosi* the importance of a righteous cause. As freemasons, they taught them hierarchy, and the power of legend and ceremony.

When Sicily simultaneously unified with the north of Italy and ended feudalism, the ensuing chaos gave Sicily's criminals a chance to put these new lessons to work. Though the northern dukes and generals leading unification described it as an act of modernisation, many southerners regarded it as another foreign conquest. Adding to the discontent, the immediate effect of the advent of private property in Sicily was a rash of property disputes. To protect themselves, landowners, towns and villages set up vigilante groups who, for a fee, protected their assets, hunted down thieves and settled disputes. To be effective, these groups required men who could intimidate others. Jail-hardened criminals were a natural choice.

Soon these bands of enforcers were calling themselves *mafiosi*, a term derived from the Sicilian word *mafiusu*, meaning swagger or bravado. Their new name was, in effect, a rebranding. Violent criminals had always been able to inspire fear. The *mafiosi* wanted respect, too. While they didn't deny a criminal self-interest, the *mafiosi* insisted theirs was an honourable endeavour: protecting poor southerners from rapacious landowners and an oppressive north. Of course, Sicilians soon learned that the people from whom they needed most protection were the *mafiosi* themselves. The protection 'racket' was born.

When organised crime reached Calabria a generation or two later, Alessandra read, it had repeated many of the same patterns. Like Cosa Nostra, Calabria's mafia began in jail. One of Calabria's main administrative centres was Palmi, a hill town with views out over the east coast that, as the provincial capital of the Gioia Tauro *piano*, the estuary plain, possessed a police station, a courtroom and a prison. In the spring of 1888, gangs of hoodlums, many of them graduates of the town jail, began staging knife fights in Palmi's taverns, brothels and piazzas. As the heat rose with the coming summer, it seemed to stoke a violent hooliganism among the ex-cons, who began rampaging through the streets, slashing citizens with knives and razors, extorting money from gamblers, prostitutes and landowners, rustling cattle and goats, and even threatening magistrates, the police and newspaper editors.

In those early days, the prototype gangsters called themselves *camorristi*, a straight copy of the Naples mafia, or *picciotti*, a word that the British historian John Dickie translates as 'lads with attitude'.[1] If they were united, it was chiefly by their dandyish style: tattoos, extravagant quiffs, silk scarves knotted at the neck and trousers that were tight at the thighs and flared at the ankle. In his history of the three big Italian mafias, *Mafia Brotherhoods*, Dickie describes how *picciotto* culture spread across Calabria in months.[2] Like all young male fashions, it might have died just as rapidly had it not penetrated the hill valleys. There the families had little taste for the *picciotti*'s dress. But the remote and defensive interior of Calabria was fertile territory for a movement whose methods were mostly physical and whose distrust of the state was pronounced. And just as they ran everything in the valleys, the families were soon running the *pic) ioterria*.

A central goal for all mafias was to create a consensus around power. Whenever the question of power arose – political, economic, social, divine – the answer had to be the mafia. It was the peculiar luck of the Italian mafias that circumstances conspired to graft their enterprise onto the most durable of southern Italian power structures: the family. In Sicily, the mafia came to be known as *Cosa Nostra*, meaning 'our thing', and Our Thing was, really, Our Family Secret, an outsmarting of the northern state built on the intimacy and obedience of kin. Likewise in Calabria, the valley families gave the *picciotti* a ready-made hierarchy, order, legitimacy and secrecy. It was this – loyalty to blood and homeland – that was the foundation of all the horrors to come.

By the turn of the twentieth century, Calabria's street hoodlums had been organised into local cells called *'ndrine*, each with their own turf, ranks and boss. At first, *picciotti* were useful for small matters: appropriating a neighbour's field for the boss's cows, resisting rent demands from fussing landlords or extracting protection money from the neighbourhood *trattoria*. Highway robbery, smuggling, kidnapping and loan-sharking were lucrative earners for more enterprising *picciotti.* Bosses also took on additional duties like adjudicating property disputes or defending women's honour.

But as the *picciotti* endured successive crackdowns by the authorities, some wondered how they might turn the tables on the state. If the source of the wider world's power came from money, they reasoned, then maybe the way to attack that outside world was to venture out into it, steal its money and take its power?

The Calabrian mafia was soon using its money to buy favours from the *carabinieri* and the judiciary. After that came bribes to political parties, mayors' offices, the state bureaucracy and the Italian parliament. In time, the families were also able to infiltrate these institutions with their own men. The insiders then defrauded and embezzled, diverting public funds to mafia-owned contracting businesses such as construction firms, refuse collectors and dockers. Elections were rigged and more allegiances bought. Those who could not be corrupted or intimidated were beaten, firebombed or killed.

All this felt familiar to a Sicilian like Alessandra. But the Calabrians outdid their peers in two respects. Where the Sicilians recruited from a particular area, the Calabrians relied on family: almost without exception, *picciotti* were either born into an *'ndrina* or married into it. And while the Sicilians certainly spun stories about themselves, the Calabrians dreamed up legends that wove together honour, religion, family and southern Italian separatism into an elaborate and almost impenetrable veil of misdirection.

By the early twentieth century, 'Ndranghetisti were tracing their origins to three medieval knights-errant. These figures crop up in mafia creation myths from Asia to Africa to Europe.[3] In the 'Ndrangheta version, the knights were Spanish brothers – Osso, Mastrosso and Carcagnosso – who had fled their homeland after avenging their sister's rape. Landing on the tiny island of Favignana off Sicily's west coast and taking shelter in damp and cold sea caverns, the trio nursed a sense of righteous grievance and steadfast family loyalty for twenty-nine long and uncomfortably damp years.

Eventually their discussions became the basis for a brotherhood founded on mutual defence. With the Honoured Society sworn to protect all members, and they it, no outsider would ever think of shaming the brothers and their families again. And when the brothers felt ready to take their creation to the world, Mastrosso travelled to Naples to set up the Camorra in the name of the Madonna, Osso sailed to Sicily and founded Cosa Nostra in the name of Saint George and Carcagnosso took a land between his two brothers – Calabria – where he established the 'Ndrangheta in the name of Saint Michael, the Archangel.

The story is, of course, bunkum. The Calabrian mafia is not hundreds of years old but barely a hundred and fifty. The story of the three knights also seems copied from that of the Garduña, a mythical fifteenth-century Spanish criminal society whose founding legend would have been familiar to 'Ndranghetisti from the time when Spain ruled Calabria. The irony is that most historians have concluded the Garduña was itself a fabrication.[4] This, then, was *mafiosi* trying to fool others with a piece of gangster fiction which had, in fact, fooled them.

This was far from the only example of mafia make-believe, however. The 'Ndrangheta's ancient-sounding name did not derive from a venerable heritage but, as Dickie uncovered, was a modern artifice that first surfaced in police reports in the 1920s and in newspaper stories in the 1950s.[5] Alessandra found more recent mafia fictions in the form of internet videos ripping off scenes from American gangster movies like *The Godfather* and *Goodfellas* and set to Calabrian folk songs. The lyrics to these melodies were hardly poetry but no less chilling for that:

Keep the honour of the family.
Avenge my father.
I have to get good with guns and knives
Because I can't stop thinking about it.

The pain in my heart –
It can only be stopped if I avenge my father.

Then there were the 'ancient' rituals. For a boss's son, Alessandra read, these could begin soon after birth. A new-born boy would be laid kicking and screaming on a bed, a key next to his left hand and a knife by his right, denoting the state and the mafia. An 'Ndrangheta mother's first duty was to ensure, with a few careful nudges, that her boy grasped the knife and sealed his destiny. In *Tired of Killing: The Autobiography of a Repentant 'Ndranghetista*, Alessandra read about the early life of Antonio Zagari, the son of an 'Ndrangheta boss who turned super-grass in 1990.[6] In his book, Zagari described a probation of two years, during which a teenage *picciotto* was expected to prove his worth by committing crimes and even killing, as well as learning by heart the fable of Osso, Mastrosso and Carcagnosso and a set of rules and social prescriptions. After that came a formal initiation ceremony. The ritual began when Zagari was led into a darkened room in which a group of 'Ndranghetisti were standing in a circle. At first, Zagari was excluded. The boss addressed the 'Ndranghetisti, asking if they were 'comfortable'.

'Very comfortable,' they replied. 'With what?'

'With the rules,' said the boss.

'Very comfortable,' came the reply once more.

The boss then 'baptised' the meeting in the name of the Honoured Society 'as our ancestors Osso, Mastrosso and Carcagnosso baptised it … with irons and chains'. He ceremoniously confiscated any weapons. The congregation confirmed their loyalty to the society on pain of 'five or six dagger thrusts to the chest'. The boss then likened their common endeavour to 'a ball that goes wandering around the world as cold as ice, as hot as fire and as fine as silk'. After the members of the circle affirmed three times that they were ready to accept a new member, they opened their ranks to admit the newcomer. The boss then cut a cross on Zagari's finger so that it bled over a burning image of Saint Michael while he intoned: 'As the fire burns this image, so shall you burn if you stain yourself with infamy.'

That was the cue for Zagari to take his oath: 'I swear before the organised and faithful society, represented by our honoured and wise boss and by all the members, to carry out all the duties for which I am responsible and all those which are imposed on me – if necessary even with my blood.'

Finally, the boss kissed Zagari on both cheeks, recited the rules of the society and delivered a homily to humility, the island of Favignana and blood – which, in case anyone was lost, was the essence of the icy, fiery, silky and world-wandering ball he had mentioned earlier.

It was a wonder anyone kept a straight face, thought Alessandra. Certainly, the cod-medievalism of the 'Ndrangheta's performances made serious historians choke. Dickie likened the 'solemn ravings' of its initiation ritual to a scout ceremony that crossed *The Lord of the Flies* with *Monty Python*. One of Italy's most eminent mafia historians, Enzo Ciconte, was just as dismissive of the 'Ndrangheta's 'Red Riding Hood fantasies'.[7] But Ciconte cautioned that ridiculous did not mean meaningless. 'No group of people can last long just by using violence, just by killing, stealing and rustling – they need some sort of faith or ideology,' he said. 'The 'Ndrangheta had no tradition. They had to invent one.'

It was a good point, thought Alessandra. What mattered with faith was not plausibility but belief. Most of the main religions clung to unlikely myths and holy stories, which they called miracles or acts of God. Few of them were ever hurt by others laughing at them – quite the opposite. More to the point, a lie was just that: a fib, a fiction, a deceit. No one was claiming the 'Ndrangheta's bosses believed it. After all, they were the ones telling it.

A better question was why the 'Ndrangheta chiefs found such decorous fantasies expedient. The answer was to be found in their spectacular rise. However contrived and derivative the cult of the 'Ndrangheta might appear to academic examination, it had gained the organisation the loyalty and secrecy of its members, the fear and respect of ordinary Calabrians and, as a result, a thick cloak of opacity under which it hid from the world. The 'Ndrangheta's stories might have appealed to Calabrians because of their own distrust of the state or their sense of theatre, or simply because they were handed down from father to son with the solemn conviction of a sacred truth. The point was they worked. Myth was how the 'Ndrangheta assumed a moral purpose when it was self-evidently immoral, how it coloured itself romantic and divine when it was base and profane and how it convinced others it was their righteous champion even as it robbed and murdered them. Myth was how those inside the organisation were persuaded they were following a higher code and those outside it found themselves stumped by even the simplest questions, such as who was who. It was all an enormous lie. But it was a lie that explained how, almost without anyone noticing, a small group of families from the wild hills of Italy's south had become the twenty-first century's most formidable mafia.

Alessandra became fascinated by the intricacies of the deception. The 'Ndrangheta was an extraordinary puzzle, a multi-level mosaic. From transcripts of tapped phone calls and bugged conversations, she discovered 'Ndranghetisti had their own language, *baccagghju*, a slang based on Grecanico whose meaning was obscure to almost everyone but initiates. Even when they spoke Italian, 'Ndranghetisti used a code of metaphors to disguise their meaning. An 'Ndrangheta family in criminal partnership with another would describe itself as 'walking with' that other family. Rather than demand protection money outright, 'Ndranghetisti would request a 'donation for the cousins', an allusion to those men in jail whose families needed support. For a boss to describe a man as 'disturbing' or 'troubling' was for him to pass an oblique but unequivocal death sentence on him. The euphemisms could be highly contorted. *Pizzo*, the word for an extortion payment, was a term whose origin was the 'piece' of ground on which a nineteenth-century prisoner had slept in jail, which were ranked according to their proximity to the boss. Outside jail in the twentieth century, it had come to denote the tribute that a boss expected from real estate inside his territory.

Deciphering the true meaning of 'Ndrangheta speak was a constant struggle. 'You have to become more perceptive, more capable of decrypting,' Alessandra would tell Paolo over dinner in their apartment. '*Mafiosi* very rarely make a direct threat. Instead, they send messages with a dual meaning.' Even the smallest gesture could carry the utmost importance. 'They can order a murder just by looking at someone from the prisoner cage in court,' she said.

One of the 'Ndrangheta's most audacious lies was its relationship with the church. The 'Ndrangheta was plainly an unChristian organisation. But since it came from the most Roman Catholic of lands, it simply insisted the opposite was true. It invoked the saints, especially the Madonna and Saint Michael, the Archangel. It mimicked prayer and church services in its rituals. And it co-opted and bred priests. At mass, some priests in 'Ndrangheta areas would exhort their congregants to resist outsiders. On saints' days, they directed celebrants to bow to statues of the Madonna before the *capo*'s house while at Easter, the honour of bearing statues of Jesus, Saint John and the Virgin was reserved for *picciotti*. The most stunning example of the 'Ndrangheta subverting Christianity happened on 2 September every year when crowds of thousands gathered at the small town of San Luca in the Aspromonte mountains for the festival of the Madonna di Polsi. Among the pilgrims were hundreds of 'Ndranghetisti, including the heads of all the clans, who since at least 1901 had used the event as a cover for the 'Ndrangheta's AGM, the *gran crimine*. In plain sight, the bosses would sit at a table laden with pasta and goat sauce, present their annual accounts – what they had earned, who they had killed – and elect a new *capo crimine* for the coming year. 'The church is very responsible in all of this,' Alessandra would tell Paolo. 'It's guilty of some terrible, terrible, *terrible* things.'

Though the organisation found Christianity useful, Alessandra concluded that at its core the 'Ndrangheta was more of a blood cult. Blood was the bond between families that was the 'Ndrangheta's strength. The act of spilling blood was also revered as a source of fearsome power. That had led to some unforgiving 'Ndrangheta feuds. The Duisberg massacre of 2007 – which police identified as an attack on an 'Ndrangheta initiation celebration when a burned picture of Saint Michael was found in the pocket of the dead eighteen-year-old – was the latest atrocity in a quarrel between two clans from San Luca. The feud had begun in 1991 when a group of boys from one family threw rotten eggs at the window of a bar owned by another. Including Duisberg, nine people had since died. Many more had been injured. To avoid being shot, 'Ndranghetisti in San Luca would hide themselves in the boot of a car just to travel 100 yards. Killings were timed for maximum horror. The year before Duisberg, a boss from one clan was paralysed by a bullet that passed through his spine as he stood on a balcony cradling his new-born son. In revenge, a rival boss's wife was shot dead in her family home on Christmas Day.

Why the ruthlessness? For the 'Ndrangheta, the answer was easy: to instil fear and reap power. For individual 'Ndranghetisti, the question was more vexed. Why be an 'Ndranghetista if your fate was to spend lengthy stretches in prison, inflict unspeakable violence on your neighbours and, in all probability, die young? Alessandra decided it came back to the lie. The 'Ndrangheta had used its fantasies about honour, sacrifice, loyalty and courage to build a prison around its young men, trapping them in a claustrophobic sect based on blood and butchery. Pride in the 'Ndrangheta's rural heritage even encouraged some 'Ndranghetisti to imbue their violence with a rustic aesthetic. Pigs often featured. A family targeted for intimidation might discover the throats of all its male pigs had been slit. On one occasion, the *carabinieri* recorded an 'Ndranghetista boasting how he beat another man unconscious, then fed his living body to his own pigs. The bloodthirstiness could also be literal. More than once, men loyal to an assassinated boss were observed to rush to the scene of the killing, dip their handkerchiefs in the departed *capo*'s blood and press the dripping cloth to their lips.

Alessandra realised that the 'Ndrangheta's phoney cult of blood, family and tradition also accounted for its oppression of its women. That misogynist tyranny was real enough. Driving through small town Calabria, Alessandra rarely saw women out of doors and almost never unaccompanied. Nevertheless, it was with a sinking sense of inevitability that she read that the 'Ndrangheta's conservative values were yet another affectation.

As long ago as 1892, the 'Ndrangheta had admitted two women highwaymen into its ranks. John Dickie found court records from the 1930s showing that the *picciotti* once had a pronounced personal and professional attachment to prostitution as both pimps and johns. But it seemed that the 'Ndrangheta later dispensed with prostitution because, though the trade was lucrative, it was built on qualities like infidelity, loose discipline and double standards which were inimical to order and control. The closed, buttoned-up, isolated family culture of traditional Calabria, on the other hand, was perfect for organised crime. Family ties were also how the 'Ndrangheta fashioned a global criminal octopus out of the pattern of Calabrian emigration to the US, Canada, Australia, South Africa and Latin America in the 1920s.

The more she read, the more Alessandra realised that the 'Ndrangheta's true genius had been in co-opting the Italian family. The more the 'Ndrangheta made itself indistinguishable from traditional, family-based Calabrian culture, the more anyone thinking of leaving the organisation had to consider that they would be abandoning all they knew and all they were. For most, it would be impossible to see beyond it.

But by basing itself around family, the 'Ndrangheta hadn't merely been bolstering secrecy and loyalty. It had understood that family itself was a kind of corruption. The undeniable love of a mother for a son or a daughter for a father – these were the sorts of bonds that ensured even the most law-abiding broke the law. Fathers would advantage their families however they could. Children would never betray their parents. Mothers, above all, would do anything to protect their children and wreak terrible revenge on those that harmed them. The 'Ndrangheta was the family augmented and accentuated into a perfect criminal entity. It was, of course, a diabolical transformation. The use of children was plainly child abuse, while to pervert the family in a country like Italy was to poison the soul of a nation. But it was also a masterstroke. If family was corruption, and family was the essence of Italy, then family was how the 'Ndrangheta could subvert and even own Italy.

For such a family endeavour to work, Alessandra was convinced women had to have a role. And from her reading of case files and investigations, she soon discovered they had several. Women acted as messengers between men on the run or in jail, passing along tiny, folded notes – *pizzini* – addressed by the use of a code of numbers. If a man was killed or inaccessible in jail, his widow could become his de facto replacement and continue the family business. Some women acted as paymasters and bookkeepers.

Most significantly, women ensured the future of the 'Ndrangheta by producing the next generation of 'Ndrànghetisti, raising children with an unbending belief in the code of honour, *vendetta* and *omertà*, and a violent loathing of outsiders who, the mothers whispered, were weak and without shame with their loose talk and looser women. 'Without women performing this role, there would be no 'Ndrangheta,' said Alessandra. Secrecy and power were the goals. Male misogyny and female subservience, forced or even willing, were the means.

What confirmed women's influence inside the 'Ndrangheta was that, though they were often the victims of its violence, they also instigated some of it. Studying transcripts of phone taps, Alessandra was astonished to discover one mother from the Bellocco clan who outdid all the men for bloodthirstiness. The *carabinieri* had managed to bug a family meeting convened to discuss how best to avenge the death of one of their men, killed in a clan feud. The men proposed killing their rivals' boss or even a number of their men. Then the mother of the dead man spoke up. 'Kill them all,' she said. 'Even the women. Even the kids.' The woman wanted an entire family of thirty wiped from the face of the earth.

There was no way any of it worked without the mothers, thought Alessandra. And to a resourceful and open-minded prosecutor, that held out an enticing possibility. In the twenty-first century, there had to be other Lea Garofalos out there, mafia mothers who were unhappy with their lives and the destiny of their children. The mother, the madonna, was a holy figure in Italy and the 'Ndrangheta had corrupted her and bent her to its criminal will. There had to be women inside the organisation who hated the way they were being used. It had to be possible for Alessandra to offer these knowledgeable figures a different life and persuade them to betray their husbands and fathers. And imagine if she could. 'It would break the chain,' she told her fellow prosecutors. 'It would remove the guardians of the 'Ndrangheta's traditions. If they took their sons too, then they would be removing future soldiers. It would be very special, very important. It would impoverish the entire mafia family. It would undermine the whole culture and the mindset.'

Alessandra was refining her theory. The way to destroy The Family, she was beginning to realise, was through its *mamas*.

VI

In January 2010, Pignatone and Prestipino finally gave Alessandra the job she wanted.[1] From the New Year, she would be lead anti-mafia prosecutor for Calabria's west coast, taking in the villages on the Gioia Tauro *piano*, the town of Rosarno and the port of Gioia Tauro. She would report directly to Pignatone and Prestipino. She would also have a second prosecutor as her junior, Giovanni Musarò, a thirty-seven-year-old on his first big posting.

Like Alessandra, Musarò was attracted by Pignatone's and Prestipino's dynamism. 'I was very young, they had this huge experience from Palermo and they brought with them a completely different way of working,' he said. Borrowing from Falcone and Borsellino, the old model of prosecutors as 'lonely heroes' was out, said Giovanni. The new watchword was collaboration. 'They put a great effort into creating a team, sharing information with colleagues and behaving like a democracy,' he said. Each member brought different strengths. 'Alessandra was driven by ethics and very determined. Pignatone had a great ability to predict events. Prestipino was very clever and very pragmatic. He knew all his investigations and all his investigators. He was able to go to each of us and say: "Maybe go to Alessandra and you'll find this. Or maybe go here and ask this investigator, and they'll help you with this."'

For Alessandra, the prize was her new territory. Palmi, on the southern end of the Gioia Tauro estuary, was where the 'Ndrangheta was born. A century and a half later, the *piano* remained the heart of the empire. Though you wouldn't know it to look at the place, thought Alessandra. The 'Ndrangheta was richer than most global corporations and in Rosarno even the most minor 'Ndrangheta family was thought to have three, four or five million euros stashed away. Yet somehow in a country of amber cornfields, olive hills and blue mountains sprinkled with red-roofed villages and magnificent Roman and Renaissance cities, the 'Ndrangheta had contrived to make their towns into verrucae of unkempt, concrete ugliness. Touring Rosarno for the first time, Alessandra felt like she'd arrived after an apocalypse. Everything looked scorched. The trees were blackened and their leaves orange and brittle. The single park was just chalky pebbles and dry spiky weeds. The streets, whose asphalt resembled spilled lava, were strewn with refuse. Everything was covered with crude graffiti. And the town was dead. Shops were shut or deserted. Many of the breeze-block houses were unfinished and empty, their gardens building sites and their glassless windows as vacant as the eyes of a skull. In the main piazza, no one sat on the benches, no one ate in the restaurants. To one side, a children's playground consisted of a rusted swing, a broken slide and a shattered piece of concrete littered with wrappers, cigarette butts and broken glass. Alessandra could feel it. The fear. The *omertà*. It reminded her of the Messina of her childhood.

Unpicking the paradox of how this desperate place could be home to such a rich criminal empire was key to the story of the 'Ndrangheta's modern rise. It began at 3 a.m. on 10 July 1973, when a small gang of 'Ndrangheta toughs from the villages around Gioia Tauro kidnapped John Paul Getty III, the sixteen-year-old grandson of the billionaire John Paul Getty, from outside his home in Piazza Farnese in central Rome. The gang held the boy in the Calabrian mountains for five months. His father, who had been in a heroin-induced haze at the time his son was taken, initially thought the kidnapping was a hoax staged by his son to obtain money. The kidnappers called the family patriarch, John Paul Getty Snr, and threatened to cut off his grandson's fingers unless they received a ransom of $17 million. The elder Getty refused, arguing: 'If I pay one penny now, I'll have fourteen kidnapped grandchildren.' To press their case, the gang cut off John Paul III's left ear and sent it to a newspaper in Rome. It was accompanied by a note threatening that the second ear would be arriving in ten days unless the ransom was paid. Getty Snr relented and paid $2.2 million, the maximum his accountants advised him was tax-efficient. He loaned the final ransom balance of $700,000 to his son, the boy's father, at 4 per cent interest.

John Paul Getty III never recovered from his abduction or his grandfather's indifference. He died at fifty-four, an alcoholic and drug addict in a wheelchair, having been crippled at the age of twenty-five by a near-lethal combination of Valium, methadone and cocktails. But for the west coast 'Ndrangheta, these grubby beginnings were the seeds of an empire. They went on to stage 150 more kidnappings. In Gioia Tauro, they used the ransom money to buy construction trucks. 'Ndrangheta men inside local government ensured these trucks were contracted for the building of a steel plant near Gioia Tauro port. When the government abandoned that project as uneconomic, the trucks went to work on a bigger site: the expansion of the port itself.

State construction contracts – building motorways, high-speed rail links, and even wind and solar farms, while loan-sharking at extortionate rates to force rivals out of business – went on to become a giant, profitable 'Ndrangheta business in its own right. By the time Alessandra was posted to the west coast, a project to widen and repair the arterial highway running from western Calabria up Italy's coast to Salerno had somehow ended up costing the state $10 billion in three decades for what was still little more than a succession of roadworks.[2] The biggest earner, however, was Gioia Tauro port itself. Once its expansion was finished, the port was the largest container facility in Italy and the sixth largest on the Mediterranean, with a capacity to load and unload millions of containers a year on a quay that ran for three and a half kilometres and was backed by an avenue of towering cranes. The 'Ndrangheta, as the only power in the area, had total control. The group 'taxed' every container passing through the port at $1.50 a time. It charged the port operators fees amounting to half their profits, an annual income that ran into several billion dollars. It used the port to send weapons around the world. And in the 1980s and 1990s, during *la mattanza*, it was through Gioia Tauro that the 'Ndrangheta built its cocaine empire.

But aside from a single street of new houses in San Luca nicknamed Via John Paul Getty, there was no sign of the 'Ndrangheta's wealth. To the 'Ndrangheta, a façade of poverty was crucial to the lie. It helped it escape the attention of the state and added credibility to its claim to be championing a deprived south against an oppressive north. The 'Ndrangheta went to mulish lengths to service its pretence. When Alessandra first visited Rosarno, Domenico Oppedisano, a seventy-eight-year-old 'Ndrangheta big shot, could still be seen in his battered trilby and dusty suit, driving around in a three-wheeled van and delivering his oranges and lemons to market.

For the 97 per cent of Gioia Tauro's population who were not 'Ndrangheta, however, the deprivation was real. Calabria was the poorest province in Italy. Incomes were around half those in the north, unemployment ran at 28 per cent and even in 2009 roasted dormice were considered a delicacy. The provincial government, meanwhile, was so dysfunctional that in 2008 a US embassy fact-finding mission concluded that, were it an independent state, Calabria would be a failed one.

Driving around the estuary delta between Rosarno and the port, Alessandra found it easy to guess who had ruined it. The area was latticed by a series of two-lane highways connected by a spaghetti of looping off-ramps and roundabouts, a modern industrial grid built with tens of millions of euros donated by the European Union and the Italian government. Economists and bureaucrats in Brussels, it seemed, had imagined a new warehousing zone to support the port that would single-handedly reverse the economic fortunes of one of Europe's poorest areas. Initially, 'Ndrangheta construction companies had been happy to take what public money was on offer. Then the 'Ndrangheta squashed the project. Threats, violence and demands for crippling protection payments had ensured all but one of the international transport and logistics businesses proposed for the site had either closed or never opened. Weeds and thickets of bamboo edged far out into the road. Tarmac roads and concrete bays cracked and splintered in the sun. Giant bougainvilleas surfed out over the walls of empty business parks. Once-luxuriant palms were grotesquely overgrown, their green starbursts turned sickly yellow by a layer of sticky dust. Street lights were ubiquitous but lifeless, connected to a field of large black solar panels fast disappearing under long grass. Rusted signs, some peppered with shotgun blasts, pointed the way to now-defunct enterprises whose gates were decorated with sun-bleached strings of international flags. In front of one grand entrance, a giant brass globe on a spike stood at a crazy angle, a dream of world domination turning, continent by continent, into a small pile of rusted metal on the ground. The only sign of life was a herd of goats grazing in drainage ditches choked with poppies, buttercups and pink and purple flowers and, to one side, a tented camp of several thousand African migrants, whom the authorities, or possibly the 'Ndrangheta, had peevishly kept off site.

The place felt like a war zone. And in a way it was. Covering the entire summit of a hill high above the port was a complex of sprawling villas and gardens once owned by the Piromalli clan, in whose territory the port lay. From here, the Piromallis had surveyed their empire like generals. The state had eventually confiscated the property but, since no one was willing to buy it, the houses and gardens were empty, an obstinate and unmissable reminder of where real power lay. Below the villa walls was a chapel and graveyard filled with baroque 'Ndranghetisti graves. Since it had been built without permits, the local authority had ordered the chapel demolished, only to discover that no local contractor was available to do the work.

In all of Gioia Tauro, a few lone entrepreneurs had taken a stand. One was Antonino de Masi, who in the 1990s decided to diversify the family agricultural machinery conglomerate into transport logistics. The business had foundered under 'Ndrangheta pressure and de Masi now pursued other ventures, such as marketing earthquake shelters and smokeless pizza ovens, both of which he had invented himself. But he refused to leave his offices. That simple act of defiance had cost him dearly. After receiving numerous death threats, de Masi had sent his family to live in northern Italy. De Masi himself was obliged to move around in an armoured car, flanked by two bodyguards. Two uniformed Italian army soldiers with automatic rifles and a camouflage jeep stood guard in his office car park. De Masi described himself as 'living in enemy territory'.[3]

Why would the 'Ndrangheta ruin its own homeland? Because de Masi was right. As a wealthy businessman with the means to pursue his ambition and the courage not to ask the 'Ndrangheta's permission, he was its sworn foe. It wasn't that the 'Ndrangheta hated development. It was that it tolerated no power other than itself. Inside its territory, there could be no intrusion by the outside world and no escape from the world the 'Ndrangheta had created. Education, especially the kind that encouraged free thinking, was discouraged. The sort of exit offered by gainful employment with a figure like Antonino de Masi also had to be crushed. The 'Ndrangheta even restricted physical ways out of the place. There was just one bus a day to Reggio Calabria. Roads built by 'Ndrangheta construction firms didn't connect to provincial highways, or to each other. Bridges over highways and rivers joined nothing to nowhere. The railway that connected Gioia Tauro to Europe stopped 1.5 kilometres short of the port, meaning all the cargo from one of Europe's biggest Mediterranean container ports had to be loaded onto mafia-owned trucks and driven three minutes to the station. This was the suffocating magnificence of the 'Ndrangheta. The point wasn't money. The point was power.

By 2010, the Calabrian anti-mafia prosecutors were finally piecing together quite how much influence the 'Ndrangheta had accumulated. Even veterans of *la mattanza* like Pignatone and Prestipino were astonished. Where once the 'Ndrangheta had been outmatched by Cosa Nostra in drug smuggling, it now dominated the entire European trade in illicit narcotics. Cocaine was produced and refined in Colombia, Peru or Bolivia, transported east, generally to Brazil or Venezuela, and from there across the Atlantic to Europe via the Caribbean or West Africa, before being landed in Holland, Denmark, Spain or Italy. Though other criminal groups were involved at each stage of its journey as producers and traffickers, the 'Ndrangheta had assumed a position of broker, overseer and employer across the entire supply chain.

Inventiveness was a consistent characteristic of this empire, especially in trafficking methods. For sea routes through the Caribbean, the 'Ndrangheta or their partners would conceal cocaine under trawlers full of frozen fish or inside tins of pineapple, or by sewing it into bananas or even dissolving it in bottles of whisky. Another trick was to secrete a load together with duplicate security tags inside a shipping container carrying other cargo. The drug could then be removed after crossing the Atlantic, generally in customs storage or at a refuelling stop, and the containers resealed with the copied tags and sent on their way without detection. To further confuse customs agents, two ships might rendezvous in the middle of the ocean and make a further swap between containers.

Aircraft offered further options. On commercial flights – across the Atlantic to West Africa, and from West Africa to Europe – the smugglers used passengers who would swallow up to thirty plastic bags, amounting to a total load of a kilo each. They would then pack as many as forty 'swallowers' onto a plane, sometimes using an entire class of African exchange students who could pay for several years at a foreign university with one trip. Plane crews, who generally sailed through customs without checks, were another good option. Mostly the traffickers would enlist individual stewards but on occasion they recruited entire crews, including the pilots. When private planes were available, freelance pilots flew small props fitted with custom-enlarged fuel tanks at low altitude thousands of miles across the Atlantic from Latin America to touch down in West Africa. A few times, the smugglers had used an ageing Boeing 727, which could take ten tons of cocaine at a time and which in 2009 had been found by the authorities in Mali in the middle of the Sahara, abandoned and torched by the traffickers after snapping its wheels on landing. The onward land route through the Sahara to the Mediterranean was perhaps the most dramatic drug lane of all, involving convoys of twenty to thirty 4×4s driving north for four or five days right across the desert, navigating by the stars and refuelling at a string of camouflaged outposts.[4]

Once the drugs reached the Mediterranean, they might be taken from Tunisia to Europe on cruise ships or driven anti-clockwise around the coast, across Libya and Egypt and on through Israel and Turkey, a journey facilitated by border guards and army officers. To move cocaine across Europe required a high degree of subterfuge. Tons of cocaine were trucked from Gioia Tauro to Holland hidden under flowers destined for Europe's biggest flower market, where florists served a second purpose as 'Ndrangheta money launderers. Payment going the other way was also disguised. Billions of euros in credit might be uploaded to hundreds of online betting accounts. One time, €7.5 million was sent in the form of 260 tons of Lindt chocolates.[5]

The prosecutors knew which 'ndrine were so trusted by the Colombians that they were allowed cocaine on credit. They knew which families had diversified into dealing arms. They'd investigated who used smuggling ships on their return journey to dump hazardous chemicals and nuclear waste by sinking boats off the coast of Somalia.

Along the smuggling routes, the investigators knew which customs services, armies, rebels, Islamists, officials, ministers, prime ministers and presidents took a cut of the profits. Mozambique's customs, the mid-point on an otherwise little travelled, entirely Portuguese-speaking route from Brazil to Portugal via Africa, had been bought almost whole. So had the entire government of Guinea-Bissau, a tiny West African state and another former Portuguese colony, where soldiers would clear traffic from public highways to allow narco-planes to land.

What gave the prosecutors most pause was how, as the rewards of power had multiplied, so had the struggle for it. As 2010 dawned, West Africa was in the midst of an unprecedented wave of coups, civil wars, revolutions and assassinations driven by the struggle to get rich from drug smuggling. Surveying the chaos created by cocaine, the prosecutors realised the 'Ndrangheta hadn't just ruined Calabria and undermined the Italian state but had done the same to large parts of the planet. This lent new urgency to their mission. This wasn't the old story about how drugs messed you up. This was about how the 'Ndrangheta's drugs had messed up the lives of hundreds of millions of people in countries on the other side of the world, places which few Europeans had even heard of.

Nor was even that the most worrying part. By 2010, Calabria's anti-mafia prosecutors were picking up indications that the 'Ndrangheta's money-laundering operations were undermining the world's financial markets and even the sovereignty of nations. Giuseppe Lombardo, a prosecutor who specialised in tracking its money, said that alongside the 'Ndrangheta's growth had come increased financial sophistication. Faced with a need to launder ever-increasing amounts of money and observing how the world's stock markets were increasingly lightly regulated, a few 'Ndrangheta families had made a first few forays into the world of international finance in the mid-1980s. A generation later, what had begun as an experiment in diversification and legitimisation was now a giant multinational asset management business run by 'Ndrangheta lawyers, accountants and bankers in Milan, London and New York through a maze of offshore financial centres that specialised in secrecy and low tax: Cyprus, Malta, Gibraltar, Mauritius, Switzerland, Luxembourg, Holland, the British Virgin Islands and other British dependencies. The global recession of 2007–9 had been a particular boon. As legitimate finance dried up, businesses, banks, stock markets and even political parties found themselves suddenly short of money. For the 'Ndrangheta, this credit crunch had proved to be a once-in-a-lifetime chance to convert criminal power into legal economic and political might around the world.

The 'Ndrangheta was driven by two motivations. It needed to safely launder its riches. And it wanted to become so indispensable to the international economy that tackling it would be an act of self-harm for any government. According to Lombardo, the 'Ndrangheta had largely succeeded in both endeavours. 'They have become one of the main interlocutors in the criminal field,' he said. 'But much more broadly, they have become a world power.'

Initially, said Lombardo, the 'Ndrangheta had bought politicians who offered state protection, and created a network of accountants, lawyers, traders and other facilitators inside the banking system which allowed the 'Ndrangheta to clean and invest its money. But in a crucial second stage, the 'Ndrangheta had opened its financial structure to organised crime groups around the world: Cosa Nostra and the Camorra, but also Chinese triads, Nigerians, Russians, Colombians, Mexicans and criminal groups from every part of the planet. 'The 'Ndrangheta plays the role of service agent to the other mafias,' said Lombardo. 'They make this network of financial professionals working for them available to other mafias. And after that, when it comes to finances, all the mafias move together as one big mafia.'

That meant the 'Ndrangheta had trillions of euros at its command. Such a tsunami of money had elevated it to a 'fundamental and indispensable position in the global market', said Lombardo, one that was 'more or less essential for the smooth functioning of the global economic system'. This new centrality afforded the 'Ndrangheta the level of protection it sought. It also offered it an opportunity to indulge in typical mafia behaviour – bullying, intimidating, extorting and blackmailing – on a whole new scale. Lombardo had indications that the 'Ndrangheta regularly manipulated stock prices or markets to its advantage and had even caused mini financial crashes to create buying opportunities for itself.

Most remarkable was what the prosecutor had discovered about the mafia's taste for government debt. 'I found a huge amount of capital deployed by the mafia to buy government bonds and Treasury debt,' he said. At first, this revelation confused Lombardo. There was no sound financial imperative to buy bonds: yields were typically low and far better opportunities were available in other financial instruments. But then he realised the 'Ndrangheta's motivations were more than merely financial. 'They don't need to become any richer,' he said. 'They're rich enough. But alongside the goal of making money is the goal of limiting national sovereignty.' The 'Ndrangheta had always sought to undermine Italian state power and authority. Now it was doing the same across the world. It did this by buying up large tranches of foreign countries' debt, then threatening those countries with dumping their debt and prompting a financial default. A debtor nation's only option was to allow the 'Ndrangheta to use its territory as a base and a money-laundering location. So far, the prosecutors had collected evidence that the 'Ndrangheta had blackmailed Thailand and Indonesia in this way. Lombardo expected China and India to be next. 'This is about conditioning the global economic system, conditioning the global citizenry and conditioning the political choices of nations,' he said. 'This is how the 'Ndrangheta become the rulers not just of territory in Italy but whole other countries.'

Lombardo's investigations revealed the 'Ndrangheta not merely as a menace to southern Italy but a global monster. Though other mafias were better known, the 'Ndrangheta was the most powerful. In the name of profit and power, it was sowing the seeds of war, chaos and corruption from Rio to Rotterdam to Reykjavík. It was the dark underside of globalisation made real in flesh and blood. Of paramount importance to Italy's anti-mafia prosecutors, however, Calabria remained the key to the entire enterprise. Any big business decision – to expand territory, to enter a new business, to eliminate a rival – was referred back to the old country. In their bunkers buried beneath Reggio Calabria and Rosarno and the orange groves of Gioia Tauro plain, the bosses were deciding the fate of nations. As she read through the latest case files, it dawned on Alessandra that with their new crackdown on the 'Ndrangheta, the prosecutors held the destiny of hundreds of millions of people, pehaps even billions, in their hands.

The stimuli to the Italian state's new campaign against the mafia were various: the outcry at the Duisberg massacre of 2007, the 2008 election of a new government publicly committed to ending the threat from organised crime and, the same year, the arrival in Calabria of Giuseppe Pignatone and Michele Prestipino, the destroyers of Cosa Nostra. The fight against the mafia was quickly reinvigorated with fresh energy and resources. Over 2008 and 2009 the *carabinieri* bugged millions of conversations. 'Ndranghetisti still habitually spoke in riddles and metaphors, and in isolation the meaning of any one conversation was obscure. But taken together and over time, the mass of recordings added up to a true revelation: the authorities' first ever complete picture of the internal structure and dynamics of the 'Ndrangheta.

There were several surprises. Hitherto, the prosecutors had understood the 'Ndrangheta as a loose alliance of family firms, each with its own territory. Surveillance of Reggio Calabria and the surrounding towns and villages revealed that the horizontal structure of hundreds of *'ndrine*, each run autonomously by a family boss, was still the 'Ndrangheta's foundation. But it emerged that above it was a new vertical, unifying hierarchy of eleven ranks. Several *'ndrine* together made a grouping called a *locale* or *società*, managed by a paramount chief, assisted by an accountant and a 'head of crime' who oversaw all illegal activities. Above the *locali* were three regional authorities called *mandamenti*, one each for the Tyrrhenian and Ionian coasts and another for Reggio Calabria. Together these three groups made up a council variously called *la provincial* or *il crimine* or – something that made Alessandra do a double-take – *La Mama*. Overseeing all of it was a *capo crimine*, or boss of bosses, who could convene a court, or *tribunale*, of senior bosses to judge a peer accused of transgressing the code.[6] 'We'd always thought of the 'Ndrangheta as a lot of local, smaller organisations,' said Alessandra. 'Suddenly we realised it had a federal structure and was being run almost like a military organisation.'

In the 1990s, *carabinieri* had picked up word of an attempt by the 'Ndrangheta to unite the clans. That had ultimately failed. From what the *carabinieri* were hearing now, this time the reorganisation had succeeded. Why? The old arguments in favour of better coordination to improve efficiency and discipline still stood. But in 2009 the *carabinieri* were detecting a more ominous motivation: to coordinate a concerted assault on the authorities through a series of assassinations and bombings. On 31 October 2009, the *carabinieri* filmed an especially brazen 'Ndrangheta summit outside Milan at which twenty-two bosses raised their glasses to toast the new city boss inside a memorial dedicated to Giovanni Falcone and Paolo Borsellino.[7] The 'Ndrangheta was abandoning its decades-old policy of discreet infiltration in favour of direct confrontation. Why the change? From what the *carabinieri* could gather, the 'Ndrangheta felt their hand was being forced. The new push against organised crime had resulted in the arrests of hundreds of *mafiosi*, including twenty-one of Italy's thirty 'most wanted', and the confiscation of assets and businesses worth nine billion euros.[8] Though the operations had hurt the Camorra most of all, the 'Ndrangheta knew it was next. Its bosses had decided on an aggressive and unified response.

For Alessandra, one episode captured by the new intelligence was especially significant. Officers watching a mafia wedding in the hill town of Plati on 19 August 2009 between two powerful clans, the Pelles and the Barbaros, were amazed to spot a who's who of the 'Ndrangheta among the two thousand guests. These included bosses not only from across Calabria, but also from northern Italy, Europe and as far away as Canada and Australia. 'They came from all over the planet to this tiny little town in the middle of nowhere,' said Alessandra. The reason for this unprecedented summit was soon clear. Wiretaps and bugs picked up numerous references to the election of a new *capo crimine*, Rosarno boss Domenico Oppedisano, appointed to spearhead the 'Ndrangheta's war on the state. That seemed to confirm the importance of a well-attended meeting of bosses held a few days earlier in Oppedisano's orange orchard. Two weeks after the wedding, Oppedisano's promotion was formally confirmed at the annual 'Ndrangheta meeting, held at the festival for the Madonna of Polsi at San Luca.

What interested Alessandra was not Oppedisano himself but who he represented. She knew the *capo crimine* was elected by a kind of criminal meritocracy, based on who inside the organisation was deemed 'most charismatic, most admirable and most ruthless'. The boss had to be someone the entire 'Ndrangheta could agree outdid them all for criminal excellence, a leader who would ensure they wasted no more time and blood fighting each other.

On the face of it, seventy-eight-year-old Oppedisano, with his farmer's tan and a family that was outranked by at least two others in Rosarno, was an eccentric choice. But with her burgeoning knowledge of the clans, Alessandra could see its logic. More than advancement for the Oppedisanos, Domenico's new position confirmed the ascendancy of the west coast clans inside the 'Ndrangheta. Specifically, it attested to the dominance of a particular Rosarno crime family to whom Oppedisano was related by marriage. It was this family's domination of the cocaine trade with two other Gioia Tauro families that, more than anything, accounted for the 'Ndrangheta's spectacular growth over the last three decades. Its reputation for ruthless violence ensured that as well as being one of the richest and most powerful crime families in all Italy, it was also one of the most feared. 'Through Gioia Tauro, they were running all the drugs and all the arms,' said Alessandra.

So spectacular had been this family's progress and so naked their ambition to dominate the 'Ndrangheta, however, that they were resented by almost every other *'ndrina*. An earlier attempt to force the election of their own family *capo* had been fiercely resisted on all sides as an unacceptable affront. The other families might be diminished by comparison but honour demanded they save face by pretending otherwise. Nominating Domenico Oppedisano was a shrewd compromise, combining the signature 'Ndrangheta characteristics of strategy and wilful delusion.

Still, Alessandra had no doubt who now held power inside the 'Ndrangheta. She had seen video surveillance of family members toasting Oppedisano with champagne on the night he was elected. In any new war on the 'Ndrangheta, this family would be target number one. They were called the Pesces.

VII

Lea Garofalo wasn't the first 'Ndranghetista to turn on the organi-sation, nor even the first woman.[1] But she was one of a mere hand-ful of 'Ndrangheta *pentiti*, and only the second woman, and the story of the Pagliarelle *mama* and boss's daughter who had crossed over to the state had reverberated like a cannon blast around the valleys. Seven years later, Lea was most likely dead. The message that sent to places like Pagliarelle and Rosarno was that there *was* no alternative to the 'Ndrangheta. You leave, you die. It was a disaster for the Italian state's new war on the mafia. What had gone wrong?

Like the officers investigating Lea's disappearance, Alessandra discovered that Lea's long struggle with Carlo and the 'Ndrangheta was well documented. Lea had made lengthy statements against the 'Ndrangheta and Carlo three times, in 1996, 2002 and 2008. From these, the picture that emerged of the rural Calabria where Lea and Carlo had grown up was of a lost world, cut off from the rest of humanity by a wall of violent tyranny. For most 'Ndrangheta children, it was enough just to be born in a place like Pagliarelle to know their destiny.

But Lea had been different. Her father, an *'ndrina* boss called Antonio Garofalo, was killed by three brothers from a rival clan on New Year's Eve 1974, when he was twenty-seven and Lea was just eight months old – and, for Lea, none of it made sense after that. The feud, or *faida*, that her father's murder set off between the Garofalos and the Mirabellis, another Pagliarelle family, lasted all through her childhood until Lea was eighteen. When she was seven, in 1981, Lea's uncle Giulio tried to avenge his brother by opening fire on a Mirabelli funeral. A few months later, Giulio was killed in retaliation. In 1989, when Lea was fifteen, another of her cousins was shot dead, right in front of her and in broad daylight, in the centre of Petilia Policastro. That same year, the Garofalos began taking their revenge, killing one of the three Mirabelli brothers. They shot a second in 1990 and the third in 1991, then in 1992 they murdered Mario Garofalo, a cousin who – illustrating the incestuous nature of the feud – worked for the Mirabellis.

Lea's older brother, Floriano, directed much of the bloodletting. He involved his nine-year-old sister, asking her to hide a pistol belonging to their uncle when a police raid was imminent.[2] But despite Floriano's instruction in the duties of *vendetta*, despite Marisa's warnings about the need at least to pretend, despite all the anger she felt over her father's death, and barely knowing that any other life even existed, Lea couldn't remember a day when she hadn't seen through the lie. 'Lea was born into a family where violence was the rule,' said her former lawyer Vincenza Rando, known to everyone as 'Enza'. 'It was "Kill one of mine and I'll kill one of yours."' Lea saw the world differently, said Enza. To her, 'the 'Ndrangheta was a cult of death and Lea was a woman who loved life. The 'Ndrangheta writes your destiny for you. Lea wanted to write her own.'

Lea's independence might have come from her mother. Though her mother had married an 'Ndranghetista, she had always worked, mostly as a cleaner at a school in Petilia. 'Our mother had a completely different mindset to people around here,' said Marisa. 'She was a decent woman.' It was Lea's mother who taught her what Lea always used to tell Denise: that education was freedom; and that providing for her family was what gave a woman dignity.

Still, their mother wasn't affectionate, said Marisa. She, Floriano and Lea grew up mostly in the care of their grandparents, who might as well have been from another century. Of the three children, Marisa said it was Lea, the youngest, who felt their parents' absence most keenly. She was always asking for pictures of her father who, since she had never known him, she was free to imagine as perfect: caring and loving and cruelly taken from the daughter he adored. As a teenager, Lea had a small 'A' for Antonio tattooed onto her hand. While the violence raged on around them, Lea couldn't imagine her father wanting her to spend her life carving out brief moments of peace in a dead-end job as her mother had done. 'You don't *live*,' Lea told the *carabinieri* in 2002. 'You just survive in some way. You dream about something – anything – because nothing's worse than that life.' As Lea grew up, it dawned on her that the freedom she craved would be impossible unless she left Pagliarelle.

Lea's tragedy was that, like many 'Ndrangheta women, she thought love was her way out. When she was fifteen she fell for a village boy she had known all her life, a thick-set bruiser with a flattened nose and cropped hair called Carlo Cosco. Carlo, nineteen at the time, was back from his new life in the north and visiting Pagliarelle for the holidays. What Lea especially liked about him was that he seemed to have no ambition other than to work at an honest job and raise a family. And he lived in Milan, 'a big city where she could start again', said Enza. Lea and Carlo eloped after a few weeks. When she was sixteen, in 1991, they married and moved to Milan, where Carlo had an apartment in a large, drab building on Viale Montello.

Almost immediately, Lea realised her escape was a mirage. No. 6 Viale Montello was in the possession of the 'Ndrangheta and Carlo turned out to be one of several 'Ndranghetisti using it as a base from which to traffic cocaine and heroin. Lea had rejected the 'Ndrangheta code but it transpired that her new husband's embrace of it had been so wholehearted, he thought nothing of tricking Lea into marrying him. Worst of all, it emerged that Carlo was working for Lea's brother,

Floriano, whose bloodthirstiness in Pagliarelle had propelled him to the head of the Garofalo *'ndrina*. Lea had thought she courted Carlo. Now it occurred to her that Carlo had sought her out – because she was the sister of an 'Ndrangheta boss. Marriage to her had been a promotion for Carlo. For Lea, the love she had imagined would free her had trapped her even deeper.

Lea sank into depression. According to Enza, she made several attempts at suicide. When she fell pregnant in the spring of 1991, Lea tried to abort. 'She did not want to give her son or daughter the same future,' said Enza. In December, heavily pregnant, she left Viale Montello and took a bus to a hospital deep in the country. She gave birth alone, to a baby girl. Lea had imagined she might give her baby up for adoption, somewhere Carlo would never find the child. 'But when Denise was born,' said Enza, 'Lea fell in love all over again. Denise gave Lea a reason to live.'

Alessandra found much in the Garofalo files that felt recognisable. Like everyone who had worked mafia cases in Milan, she knew all about No. 6 Viale Montello. A vast and historic building in the middle of the Italian business capital, *il fortino delle cosche* (the fort of the clans) wasn't just a mafia base but a six-storey challenge to Italy's claim to be a modern, unified, lawful state. The 'Ndranghetisti paid no rent on its 129 apartments, nor any tax, nor any bills for municipal services like water or electricity. They treated the Renaissance mansion with disdain. A spaghetti of wires hung from its walls and collapsing balconies. Its courtyards and central garden were filled with refuse and rusted, broken appliances. The stairwells and corners stank of urine. Not only was the building a hub of the European drug trade, it was the source of supply for hundreds of Milan's street dealers, especially those in the notorious Piazza Baiamonti, and a focal point for other criminals of every type: enforcers, smugglers and killers; political corrupters and state contract fixers; wayward policemen, judges and politicians. And all of it in flagrant plain sight. Viale Montello was an arterial thoroughfare just a kilometre from the city centre and yards from a city police station. Unsurprisingly, No. 6 Viale Montello was something of a preoccupation for Milan's anti-mafia prosecutors, who had it under near-permanent surveillance.

For the prosecutors, the relationships inside No. 6 Viale Montello in the 1990s – between brothers, in-laws and even husband and wife, and the way those dynamics eventually played out – became an important early case study of this newly ascendant mafia. It was from watching events there that the prosecutors would be able to assemble a picture of what Alessandra described as a 'modern, efficient, present-day organised crime syndicate' whose strength lay in 'enforcing a respect for medieval rules'. In the end, the prosecutors would conclude that they were fighting a culture, and that in No. 6 Viale Montello they had a peculiarly instructive Petri dish. Among the most informative events they watched there was the rise of an ambitious young 'Ndranghetista called Carlo Cosco, and his eventual undoing by his wife.

Carlo's first big step up the ladder had been to marry the boss's sister. On his return to Milan in 1991, the surveillance teams watched as Floriano's lieutenants in Milan, Silvano Toscano and Thomas Ceraudo, duly catapulted Carlo and his brothers, Vito and Giuseppe, to prominence, granting them control of the lucrative dope and protection rackets in Piazza Baiamonti and nearby Cuarto Oggiaro. As a medium-level drug smuggler, dealer and extortionist, Carlo wasn't above manual tasks. Sometimes he would ask his new wife, Lea, to help cut and package heroin, cocaine and hashish. He asked her for other favours too, like spying on Antonio Comberiati, a rival 'Ndranghetista who lived in the building with his wife, Gina.

Comberiati was a hothead and troublemaker. His nickname was *il lupo*, 'the wolf'. He resented most of the families in Viale Montello, seemingly aggrieved by his and Gina's inability to conceive. But he was especially incensed by Carlo's promotion.

One day in February 1994, Lea was dressing Denise, then two, for her first Milan city carnival, when Carlo interrupted to say he had seen Comberiati talking to the Chinese shop owner who 'employed' Carlo as a security guard. This arrangement was standard for the men at Viale Montello. Whenever *carabinieri* asked for proof of occupation, they would be shown contracts of employment claiming a job providing security for the Chinese traders on the ground floor. Carlo was concerned by what might be transpiring between his sponsor and his rival and asked Lea to listen in from the street. Lea soon overheard Comberiati insisting that the store close because it was being watched by the *carabinieri*. If Carlo lost his 'job', said Comberiati, that was too bad.

This was too much for Lea. 'I couldn't help myself,' she said in testimony years later. 'I interrupted and tried to defend Carlo, saying we had a daughter and Carlo had the right to remain there to work.' Comberiati, outraged at being confronted by a woman, and his rival's wife to boot, shouted back that he outranked Carlo. Then he threatened to kill Lea for daring to face him. 'I'm the boss around here!' he shouted. 'I'm in charge! It's my right!'

The fight continued inside the courtyard of Viale Montello. Eventually, Gina and several other women intervened. Lea ran back up to her apartment. Carlo was waiting. He had heard everything. 'Don't worry,' he reassured Lea. 'One day Comberiati will pay.'

In the event, it was Comberiati who made the first move. In simultaneous assassinations on the night of 30 November 1994, Thomas Ceraudo was gunned down in Cuarto Oggiaro and Silvano Toscano was abducted from his mother-in-law's house in Petilia and killed, his body dumped in a field outside town. Comberiati barely bothered to deny he was to blame. The surveillance teams at Viale Montello reported that he immediately installed himself as the new king of Milan.

But with Carlo's backers dead and Floriano looking weak, Comberiati was daring Carlo to respond. Six months after the double murders, just after midnight on 17 May 1995, Lea was sleeping in bed with Denise when she heard several shots ring out in the courtyard below. When she opened the door, she could see Comberiati's body lying prone on the concrete. It was raining. Gina was screaming for an ambulance and shouting that the killer was still in the building. She started smashing the windows of a Chinese shop in which she was convinced the gunman was hiding. Lea observed her. Then she watched the ambulance and *carabinieri* arrive. After twenty minutes, Carlo's brother Giuseppe appeared at her door, exhilarated.

'He's dead,' said Giuseppe.

'You sure?' asked Lea.

Giuseppe giggled. 'The bastard just wouldn't fucking die,' he said. 'It was like he had the devil in him or something. But, yeah, he's dead now, for sure.'

Giuseppe left for his apartment. Carlo arrived seconds later.

'Where were you?' asked Lea.

'Karaoke,' replied Carlo.

'Liar,' Lea shot back.

Carlo laughed. 'Well, then, I've been over at the shop getting a sandwich.'

Lea later told the *carabinieri* that she had surmised that Carlo had stood watch for Giuseppe while his brother shot Comberiati, then the two men had dumped the gun in the street. It made sense for Giuseppe to pull the trigger, said Lea, because he 'needed the points'. 'Carlo doesn't need them,' she explained to the prosecutors. 'He's already Floriano's brother-in-law. But Giuseppe's no one. A killing like this gives him position. He becomes somebody.'

With his rival dead, Carlo's accession, and the elevation of the Cosco family, was complete. Previous generations of Coscos had been goat herders and fruit farmers. Now, through luck and ruthlessness, they were players in an exploding international criminal empire. Carlo himself was right hand and brother by marriage to Floriano Garofalo, one of the most powerful *'ndrina* bosses in all Calabria.

For Lea, however, something died with Comberiati. Her husband had brought violence into the home where she lived with their daughter. Years earlier, she had tried to escape and it hadn't worked. For Denise's sake, she had to try again. Looking at her daughter was like looking at herself in the third person, thought Lea. She could see everything clearly: all the troubles around the two of them and what they needed to do to move past them. 'She wanted Denise to have other possibilities in her life,' said Enza. 'The chance to be part of the cult of life and friendship and respect and to be part of another kind of family.'

Lea tried one more time to convince Carlo to leave the 'Ndrangheta. The three of them could begin again somewhere new and raise their baby to be anything she wanted to be, she said. Carlo's response was to beat her. That was the last straw for Lea. 'So she decided to go to the *carabinieri* and tell them all about the drug trafficking,' said Enza.

In May 1996, Carlo, Floriano, Giuseppe and several others were arrested at No. 6 Viale Montello. The operation to detain them – using four hundred men to seal off the street and storm the building – confirmed the Coscos' new status in the European drug trafficking elite. Carlo was transferred to San Vittore prison, on the other side of town.

Though she had played a key role in his arrest, Lea decided she would give Carlo one last chance. In September 1996, Lea, now twenty-two, took Denise, five, to see him in prison. 'I want to stay with you,' she told him, 'but on one condition: you collaborate with the *carabinieri* and denounce the 'Ndrangheta. When you come out of jail, we can start a new life. Or you continue this life and you will never see me or Denise again.'

Carlo leapt over the screen between them and grabbed Lea. He had his hands around her throat by the time the prison guards pulled him off. He expected his wife to stand by him. After all the work and all the blood, Carlo's manoeuvring had paid off. He was king of Milan. Now Lea was betraying him and taking it all away: his link to the boss in the old country, his standing in the brotherhood, even his self-respect as a man. Lea had broken the code. There was only one remedy. From that day, said Enza, Lea knew she was living under 'a death sentence'.

Lea returned to Viale Montello for a final time. She packed a suitcase, then called a friend to drive her and Denise to a convent in Bergamo where they would be safe. Renata, Giuseppe Cosco's wife, saw Lea leave. 'I remember the day Lea left Milan well,' she said in court fifteen years later. 'Lea looked at me with anger. She spat on the ground. She swore she would never again set foot in that shitty place. She yelled that she wanted a different future for herself. A different future for her daughter.' And just like that, Lea and Denise were gone.

The next six years were the happiest of Lea's and Denise's lives. Initially, the pair stayed in an Ursuline convent in Bergamo, dedicated to the education of women and girls. In Mother Grata, who ran the convent, Lea seemed to discover the parent she'd never had. She began reading for the first time in years, learning about Giovanni Falcone, Paolo Borsellino and Giuseppe Impastato, a Palermo anti-mafia activist who had been born into a Cosa Nostra family and was assassinated by them at thirty. After a few months, Lea and Denise moved into a small apartment on Via Alfieri, a quiet street of bungalows and two-storey houses painted yellow and pink, not far from Lake Iseo. Later they moved into town to another small place on Via Mose del Brolo, a dead-end street full of pensioners and students. Lea found work in factories and bars. She met a man. She and Denise adopted a dog. Lea even went skydiving.

Every June, Lea and Denise would go down to Pagliarelle to spend the summer holidays with Marisa and their relatives. Perhaps it was those breaks in Calabria, unmolested by Carlo's men, that lulled Lea into thinking her escape was real. When they were back home, Lea even allowed Denise to visit Carlo in Catanzaro jail, to which he had been transferred from Milan.

But Carlo never had Lea out of his sights. When the officers investigating Lea's disappearance tracked down Salvatore Cortese, an

'Ndrangheta killer who had shared a cell with Carlo in Catanzaro from 2001 to 2003 and had since turned *pentito*, Cortese told them Carlo never forgave Lea. Carlo, he said, was always talking about how Lea had betrayed him and betrayed the 'Ndrangheta. Carlo was especially incensed that she still stayed with her family in Pagliarelle and walked around the village alone and in front of everyone. She was flaunting her freedom, said Carlo. He knew about her affair in Bergamo and suspected, since Lea never came to visit, that the other inmates in Catanzaro had deduced the same thing. Worst of all, her brother Floriano was doing nothing about any of it. Carlo had been wronged and wronged again. It was intolerable. 'And,' said Cortese, 'according to the 'Ndrangheta's rules, Floriano's silence allowed Carlo to appeal to other men of honour for permission to kill Lea.'

Nonetheless, killing the sister of a boss was a tricky business. Carlo told Cortese that Lea had to be dispatched in such a way that Floriano would believe she had run off with her new lover. 'The plan to physically eliminate Lea Garofalo and get rid of her body by dissolving it in acid grew in Carlo's mind since at least the early 2000s,' said Cortese. How did Cortese know that, asked the *carabinieri*? Because, Cortese replied, he was among those Carlo asked to help him.

Carlo knew he might fool Floriano but not the entire 'Ndrangheta. If he was to pull off such an audacious killing, he would need approval from higher up. Approaching two bosses in the prison yard, he explained how his honour and that of the wider 'Ndrangheta had been so impugned that it could only be restored by washing it in blood. The two bosses knew Carlo was right. But they had their own clan feuds to pursue. Calculating that Carlo's *vendetta* would anyway have to wait until he was released from jail, they stalled.

Carlo still held out hope that Floriano would choose his duty over love for his sister. Getting his brothers to set Lea's car alight in Bergamo in 2000 was Carlo's way of reminding Floriano of his obligation. It had some effect. One summer's day two years later, when Lea and Denise were back in Pagliarelle, Lea took Denise to buy a *gelato* from the shop off the main piazza. Vito Cosco drove up in his car. He was agitated. He told Lea he was tired of taking Denise to see Carlo. Carlo was sick of it too. It wasn't right, said Vito. Lea had to get in line.

Lea refused. As the argument grew more heated, Floriano, by then out of prison and back in Pagliarelle, arrived. Vito was right, Floriano shouted at Lea. What kind of woman let her husband rot in jail alone? What kind of sister was she to him, Floriano, an *'ndrina* boss? Then, in the middle of the square, Floriano held Lea by her shoulders and slapped her across the face for everyone to see. He leaned over his sister, looking as though he was about to strike her again. As he did so, however, he whispered in her ear: 'Lea! You have to escape! Because, really, I have to kill you!'

Twice Lea had run from the 'Ndrangheta. Twice it had clawed her back in. For choosing freedom over murderous criminality, her husband wanted her dead, the 'Ndrangheta required it and her brother had told her he would be the one to do it. Lea felt like the world was closing in on her. On 29 July 2002, a few days after the argument with Vito and Floriano, the door of Lea's grandmother's house was set alight while Lea and Denise were inside. It was an especially blunt 'Ndrangheta message. There was no way out.

Perhaps because it was so unthinkable, the 'Ndrangheta had over-looked one exit, however. On the morning of 29 July 2002, Prosecutor Salvatore Dolce in the nearby city of Catanzaro received a call from the chief of the *carabinieri* in Petilia Policastro. 'He told me that in front of him stood the sister of Floriano Garofalo. She had a ten-year-old girl with her. She wanted to give evidence about a number of facts and events concerning her family. She wanted to break with her past and the environment in which she had been living.'

Dolce immediately understood the significance of what he was hearing. In 2002, the authorities knew very little about the 'Ndrangheta. Despite prosecuting several 'Ndranghetisti for their roles in the Pagliarelle feud, their knowledge of what had happened barely extended beyond the body count. Though they had successfully prosecuted Carlo and Floriano for drug trafficking, they also knew little about the structures and hierarchy of the wider 'Ndrangheta. 'Up until that time, we had very poor knowledge of the workings of the 'Ndrangheta,' said Dolce. 'State witnesses are our main source of knowledge for any mafia and we just hadn't got that many from the 'Ndrangheta. The 'Ndrangheta was known, of course – its existence was no big secret – but its internal dynamics were not known.'

Dolce knew immediately what he had to do. 'I did not go to Petilia,' he said. 'It's a small town. The fact she had gone to the *carabinieri* would have already alarmed people there. So I could not go personally to listen to her statement there. Instead, I had the *carabinieri* move her urgently to a hotel 100 kilometres away and I went to see her there. And I did nothing but listen to her talk for two days.'

What particularly impressed Dolce was how different Lea was to the stereotype of an 'Ndrangheta woman. Most were submissive, ignorant and poorly educated. Lea was assertive, knowledgeable and articulate. 'She had a different outlook,' said Dolce. 'She was open-minded. She wanted her own life. She did not want to depend on a man or to stay at home. She wanted her independence. She wanted to be the protagonist and the subject in her own life. Lea had grit.' Just as impressive, said Dolce, 'she was very honest. If she hadn't told us she had been involved in the drugs, we'd never have known.'

Lea's testimony began from her father's death when she was eight months old and ran through everything that had happened in the past twenty-eight years. She spoke about the Pagliarelle feud. She gave an account of all the murders and named all the killers. She detailed how her brother Floriano had shot and knifed his way to the top, and how that had enabled him to take over the protection and cocaine rackets in Milan, especially Cuarto Oggiaro. She talked about packaging and distributing cocaine inside No. 6 Viale Montello. She described Antonio Comberiati's murder and how Carlo and Giuseppe had spoken about killing him. Finally, she said she had decided to turn state's evidence because she felt time was running out. Her greatest fear was that someone would break into her house and shoot Denise.

Reading through Lea's statements years later, Alessandra was amazed by the detail. Dolce had reacted the same way at the time. 'I have had experience of false *pentiti* – men who just say a few things but not everything,' he said. 'They make a utilitarian choice. They decide to collaborate because they are facing life sentences.' But Lea was different, he said. Her collaboration was 'more genuine, and more effective. She said everything she knew. She hid nothing. You could feel how her choice had put her through suffering and pain. But she had a very dignified look. She was very determined and proud of what she had done.'

The more Alessandra read about Lea, the more she was struck by how, seven years before, in two days of interviews and on her own initiative, Lea had single-handedly proved her theory that mothers were the key to undoing the 'Ndrangheta. Lea's testimony amounted to an unprecedented insight into the 'Ndrangheta. Her motivation – to give Denise a better life – was untainted and unstoppable. Lea should have prompted a complete rethink inside the Italian judiciary of the value of women in the fight against the mafia. There was certainly every reason to imagine that July 2002 had been the start of a whole new chapter in the war on the mafia. That made the investigation into Lea's disappearance even more critical. What had happened?

VIII

L ea was a beguiling mix of the carefree and the purposeful.[1] She laughed easily, because life was for living, but she would erupt if she felt her freedom or Denise's were threatened. She and Denise would have been safer, she knew, if she had been able to accept the meek, servile existence of an 'Ndrangheta mother and wife. But to Lea, that meant dying anyway. If the happiness she enjoyed as a free woman and the possibilities Denise enjoyed outside the 'Ndrangheta were often eclipsed by terror, it was a price Lea felt they had to pay.

The day Lea walked with Denise into a *carabinieri* station in July 2002, she was petrified. Annalisa Pisano, then thirty-four, was a public defender on call. 'There was a list of lawyers to deal with witness cooperation,' she said. 'I think they picked me because I lived close by and I was a woman.' Tall with short blonde hair and the businesslike bearing of a young criminal lawyer with her own practice, Annalisa arrived at the station, rang the bell in the waiting room and sat down, unaware that the mother with a small child sitting quietly next to her was her new client. 'But then the *carabinieri* officer came and said: "This is the girl who has asked for your help. She has made the choice to talk." And we had fifteen minutes to prepare before the procedure began.'

Annalisa remembered thinking how Lea was 'so small, so skinny, and Denise so tiny'. She wondered how they would handle the giant step they were taking. 'There's almost no words to describe the choice Lea was making,' said Annalisa. 'I could see she was blinded by terror, in a condition of high anxiety and stress. She had an idea about her brother, that he could take some action to reconcile with Carlo and preserve the status quo. But she was trying, like all mothers, to be courageous because she had her daughter with her.' Annalisa tried to be sympathetic, telling Lea that she would get help and support from the state. The provincial *carabinieri* guarding her were no help. 'Are you really interested in cooperating?' asked one officer, gruffly. 'Because if not, you'll stay here.'

The state's first task was to assess whether Lea and Denise were worth protecting. After two days of testimony, Lea was judged genuine, and she and her daughter were granted state protection. The process, bureaucratic and banal, was at odds with the momentous nature of what was happening. This, after all, was how a *pentita* gave up allegiance to family and homeland, abandoned everything and everyone they had ever known, accepted that for ever after they would be at war with one of the world's most ruthless mafias and put their faith in a state that they had been taught to despise from birth.

Initially, Lea and Denise were moved to Ascoli Piceno, a small, quiet province east of Rome. Lea told Denise they were to pretend they were sisters. They'd even had new make-believe names: Alessandra de Rossi and her younger sister Sara. But Denise kept forgetting the rules, calling Lea 'mama' or 'ma', and after a few weeks, Lea changed their names to Maria and Denise Petalo so that anyone overhearing them could excuse 'ma' as Lea's nickname.

Though safe from harm, Lea and Denise found their new life hard. They were rarely in one place long enough to put down new roots, moving six times in six years. Lea, for whom freedom meant the opportunity to be gregarious, found the isolation especially difficult. Her one connection to the outside world was a mobile given to her by the prosecutors, which she used to talk to Annalisa. 'We spoke every day for the next six years, even on Saturdays and Sundays,' said

Annalisa. 'For all that time, I was her only point of contact on the outside.'

Despite the state's efforts, Lea also felt a constant threat around the corner. One day in August 2003, she read in the newspaper how Vito Cosco, then thirty-four, had shot and killed two small-time drug dealers who had insulted him. One of Vito's shots had also killed a two-year-old girl. A fourth victim, a sixty-year-old man who witnessed the shooting, had collapsed and died on the spot. Vito holed up at No. 6 Viale Montello for three days before phoning the *carabinieri* and telling them to come and arrest him. The newspapers called the killings 'the massacre of Rozzano' after the small town outside Milan where they took place.

The Garofalo–Mirabelli *faida* raged on as well. In September 2003, Lea's cousin, Mario Garofalo, was shot in his car at a junction outside Pagliarelle. In June 2005 Floriano, by then forty, was walking to his front door in Pagliarelle when a man stepped out of the shadows carrying a shotgun. Floriano ran. Sprinting through a vegetable plot, he tore across the main road and up a side street. The gunman ran after him and shot him in the back. Floriano fell against a fence. The gunman reloaded, walked up to Floriano and shot him several times in the face, blowing his head back to a stump.

Though Lea had often lived in fear of Floriano when he was alive, now she was convinced her brother had died because he had refused to kill her. Carlo had been released from prison in December 2003. Floriano's murder eighteen months later couldn't be a coincidence. 'It's my fault they killed him,' she told Marisa. The guilt destroyed her. Just as bad, in her safe-house her protection officers would grin at her and tell her that the threat to her life was gone. They didn't understand anything. Not that it had probably been Carlo who had killed Floriano. And not that with Floriano dead, Carlo now not only ruled the Pagliarelle 'Ndrangheta but had also inherited the task of restoring its honour by killing Lea. The threat to Lea had soared. She took to staying awake through the night and sleeping during the day while Denise was at school. Even then, she kept a knife under her pillow.

Lea was right to be scared. Carlo began his search for her the day he left jail. He dropped by the convent in Bergamo, explaining he was a relative and asking the nuns if they had any contact with his cousin. In November 2004, Gennaro Garofalo, a member of Carlo's 'ndrina who had once worked as a police auxiliary, showed up at his old station in Monza, asked his old colleagues out for pizza, then casually logged onto the witness protection system to search for Denise's address, which came up as No. 9 Via Giovanni Ruggia, Perugia. Later in court Gennaro would claim he saw nothing sinister in a father's desire to know his daughter's whereabouts. 'Carlo always treated Denise well,' he explained. 'In Pagliarelle, he made sure Denise ate and dressed well. She always had earrings.'

Early in 2005, Carlo sent two of his men, Rosario Curcio and Giovanni Peci, to find Lea in Perugia. The address in Via Giovanni Ruggia turned out to be a police station. When the men returned to Carlo empty-handed, he sent them back in a fury. By then, however, word had circulated in Pagliarelle that Carlo was closing in on Lea and a cousin had travelled to Perugia to warn her. Lea and Denise were quickly moved to Florence. But Carlo was relentless. In 2006, he sent another cousin, Genevieve Garofalo, to meet Lea with a message that Carlo wanted to see her and had set aside €200,000 for Denise. 'It's a trap,' Lea told Denise. 'He's trying to get us back to Calabria.' Lea was right, no doubt. Still, Carlo's persistence was having an effect. Lea could feel herself increasingly enclosed in a prison of paranoia.

Alessandra had enough experience of witness protection not to be surprised by what she was reading. The system wasn't perfect. The mafia had always had its men inside the judiciary, passing it information on the whereabouts of *pentiti*. There was also an inherent contradiction between trying to protect someone and simultaneously giving them their freedom. Sometimes that need for personal liberation led witnesses to put themselves in harm's way. Lea's motivation was always to give Denise a different life. But she also longed to free herself – and she had hardly achieved that. She couldn't go out unaccompanied. She couldn't talk to strangers. She was to live meekly and quietly, dependent on meagre handouts. It was eerily similar to 'Ndrangheta life. Some of the officers guarding her seemed to regard her as little more than a lowlife Calabrian hick who'd conned the state and struck it lucky. The truth was that the sacrifices she had made in her fight against the mafia – risking her life, abandoning her family and friends – were far greater than any nine-to-five provincial cop would ever make.

Lea began to push back. She demanded to see her boyfriend from Bergamo. She asked not to be placed in towns with Calabrian populations. She wandered off into town without telling anyone. She refused to accept her protection officers' complaints about her behaviour. 'Why do I have to defend myself against the state that is supposed to be defending me and my daughter?' she asked. Denise, as a growing girl, was also becoming difficult. 'Lea would explain to her daughter why they were moving and why they had to change their names,' said Salvatore Dolce, the prosecutor, 'then the daughter would talk about it at school, and they would have to move again.'

As months turned to years, the state began to have doubts about Lea and Denise for other reasons, too. The procedure for mafia turncoats was to keep them closely guarded while their evidence was evaluated, corroborated and any trials conducted. Only after that would the government give them a permanent new identity, home and job. But not only was Lea proving tiresome to handle, without other *pentiti* to confirm her evidence, the investigators were having trouble building a solid case against Carlo. Lea's statements, mostly describing what she had heard but not seen, weren't enough on their own to make arrests or secure convictions. 'We investigated for a long time but we never found enough confirmation,' said Dolce. 'Then a colleague replaced me and was very severe in his assessment: how what we had was not enough for arrests, and the silly things Lea did. So in February 2006 Lea and Denise were ejected from the programme.'

Annalisa immediately won Lea and Denise a temporary reprieve while she appealed the decision to throw them out of witness protection. But Lea was shattered. The state had reneged. It had promised her and her daughter a new life. Then it had betrayed them. She had expected the state to prosecute every crime she had revealed. It hadn't prosecuted any. Worse, by taking her testimony, the state had needlessly exposed Lea and Denise to even more danger than before. The Italian state, Lea decided, was little better than the 'Ndrangheta. The irony was that if Lea had been an actual 'Ndranghetista – if she had taken part in the dealing and the thieving and the killing – she would have been more use to the authorities. It felt like they were punishing her for being honest.

That July, she phoned Annalisa. 'I've changed my mind,' she said. 'I'm getting out of the programme.' Denise said later, 'My mother decided to give up on the state. She had lost all confidence in them. Our life was exhausting and for what? Her statements turned out to be useless.'

Annalisa, aware that Lea was now suffering increasingly dramatic mood swings, managed to talk her client around. 'More and more, she was finding herself lost in a reality that was bigger than her,' said Annalisa. 'You have to remember she was just a girl, only thirty-two years old. She thought her world and all her plans were collapsing around her.' But Lea had already submitted a formal request to leave the programme and, until Annalisa could get her readmitted once again, she and Denise were on their own. It was terrifying, said Annalisa. The state had washed its hands of Lea and Denise. Her *mafioso* husband was trying to kill her. Lea had no one. 'And so,' said Annalisa, 'it fell to me.'

Annalisa did her best. In November 2006, she moved close to where Lea and Denise were living. She became, as she said, 'less a lawyer than a mother'. But Lea remained volatile and mistrustful.

Denise, who turned fifteen in December 2006, was also no longer a girl playing a game of hide-and-seek with her mother but, increasingly, a teenager with her own opinions. Lea had shielded her daughter from much of the truth about Carlo. The price of Denise's innocence was that she didn't understand why, now she and Lea were out of witness protection, she couldn't see her father. 'Denise kept asking,' said Annalisa. 'She would insist, pressing and pressing. Lea would call me every day because she couldn't manage Denise – you know how teenagers are.' Annalisa tried to mediate between mother and daughter. Denise responded by demanding that the lawyer find a way for her to meet her father. Annalisa refused point blank. 'I told Denise it was completely unacceptable for her to meet her father. I only had to see the terror in Lea's eyes when the name of "Cosco" came up. But I think Denise started hating me after that.'

Looking for help wherever she might find it, Lea briefly moved with Denise back to Bergamo, where Lea sought the advice of Mother Grata and found a job in a bar. Then they moved to Fabriano, where they had also lived before and Lea had an old boyfriend. At the end of 2007, Lea went to a café in Rome run by the anti-mafia group Libera. She met Libera's president, Father Luigi Ciotti, who put her in touch with a lawyer who volunteered for the organisation.

Lea met Enza Rando at her townhouse offices in the centre of Modena. The two women were very different. Lea, now thirty-three, was free-spirited and passionate, and the knowledge that she might die any day had given her a determination to live each one as her last. Enza was in her fifties, small, neat and conservative. But at their first meeting, Lea brought pastries, then sat down and poured out her life story. Almost immediately, Enza loved her. 'Lea was beautiful,' she said. 'Very intelligent and very courageous.'

Annalisa had often been hard on Lea, especially when it came to Denise. Though Enza couldn't offer Lea much more than Annalisa, to Lea, after six years in isolation, she was a fresh face ready to listen. And from the moment Enza appeared, Annalisa sensed a new distance between herself and Lea. 'There was a change,' said Annalisa. 'I could tell another lawyer was giving her advice. Something was wrong. I felt I was losing Lea. And I thought it was best to stop right then. Overlaps like that – inconsistencies, conflicting advice – could be very dangerous for Lea.'

Heartbroken, Annalisa wrote a letter to Lea, offering her resignation. 'In my mind, I was hoping this would shake Lea up and she would change her mind,' she said. 'We'd had ups and downs but six years is a long time.' Instead, in June 2008, Lea accepted Annalisa's notice.

In September 2008, largely as a result of Annalisa's years of appeals and applications, Lea and Denise were readmitted to the witness protection programme. They were moved to Boiano, a small town near Campobasso in central Italy. Denise settled in well at her new school, and soon had a new group of friends. But by now Lea's state of mind had graduated from paranoid to disturbed. She was still staying awake all night, sleeping through the day and keeping a knife under her pillow. Now she bought a guard dog and began taking lessons in martial arts. Nothing could soften the loneliness, however. She had no friends in Boiano and, with Annalisa gone, no one to talk to. Without government papers giving her a new identity, she also couldn't risk working, lest her name on an employee record identify her whereabouts. 'It's all been a pile of crap,' she would tell Denise. 'Just a giant waste of our lives.'

'It was so lonely for her,' said Denise. 'And without a job, she couldn't be independent, she couldn't provide for us by her own efforts and, for her, this was a real defeat.'

One day in April, Lea decided to write to the President of Italy, Giorgio Napolitano:

I am a young mother at the end of my tether. Today I find myself together with my daughter isolated from everything and everyone. I lost everything. My family. My job. I lost my home. I lost countless friends. I lost any expectations of the future. I had reckoned on all of this. I knew what I was getting when I made my choice.

But her sacrifices had been for nothing, wrote Lea. Her statements had led to no arrests and no convictions. She and Denise had suffered for seven years for no reason. And then the state cast them out. Lea wrote that she was losing her faith in justice. 'The worst thing is that I already know the fate that awaits me. After poverty comes death. Undeserved and unearned but unavoidable.' Who else would make the choice she had? she asked.

'Today, Mr President, you can change the course of history. I still believe that a person can live with integrity and decency in this country. Please, Mr President, give us a sign of hope. Help innocent victims of injustice.'

But when Lea went to post the letter in Boiano, she spotted a couple on a street corner who seemed to be watching her. The woman was wearing an earpiece. As Lea approached, the woman reached into her bag. Lea thought she was going for a gun. 'I didn't believe her,' said Denise, when Lea told her later, 'but I wasn't there and I didn't see it and my mother certainly believed there was someone who wanted to hurt her. She was very frightened. She decided not to send the letter and told me that we were leaving the protection programme once again.'

Lea's second request to leave the state programme was the final straw for its administrators. They gave her and Denise two weeks to vacate their safe house and advised her never to reapply. Lea and Denise were on their own once more, and this time for ever.

*

Lea, however, had a new plan. She phoned her sister Marisa and asked her to pass on a message to Carlo. 'She basically said: "OK, I said some things that were inconvenient for you,"' recalled Denise. '"But I retracted everything and there will be no trial and no one will be shamed. So you have to leave me alone and leave my daughter alone."'

Lea wanted out of witness protection, said Denise, because the process had been 'absolutely pointless'. The one upside was that if the state wasn't using her evidence, then Carlo had no reason to kill her. She just wanted to return to Pagliarelle and be left alone to quietly bring up their daughter. In return, she said Carlo would get to see Denise whenever he wanted. 'She just didn't want to have to worry about her life and my life any more,' said Denise.

Carlo agreed. In a few days, Marisa came to pick up Lea and Denise from Boiano and take them back to Pagliarelle. Lea refused to see Carlo and stayed in the house with the curtains drawn. For Denise, it was the first chance she'd had to see her father in nine years. 'He took me for drives, to restaurants, to see his friends, to eat at his house,' she said. 'He said we should move to Pagliarelle and that I could finish high school down there.' Denise said she wanted to finish school in Boiano, where she had friends. She asked Carlo to rent an apartment there because she and Lea had nowhere to live. Carlo agreed to that, too. After Easter, he and Denise drove to Campobasso, a short bus ride from Boiano, and rented the first apartment they were shown near the school in the old town for one month. Carlo then installed Denise, his mother Piera and his nephew Domenico – Uncle Giuseppe's son – in the apartment. Since he was paying for it, Carlo moved in himself for a few days.

Lea was furious at the way Carlo was insinuating himself back into their lives. She had no choice but to accept his money for her daughter's sake. Nevertheless, while Denise, Carlo, Carlo's mother and Carlo's nephew slept in the apartment, Lea refused to meet Carlo and spent the nights outside in the car. 'We'd slept in the same bed for years,' said Denise. 'She found it hard.'

The pressure eased slightly when Carlo returned to Milan. But the atmosphere in the apartment remained poisonous. On 24 April, Lea's thirty-fifth birthday passed without celebration. Another day, she fought with Carlo's mother Piera, saying she shouldn't be there and that she, Lea, should be taking care of Denise, seeing as she'd managed for seventeen years. Shortly afterwards, Lea had to take Piera to hospital for what looked like hypertension. When Carlo heard his mother was sick, he drove back down from Milan.

The night that Piera was released from hospital, Lea, worried about her mother-in-law and unable to deny a son's love for his mother, found herself at supper with the entire Cosco family. It was the first time Carlo and Lea had been in the same room for thirteen years. Lea was primed to explode. When Piera yelled that Lea was making her unwell – 'she's killing me with her shouting' – Lea, who was holding a bread knife, blew up. What was Piera even doing there? Why were any of them there? What the fuck was *Carlo* doing there? Lea and Denise had done fine by themselves all these years. She waved the knife at Carlo and shouted at him. You have to go, she said. Get the fuck out of here right now! Go now! Go now!

'I was crying through all of it,' said Denise. 'But my father didn't say anything. He just took the two suitcases he'd brought with him, kissed me on the cheek and left.'

Without money, Lea and Denise were still dependent on Carlo. They needed him even for small things like fixing the broken washing machine in the apartment. In early May, Denise and Lea went to a four-day pop festival in Rome, returning to Campobasso early on 5 May. At 9 a.m., Carlo called Denise to say a repair man was coming that day to fix the washing machine. Denise said OK and went to bed. Lea fell asleep on the couch.

A few minutes later, the doorbell rang. Lea stuffed a knife in her back pocket and answered the door to a clean-shaven man in jeans and a blue jacket with a tattoo down one side of his neck, carrying a tool box with a Winnie the Pooh sticker on the side. The man said he had come to fix the washing machine. Lea let him in and showed him to the kitchen. She watched him as he pushed a few buttons on the machine. He didn't open his tool kit. He asked Lea how the machine worked. Lea regarded him. 'If you have to kill me, do it now,' she said.

The man flew at Lea and she pulled the knife from her back pocket. He stuck two fingers down her throat, trying to choke her. Lea kicked him in the crotch. The tool box fell onto the floor. Upstairs, Denise heard the crash. 'I came down and this man and my mother were wrapped around each other,' she said. 'At first I thought it was my father, because he was dark-skinned and wearing the same jacket my father had.'

Denise jumped on the man and started punching and kicking him. She saw his face: it wasn't Carlo. Still, the man seemed to recognise Denise. He looked at her with shock, threw the two women off and ran for the door. Denise chased him and grabbed him by the throat. 'Who sent you?!' she shouted. 'Who sent you?!'

'Let me go!' the man yelled, and ran out.

Denise went to help Lea, who was bleeding. The two of them examined the tool box that Lea's attacker had left behind. Inside were no plumbing tools but, instead, duct tape, wire, rope, scissors, a saw and latex gloves. Lea called the *carabinieri*, who interviewed her and Denise and took fingerprints. Once they left, Lea told Denise that though it was important to have an official record of the attack, they couldn't count on the *carabinieri* to keep them safe. They packed, ran down to Lea's car and drove to a B&B, taking care to park on a different street. After staying in their room all day and all night, they left early the next morning without paying and drove to the main piazza where Lea pitched a tent opposite the town hall. They were safer where everyone could see them, she said.

Lea and Denise were convinced Carlo had sent an assassin to kill Lea. Still, when Carlo called, Denise arranged to meet her father in town. 'I had no choice,' she said. 'If a person wants to hurt you or kill you, either you let them or you pretend to be their friend.'

When Denise saw Carlo, however, she couldn't control herself. She flew at him. She accused him of trying to kill her mother. Carlo shouted back that the attack had had nothing to do with him.

'But you were the only one to know about the broken washing machine!' said Denise.

'Your phones are tapped!' shouted Carlo. 'You were in the protection programme! Anyone could have known about the washing machine! Anyone could have sent that guy!'

Denise was caught off guard for a second. Then she said: 'I never want to see you again. I'm going with my mum.'

Lea wished that the two of them could have ridden off into the sunset as Denise wanted. But with no money, no state protection and no lawyer, their only option was to follow their original plan, move back to Calabria and try again to secure a truce from Carlo. They packed up their tent, caught the train to Calabria and moved into Lea's mother's house in Petilia, all three women sharing a kitchen, a single bedroom and a tiny bathroom. Lea replaced the old wooden front door with a new metal one. Aside from walking a few metres to buy cigarettes, she stayed indoors.

For Lea, life in Petilia and Pagliarelle was more claustrophobic than ever. She had to assume that most of the village might be trying to kill her. She quarrelled with the few people she did see.

Denise quickly couldn't stand to be in the apartment with her mother. Almost without realising it, she found herself falling into the routine of clan life, taking drives into the country with her father when he was down from Milan, eating lunch with him and his friends. In Pagliarelle, there was no way to behave differently. But when she returned to the house with new jeans, new trainers or a new jacket, Lea, who had raised her daughter to despise materialism, would throw a fit.

What surprised Denise was that Carlo seemed to find the situation just as hard. One day he asked his daughter to go on holiday with him. When Denise asked Lea, and her mother initially agreed only to change her mind at the last minute, Carlo erupted. 'On that occasion, I really understood how deeply my father loathed my mother,' said Denise. 'He insulted her in front of me and said that for my entire life, my mother had made all the decisions for me and that she still did. He couldn't stand that. It was intolerable. He couldn't allow my mother to decide whether or not I spent time with him.' Marisa, who overheard, took Denise aside after Carlo left. 'He really wants her dead,' said Marisa. 'He truly hates her.'

Towards the end of summer, however, Lea began to think that Carlo might be softening. In September 2009, she asked to meet him and Carlo came to the house. Denise was there. 'They were talking for more than an hour, just the two of them,' said Denise. 'At one point, I couldn't see them anywhere and I got scared. But when I looked out from the balcony, they were in the garden under a tree, just talking. They waved at me.' Lea announced that she and Carlo were going for a drive to Botricello, a small holiday town built around a medieval castle on the coast where they used to go as teenagers. It was already 11 p.m. and she and Carlo didn't return until 4 a.m. When Denise asked Lea the next morning what her parents had been talking about for so long, Lea smiled coyly and said: 'You know, old times. Mind your own business.'

It might seem strange to others, said Denise, but she believed her parents had loved each other once. Now she began to imagine that they would again. A lot of their conversation that night had been about where Denise should go to university. Lea favoured Catanzaro while Carlo was pushing for Milan. Lea was hurt that Denise might want to leave her. 'After all she had been through, after everything she had done for me, she said I was being ungrateful,' said Denise. Still, it was everyday parent chat. Meanwhile, Denise and Carlo were getting used to each other's company again. 'We spoke on the phone, we went to the beach, we ate dinner together,' said Denise.

On 19 November 2009, Lea and Denise travelled to Florence. Lea was due in court accused of a minor assault from years earlier when she had slapped a teenage girl in the street after the girl accused Denise of trying to steal her boyfriend. The case was to be heard on 20 November. Enza had agreed to represent Lea. The day before, Denise and Lea went window-shopping in the city. Denise spotted a sweatshirt she liked, but she knew Lea wouldn't have the money for it and worried she would sell the gold necklace and bracelet Carlo had given her to buy it. So Denise called her father. Carlo said new clothes were no problem and suggested that after the case, she and Lea come to Milan and they all go shopping together.

When Enza heard about the plan, she told Lea, 'It's a bad idea. Carlo's trying to kill you.' But, said Enza, 'Lea was a strong woman and she had decided.' Lea told her lawyer, 'It's Milan, not Calabria. A big city. People everywhere. I'll never be alone and Denise will be with me. Nothing's going to happen. He wouldn't be able to organise anything in time.'

On the day of the court case, Enza managed to negotiate an official reprimand for her client. Hours later, Lea and Denise caught the evening train to Milan. Watching them leave, Enza decided she would try to stop them one last time. 'Turn around,' she texted her client. 'Get off at Piacenza. Libera has a place for you where you can be safe.'

As they neared Milan, Lea sent her reply. 'Thank you, my lawyer, thank you. But Denise and I have to try to make a life for ourselves. God bless you. God bless us all.'[2]

'And that was the last I heard from her,' said Enza.

ACT TWO

REBELLION IN ROSARNO

IX

A few minutes before dawn on the first Sunday of 2010, the rattle of a scooter could be heard curling up through the empty streets of Reggio Calabria. Two figures leaned into the windscreen to protect themselves from the January cold. In front was a woman in a dark jacket, tight jeans and stilettos, a dark helmet pushed down over her long hair. Behind her sat a man in jeans and a dark jacket. Despite the speed at which the pair were racing across the icy cobbles, the man declined to hold on to his companion. Instead in his arms he cradled a bulky canvas bag, almost as though it were a baby.

After following the shoreline for a few minutes, the pair turned away from the sea and climbed up steeply towards the centre of the old town. They passed the floodlit walls of the Castello Aragonese, built by the Normans and expanded by the Spanish in the fifteenth century. When the pair reached the castle gardens, the woman executed a wide about-turn, eased off the throttle and allowed the bike to coast gently over the cobbles back down the hill. After a few yards, she pulled up in front of an imposing metal gate, holding the bike on the slope with her legs and keeping her hand on the accelerator. Behind her the man bent over his bag and pulled his jacket around him as though he were lighting a cigarette. Suddenly there was a spark. Flames licked up out of the bag. The man jumped off the bike and ran towards the gate, swinging the burning bag high and wide like a lasso to avoid the flames. The woman revved the engine and let the bike roll slowly down the hill. The man dropped the bag, ran back to the moving bike, jumped on and the pair roared off. Seconds later, the bag exploded.[1]

In the pre-dawn calm, the noise of the blast rolled out across the Straits of Messina like thunder. The noise woke Alessandra and Paolo in their apartment. A few hours later, watching a press conference, Alessandra heard a *carabinieri* commander describe the bomb as the kind of crude device – a stick of dynamite attached to a ten-kilo gas cylinder – familiar to anyone with experience of southern Italy's protection rackets. Aside from some damage to a gate and a railing, there was little physical harm done.

That didn't mean the attack wasn't serious. The mayor of Reggio, the chamber of commerce, the president and vice-president of the Italian parliament, even Italy's head of state, President Giorgio Napolitano, sent the Reggio authorities messages of solidarity. Italy had declared war on the world's most powerful mafia. The *mafiosi* had started the New Year by signalling their intention to strike back.

The stakes in this new fight had escalated radically over the previous few months. Thanks to years of surveillance, for the first time the Italian state now had a comprehensive picture of the 'Ndrangheta's structure and its cocaine business. The prosecutors were now confronting the full scale of the mission they had undertaken. Their priority was also clear: Calabria's west coast, the heart of the cocaine business. That explained the bomb's target, detonated outside Reggio's courthouse, the seat of justice in Calabria for as long as the 'Ndrangheta had existed and, in 2010, the offices of Calabria's attorney general, who oversaw the confiscation of mafia assets. If the 'Ndrangheta liked to send messages, this was the group at its most unequivocal: Calabria's prosecutors should end their campaign or face violent consequences. But as Alessandra and her colleagues absorbed the implications of the warning, they drew a second conclusion, too. To provoke this kind of reaction, their crackdown must be having an effect.

There followed other signs that the west coast 'Ndrangheta was feeling the pressure. A week after the bomb, Rosarno erupted in three days of riots. The violence began when a group of 'Ndrangheta teenagers, apparently bored and looking for kicks, fired an airgun into the tented camp behind Gioia Tauro port where more than a thousand West African migrants lived. Hundreds of Africans marched into Rosarno, protesting, burning several cars and fighting with the police. Rosarno hoodlums armed with iron bars set up roadblocks. At least two Rosarno men tried to run over migrants in the street. More than twenty Africans were injured, many of them beaten and three shot. Eventually, riot police descended. On the orders of the interior minister, they expelled every last African – a total of 1,200 people – from the town. Rosarno and its people, said Minister Roberto Maroni, were the unfortunate victims of 'too much tolerance'.

But if the Rosarno *picciotti* considered such unashamed racism a victory, they were mistaken. Led by Pope Benedict XVI, the violence drew condemnation and outrage from across Italy. One opposition leader, Luigi Manconi, said that by expelling the Africans, the authorities had been complicit in creating 'the whitest town in the world'. The media attention also exposed the wretched hypocrisy of the 'Ndrangheta – who, it turned out, were attacking the very people they had brought to Rosarno to work as fruit pickers for as little as €3 a day. The spotlight on Rosarno also gave Alessandra's office an opportunity to score a very public victory. A day after the violence died down, with the eyes of Italy still on Rosarno, her office arrested seventeen suspected members of the Bellocco clan, the Pesces' main rival in the city, and seized assets of several million euros.[2]

Almost straight away, the 'Ndrangheta tripped up again. Nine days later in Reggio, hours before President Napolitano arrived to reinforce his support of Calabria's authorities in their new war, a telephone tip-off led *carabinieri* to a stolen car parked close to his route. The vehicle contained two bombs and two pistols. But what was intended to intimidate quickly managed to do precisely the opposite. The tipster was arrested almost immediately and charged with mafia association. Napolitano's visit went ahead, though now he was able to strike a courageous profile by defying the mafia's threat to his life and, on 'Ndrangheta turf, hailing a 'turning point' in the fight against them. As a final insult, by the end of the month Reggio Calabria had been selected as the location for a new Italian agency tasked with seizing mafia businesses and transforming them into Libera shops or offices for policemen, magistrates or the tax department. As fightbacks went, it felt uncomfortably like humiliation.[3]

But even if the 'Ndrangheta had lost the opening exchanges in its war with the state, the fight was far from over. Alessandra, in particular, was convinced that a crucial weakness in the state's strategy meant it could never win. Pignatone and Prestipino were free thinkers who had no trouble imagining a woman 'Ndranghetista could be as much use as a woman prosecutor. But among the rank-and-file, 'Italian prosecutors were still not investigating women,' said Alessandra. Many rejected outright the idea that women could serve justice in any way at all. ('I mean, *really*, women do have eyes and ears,' said Alessandra.) They also refused to see as anything other than exceptional what Alessandra was observing in Rosarno: that by early 2010, 'Ndrangheta men had realised their women were being left alone by the authorities and were starting to give them power. The scooter driver at the Reggio bomb attack had been a woman. Across the province, at least two women had become clan bosses. Nevertheless, said Alessandra, 'it was still very hard for us to make our colleagues believe that women had a role.'

Alessandra understood that if many prosecutors and *carabinieri* were barely able to conceive of a woman 'Ndranghetista, then they would dismiss out of hand the idea of an 'Ndrangheta woman with the strength to rebel against her men. 'This was another form of the same prejudice,' she said. 'The belief that no one, and certainly not a woman, is going to talk about their own family, let alone testify and accuse their own family.' She conceded that it would take unusual bravery. But to write it off as impossible was to guarantee it never happened. 'When justice shows to people that it is strong and that the state is present and can help you if you want to collaborate,' she said, 'then you find collaborators appear.'

At heart, thought Alessandra, this was a failure of perception. Whenever her male colleagues saw women and children, they saw family and nothing else. Most seemed incapable of identifying what a family might represent in a place like Rosarno or Pagliarelle: a living, breathing criminal organism. 'The entire structure, the family nature of it, makes it hard for many people even to recognise it as a problem,' she said. Once again, Alessandra was confronting the 'Ndrangheta's astute understanding of family. 'The part played by family, and by women, makes them so difficult to track.' Sometimes she felt she was the only one who could see what was right in front of them all: women who were simultaneously mothers, *mafiosi* and potential state witnesses. That had been the problem with Lea Garofalo. The state had seen her too simplistically, as a battered wife, a troubled witness, a victim. Only one prosecutor, Salvatore Dolce, had grasped everything that Lea was and everything that she offered the state. What Alessandra needed was another 'Ndrangheta mother to change her colleagues' minds.

As it happened, she would have two.

According to the precepts of clan rivalry, Giuseppina Pesce, thirty-one, and Maria Concetta Cacciola, thirty, shouldn't have been friends.[4] The Pesces led the most powerful clan in Rosarno, which had ruled the town since the 1920s. The Cacciolas were muscle for their rivals, the Belloccos. The Pesces and the Belloccos sometimes cooperated in business and on occasion their children even married each other. But as the Pesces climbed ever higher up the 'Ndrangheta's new vertical hierarchy, the Bellocco name meant ever less – and the Belloccos hated the Pesces for that.

Giuseppina and Concetta also weren't alike. Giuseppina was tough, an 'Ndrangheta wife who had pushed the men in her family to let her become an 'Ndranghetista in her own right. There were limits on what a woman could do in the organisation. Murder and violence were out, and any involvement in extortion, corruption or drug smuggling was confined to bookkeeping and passing messages between the men. But Giuseppina was dismissive of any man who imagined her to be less than him and communicated her adamant equality in a tomboyish appearance. She wore bulky woollen V-necks over cheap and baggy worker's shirts. She had no time for make-up. Her dirt-brown hair was cut in a scruffy parting at whatever length kept it out of the way, and from under it her brown eyes would stare out at the world with a blankness that conveyed an intimidating intimacy with brutality.

Concetta could not have been more different. She took no part in the men's business, and her knowledge of it extended little beyond gossip about where the bunkers were and who had killed who. Unlike the Pesces, the Cacciola men didn't accept even a hint of independence or assertion in their women, and they kept Concetta confined to the house for weeks at a time. On the rare occasions she was allowed out, Concetta's own private rebellion was to emerge immaculately dressed, as though she were a busy socialite. She favoured tight jeans with unbuttoned blouses that hung loosely across her perfumed chest. Her jet-black hair was styled in a long undulating curl that swept across her forehead, nestled over her ears and executed a jaunty ski-jump on her shoulders. She plucked her eyebrows, waxed her legs, painted her fingernails and toes and matched dark shades of plum and scarlet on her lips with heavy mascara and a brush of mauve over her eyes. If Giuseppina's appearance implied equivalence to any man, Concetta presented herself as nothing like them.

Despite their differences, Giuseppina and Concetta had been close friends since they were girls. When they were growing up in Rosarno in the 1980s, the town had been a cold, hard place of loveless lives where girls could be beaten just for stepping out of the house unaccompanied. Rosarno was also small, however, and as schoolgirls Giuseppina and Concetta would see each other every day in the playground or the street. As they approached their teens, their lives also followed an identical prescribed course, which – since the town had no secondary school and 'Ndrangheta girls weren't allowed to leave it – meant marriage quickly followed by motherhood.

Giuseppina finished her education at thirteen. By then, she had already met her future husband, Rocco Palaia, twenty, whose father managed weapons for the Pesce clan. At fourteen, Giuseppina eloped with Rocco, a common event in Rosarno, known as *fuitina*. At fifteen she gave birth to the first of the couple's three children, Angela. By then, Rocco was doing little more than smoking weed and lying around the house all day, so Giuseppina went to work in the family store. It wasn't long before Rocco was arrested and jailed for mafia association.

Concetta had always had it harder than her friend. When she was eleven, her brother Giuseppe caught her playing in the street with a few local boys. He beat her, dragged her home by her hair and forbade her to leave the house alone again. After that, Concetta never went out for pizza or *gelato*. 'You know my brother 'Peppe,' she would say. 'If he saw me, you know he'd kill me.' Concetta left school at eleven. When she was thirteen, inside a single year, she met her twenty-one-year-old future husband, Salvatore Figliuzzi, eloped with him, married him and saw him hauled off to jail charged with mafia association. A few months later, aged fourteen, Concetta gave birth to Alfonso, the first of the couple's three children.

By the time of his arrest, Salvatore was already beating Concetta regularly. One day he held a gun to her head. When Concetta complained to her father, he replied, 'It's your marriage and your life. You deal with it.' Concetta might have expected things to improve with Salvatore in jail. Instead, her father took over the role of violent disciplinarian, slapping her to the ground in the street one day when she returned late from a shopping trip to Reggio. Meanwhile, on conjugal visits to prison, Concetta conceived a second child, Tania, then a third, Rosalba, whom she named after her mother.

By their early twenties, Giuseppina and Concetta were alone, married to jailbird husbands and mothers to three children each. They would meet at the school gates or the doctor's or in the Pesce family mini-mart where Giuseppina worked, across the street from the Cacciola family home. The two women negotiated their situations as best they could. Concetta had somehow remained 'a sunny girl', said Giuseppina years later, through tears. 'Optimistic. A force of nature. She always laughed. She always cared so much.' As Lea had done growing up in Pagliarelle, Concetta sustained herself with a dream of true love that would take her away from it all. With Salvatore in jail, she began fantasising that she was not the abused wife of a violent small-time gangster at all but, rather, a woman tragically separated from her love. On prison visits, she would wear scarlet lipstick with thick eyeshadow and frame her face with thick long curls. She wrote Salvatore letters which she decorated with love hearts. 'I go out in the morning to take the children to school but I have no contact with anyone,' she wrote in 2007. 'How can I live if I cannot even breathe? If I can't even speak to anyone? My father likes to see me miserable from dawn to dusk. If only I could have a little peace of mind. I'd pay anything, take anything, for a little peace. I don't know how long I can go on without you.'

If Concetta survived by retreating into fantasy, Giuseppina endured through sheer will. Like Concetta, she was beaten by her husband. But Rocco would hit Giuseppina not because she was out on her own or because she was looking at other men, or even just because he could, but because Giuseppina insisted on speaking out of turn. 'He beat me when I said what I thought,' she said. 'He attacked me to get me to shut up.'

After Rocco went to jail, Giuseppina's father, Salvatore, told her to confine herself to the home like Concetta. He refused to let her go to college or divorce Rocco or continue her piano lessons. 'You're not going anywhere,' he shouted. 'You'll stay locked up in the house.' Giuseppina's way of conserving some autonomy was to join the family firm. Within a few years, she was running messages between bosses in jail, laundering money and overseeing the collection of *pizzo*. 'I am part of the family,' she said later. 'I lived in the family. I *know*. I lived and breathed these things, the superiority and the power and the privilege. No one had to come and tell me what to do. No one ever said they were *mafia*. But I knew because I was there. I was in it.'

With every year that passed, Giuseppina's knowledge of the 'Ndrangheta grew. She knew its power structure intimately. The nominal head of the clan was Giuseppina's uncle Antonino. Since he was in jail, however, others handled day-to-day operations. By primogeniture, Giuseppina's father, Salvatore, should have been the first choice to replace Antonino. But Salvatore had never been leadership material: since he was a boy, his nickname had been '*u babbu*', the buffoon. The mantle instead fell to Antonino's son and Giuseppina's cousin, Francesco 'Ciccio' Pesce, a hothead given to angry and violent outbursts who wielded absolute power in his father's stead.

The 'Ndrangheta was run as an autocracy. But Giuseppina would later insist it was one willingly accepted by its subjects. In the 'Ndrangheta, tyranny was what passed for effective leadership, and what it took to have and hold power. At its heart, however, Giuseppina said an *'ndrina* was a collective. 'We decided together, as a family, who took state contracts, who handled extortion, who handled the trucks, who oversaw the drug trade, how the money was shared. That's the strength of the clan – that we are all family members together.'

Inside the *'ndrina*, *picciotti* like Giuseppina were expected to help out however they were needed. Her work gave Giuseppina a comprehensive view of the Pesce empire. The house of her seventy-eight-year-old grandmother, Giuseppa Bonarrigo, often served as a base for operations and a meeting place. There the family would discuss at length the delicate question of how much *pizzo* to charge. The younger men tended to squeeze as much as they could out of everyone, once even extorting tickets for the entire family from a visiting circus. The older men would warn against overdoing it, arguing that driving a business to ruin was in no one's interest. Another point of discussion was how to divide the take. Giuseppina saw many *picciotti* try to resist handing over their revenues to a common family pot, as required. What everyone agreed, however, was that there could be no exceptions to paying *pizzo*. 'An outsider can't say no,' said Giuseppina. 'Because he is afraid. Because he knows there will be repercussions. The men would go and ask for money like they were doing people a favour. But everyone knew they couldn't refuse.'

Giuseppina got to know other sides of the business. Her father, Salvatore, her cousin Ciccio and her husband Rocco all moved cocaine through Gioia Tauro port and stashed packages in the house, ready for onward transport. Negotiating the interminable roadworks on the A3 from Reggio Calabria to Salerno one day, her brother pointed out which sites belonged to the Pesces and which to other clans. 'Ndrangheta rules also required each clan to have a stash of automatic rifles, pistols and explosives. Rocco and his brother had buried the Pesce arsenal around town – heavy automatic weapons, AK-47s, rifles, pistols, shotguns – wrapping the guns in sheets of plastic and duct tape with a round in the chamber, ready to go. 'We're prepared for a war,' Rocco liked to say.

It was the Pesces' firepower that guaranteed the family was feared or, as they liked to see it, respected. Around town, people would make way for Giuseppina. In restaurants, bills never appeared. In grocery stores, the manager would come out to serve her personally. If she went to the doctor's, she walked straight to the head of the queue and 'no one could ever say anything to me because I was part of the family'. One time she went to an ear specialist in Gioia Tauro. On hearing her name, the man asked after the health of her niece and her daughter, then knocked his price down to bargain-basement level, saying he wanted to send 'his greetings to my uncle and my family'.

But if the family enjoyed their local fame, other kinds of attention made them paranoid. The ability of the police and the *carabinieri* to listen in was unreal. They tapped phone calls, filmed the interiors of houses from several kilometres away, mounted secret cameras outside homes and schools and planted bugs almost anywhere – in cars, walls and fireplaces, in orchards and schools, even under stones in Giuseppina's grandmother's garden. The Pesces bought bug detectors to sniff out these devices, as well as jammers to block their signal and scanners of their own to monitor the *carabinieri*'s radios. Still, they were often reduced to whispering and using sign language in their own homes. Ciccio was always telling the others, 'Don't talk too much.' More than once, his paranoia led him to smash up his phone and television, unscrew every lightbulb in his house and throw everything into the street.

This mistrust forced many a boss into hiding. Most sought sanctuary in secret underground bunkers buried deep in the countryside. It wasn't as bad as it sounded. The bosses would kit out their bunkers with lights, televisions, kitchens and comfortable beds. Some had their hideouts built into the cliffs to give them a sea view and a sunset. Others enjoyed bucolic locations in orchards or olive groves. Instinctively territorial, however, the Pesces built their bunkers in town, often under their own houses. Before he was arrested in 2005, Giuseppina's father had been hiding for years in a bunker that he'd spent thousands of euros renovating under the floor of Giuseppina's grandmother's house.

If respect was everything to the Pesces, shame was unacceptable for the same reason. The treacherous and unfaithful didn't just need to be killed. They had to vanish from the face of the earth and leave no reminders of the dishonour they had brought on the family.

By 2010, Michele Prestipino was looking into twenty Calabrian 'suicides' that he suspected were actually wrongly recorded honour killings. In one of the most recent, a widow called Dominica Legato had jumped to her death from her balcony in Rosarno in 2007. At least, that was what her son told police. Giuseppina, Concetta and every woman in Rosarno suspected another version of events, as did the coroner, who found knife wounds on Dominica's hands, suggesting she had been fending off an attack when she fell. A few months later the Rosarno man with whom Dominica was said to be having a relationship also disappeared.

The full fury of the Rosarno 'Ndrangheta's rage could be terrifying. What made it even more disturbing was how the 'Ndrangheta could sustain it. In 1979, when she was twenty-five, the husband of Concetta Teresa Galluci, a mason, died in an accident, falling from the fourth floor of a building he was helping build for the Pesces. Concetta and her husband had had three children. More than a decade later, she began a relationship with twenty-three-year-old Francesco Alcuri. One night in November 1993 in Rosarno, Alcuri was shot nine times in the groin, dying eleven days later in agony. Concetta, now forty, fled for Genoa in northern Italy, where her sister lived. One evening four months after arriving, she opened her sister's front door and was shot in the head. The gunmen then shot the dead woman's seventy-two-year-old mother as she ran into the living room in her nightdress, before killing her twenty-two-year-old niece while she slept in her bed.

The Pesces were deeply secretive about their own family embarrassments. Not for them the scrutiny that accompanied the discovery of a dead body. Long ago, the Pesces had calculated that since Rosarno's graveyard was the most obvious place to dump a body, it would be the last place anyone would look. Up there somewhere, his bones mixed in with hundreds of others, was Giuseppina's grandfather, Angelo Ferraro, killed for having an affair. Under the floor in the chapel was Annunziata Pesce, Giuseppina's cousin, who had betrayed her husband and the entire 'Ndrangheta by running off with a policeman. Kidnapped off the street in broad daylight in 1981, she was shot in the head by the boss, Antonino Pesce, while her elder brother

Antonio watched. Antonio's reward for his unflinching loyalty? Promotion to a dominant position inside the *'ndrina* for him and his immediate family.

Killings like these left no doubt about the price of betrayal. It was a measure of the desperation of many 'Ndrangheta women that the men kept finding it necessary to carry them out. Perhaps it was inevitable. 'Ndrangheta mothers knew their sons would grow up to be killers and drug dealers destined for prison and an early grave. They knew their daughters would be married off as they had been, barely pubescent, to an older, abusive, criminal husband. They expected to lose their own abusive, criminal husband to death or jail. Faced with a life in which what Concetta called Rosarno's 'stone-hearted men' extinguished all the light and joy in the world, it was hardly surprising that the town's women grabbed what little sweetness they could.

Many of the men seemed to understand this. Their response was not to ease off but to take pre-emptive action, particularly when, with a husband dead or in jail, an 'Ndrangheta wife found herself alone. Concetta's cousin Giuseppina Multari had been locked up at home as a virtual slave since the day in 2005 that the Cacciola men had killed her husband, their cousin, for being a junkie. When her brother tried to confront the Cacciolas about the way they were treating his sister, he also vanished.

When Concetta's husband, Salvatore, went to jail, her father and brother resolved to prevent her from almost ever leaving the house. But such blinkered conservatism blinded them to the fact that they were living in the twenty-first century, in which friendship – or more – was only ever a click away. 'In the land of the 'Ndrangheta, the internet is an open window to a closed world,' said Alessandra. 'It introduces women to a free world. It tends to provoke a kind of emotional explosion.'

So it proved with Concetta. 'She began to explore the world through the web,' said Giuseppe Creazzo, a prosecutor in Palmi who would later investigate the Cacciola family. Concetta found she liked celebrity news: charming people leading beautiful lives. She imagined the famous couples watching sunsets together and going out at night. Soon, said Creazzo, she was looking for friends for herself. She joined Facebook. And slowly, a feeling began to grow inside her. 'Every day,' said Creazzo, 'Concetta felt more and more like rebelling.'

By the middle of 2009, Concetta was chatting regularly to a Rosarno man who had moved to Germany. Giuseppina, more assertive, went further than her friend, beginning a clandestine affair with a man called Domenico Costantino with whom she had worked at a family factory that made crystallised fruit. 'He was the first man who ever seemed to care for my children,' said Giuseppina. 'He was the first man to respect me as a woman, the first who ever loved me.'

Almost anywhere else in Europe, either of these liaisons would have merited condemnation or, perhaps, understanding. In Rosarno, Concetta and Giuseppina were risking death. It was a gauge of the lovelessness in their lives that both women courted that danger without hesitation.

X

In Pagliarelle, the *carabinieri* were watching another illicit romance unfold.[1]

For Denise, a birthday without Lea had been followed by Christmas without Lea, then New Year without Lea, all of them spent in Lea's apartment, upstairs from Lea's mother. One night, a friend's family took Denise to a restaurant on the coast for dinner – but someone had brought Christmas presents from Milan. Another time, when Carlo took his daughter to the dentist, Denise let herself imagine that it would be the most natural thing in the world for a daughter to ask her father if he had any news of her missing mother. 'Get it through your head: I don't know anything about your mother,' snapped Carlo. 'She left. She left *you*. You're on your own.'

Denise already had a difficult relationship with food. Now she took to binge eating to relieve the stress, gaining twenty kilos in months. If Carlo noticed, he didn't seem concerned. Denise's Aunt Marisa took her niece to a clinic but when that proved ineffective, she also offered Denise little other help.

Desperate, Denise turned to the man her father had deputed to keep an eye on her in Pagliarelle. Carlo had given thirty-one-year-old Carmine Venturino orders to escort Denise wherever she went and, above all, to keep her away from the authorities. Carmine would drive

Denise around all day. He gave her pocket money. He worked with her in the Cosco family pizzeria in Petilia. When Denise started at a new high school in January, it was Carmine who helped settle her in. Watching all this, the surveillance teams began to feel uneasy. The officers knew Carlo had told Carmine to watch Denise. But this looked like something else.

What made the officers particularly uncomfortable was what they were learning about Carmine's movements on the night Lea vanished. Phone records showed that Carmine spoke to Carlo dozens of times in the hours after Lea disappeared and in the days that followed. Carmine said little of substance in his calls. But his tone had been panicky and his movements erratic. His GPS showed him driving outside the city several times in the days and nights after 24 November. Recordings of his voice showed he'd been desperate to find the keys to a warehouse and that, once he located them, he kept going back to the place. Besides, thought the officers, Carmine was Carlo's sometime flatmate and one of his key lieutenants. He *had* to be involved.

On 3 February, the *carabinieri* in Campobasso announced they had enough evidence to arrest Carlo for ordering the attack on Lea in her apartment in May 2009. They detained Carlo just as Denise returned from school. Watching her father being led away in handcuffs, Denise recognised the look on his face as the same he'd had on the night Lea went missing. A newspaper report about Carlo's arrest the next day was accompanied by a picture of another man charged with the Campobasso attack, Massimo Sabatino. The paper said Sabatino was an associate of her father's and was already in prison on a drug charge.

Two months in, the officers investigating Lea's disappearance could be pleased with their progress. They had a prime suspect, for whom they had established motive and opportunity, and from Lea's case files, they had ample documentation to back up their allegations. Handily, Carlo was now also under arrest for another attack on Lea. But the murder case against Carlo also had a giant flaw: no body. Without it, a prosecutor couldn't even say for sure that Lea had died, let alone how.

Then the *carabinieri* got lucky. Massimo Sabatino, thirty-six, was a career criminal with a long list of convictions for robbery and drug dealing. When he was served his indictment for the Campobasso attack, he was already in San Vittore prison on a charge of dealing heroin after being arrested in December 2009. Slow and poorly educated, Sabatino handed the charge sheet to his friend and cellmate Salvatore Sorrentino, who had been picked up in Milan in January for absconding from house arrest at the end of a five-year sentence for robbery. While Sorrentino digested the document, Sabatino explained to his friend that for a few years he had been looking after weapons and cocaine for an 'Ndrangheta boss in Milan called Carlo Cosco. His connection to Carlo was through his sister Rosi, who was engaged to Rosario Curcio, one of Carlo's crew.

One day in April 2009, Sabatino said, Carlo had offered him €25,000 to drive to Campobasso and recover a drug debt from a woman living there. Carlo later refined the plan, saying Sabatino should go disguised as a washing-machine repair man and tie the woman up, drag her to his van and take her to Bari on Puglia's east coast, where Carlo and his brothers would be waiting. Carlo had also given him 50 litres of sulphuric acid to carry in the back of the van. Sabatino said he had done as instructed but failed to kidnap the woman because her daughter, who wasn't supposed to be there, had appeared from nowhere and jumped him.

Sorrentino said that according to the charge sheet, Sabatino's fingerprints had been found on the washing machine in the apartment. Sabatino agreed that was possible: he'd worn latex gloves but torn them in the struggle with the women. Sorrentino continued that the woman Sabatino had been trying to abduct was a Garofalo, a name familiar to anyone in the 'Ndrangheta. Sabatino claimed he'd never known the identity of the woman. Sorrentino said that according to the indictment, Lea had not only been Carlo's wife but also a *pentita* who had testified against him.

It began to dawn on Sabatino that he was in real trouble. He told Sorrentino that he knew of a second, successful attempt to kidnap Lea in Milan on 24 November. Though Sabatino stressed that he had played no part, he assumed Lea was now dead. He added that he had no alibi for either May or November.

Sorrentino agreed it looked bad. Sabatino had to be looking at life. Sabatino swore. Carlo was a motherfucker, he said. He hadn't paid him for the Campobasso job and had refused even to give him money for a lawyer when he was arrested in December.

Sabatino didn't know what to do. But his cellmate Sorrentino did. A day or so later, he sent a letter to the Milan prosecutor investigating Lea's disappearance, offering to relay everything his friend had told him in return for a reduced sentence. The prosecutors, sceptical at first, were reassured when Sabatino was moved to a different cell and his new cellmate made a statement confirming many of the same details. When a prosecutor confronted Sabatino, he lied so badly – initially claiming he was meant to recover a debt from Lea, then claiming he was robbing her, then admitting he was trying to kidnap her – that he managed to solidify the case against him and Carlo.

To the investigators, the case was beginning to look conclusive. But Sabatino had given them something else, too. According to Sorrentino, Sabatino claimed that the Cosco brothers had also killed two Garofalo men in the past. Sabatino even named Giuseppe Cosco as the shooter in the first killing, which he added had taken place in a Milan apartment block in 1995. Allowing for the distortion of jailhouse hearsay, this seemed to be corroboration of Lea's allegation that Giuseppe Cosco had shot dead Antonio Comberiati at No. 6 Viale Montello in May 1995. The allegation that the Coscos had killed a second Garofalo seemed to refer to the 2005 death of Lea's brother Floriano, a killing which was unsolved. Here, finally, was the evidence to substantiate Lea's allegations. Disbelieved in life, she was being vindicated in death.

*

There was still the mystery of what had happened to Lea, however. In Catanzaro, down on the coast below Pagliarelle, the prosecutor's office had informed Annalisa Pisano that her former client had disappeared. 'They told me clearly that it had to be *lupara bianca*,' she said. Though she and Lea hadn't spoken in a year and a half, Annalisa still felt a strong bond with her. That night, said Annalisa, 'I dreamed of Lea. She was in a warehouse, surrounded by flames and she was asking me for help. She was calling me by my name. "Annalisa!" But everybody was telling her "No!"' And every night from then on, to the day years later when Lea was found, Annalisa had the same recurring dream. 'People would ask me: "How do you know she has been burned?" And I'd reply: "Because I see her. You can believe me or not." And I am not the kind of person who believes in these things. But I saw her. Almost every night. She was on a chair, in a warehouse, surrounded by fire, calling for me. And at that point, I would wake up.'

For Denise, Carlo's arrest only sharpened the questions over her mother's death. *How* had Carlo killed her? Did he shoot her? Suffocate her? Slit her throat? Did he have one of his men do it? Did she scream? Was it quick or did he draw it out? Did he torture her? At what point did Lea know she was going to die? Would Denise know when her own time came?

While Carlo's arrest should have come as some relief, in Pagliarelle it just made it harder for Denise to maintain the lie. In mid-February, on the eve of her first visit to see Carlo in jail, the surveillance team picked up a text message from Denise to Carmine. Denise was losing her mind. The situation was impossible, she said. How could she keep on pretending when her father was in jail accused of trying to kill her mother? How could she face him? 'Carmine calmed me,' Denise said. 'He made me laugh. He made me feel good.'

The respite was temporary. When Denise went to Catanzaro jail the next day with her uncle Vito, she wept throughout. Vito tried to be sympathetic but didn't seem to know how. 'Crying when your father is in prison and your mother is missing is only natural,' he said blankly.

Carmine was waiting for Denise when she returned. Once inside her aunt's house, she collapsed. 'It was an hour of crying and eating at the same time,' she said later. 'I was so desperate. I wasn't thinking about who I trusted and who I didn't. I was desperate for some affection. I cried. I ate. I was shouting out: "Leave me alone! I have to go to a place where I don't want to go, live in a place where I don't want to live, with people that I suspect? What do you want me to do? Laugh?" What I suffered, nobody can understand.' In the end, Carmine just held Denise. They hugged for what seemed like for ever. Then they kissed.

Over the next few weeks, the surveillance team watched as Denise and Carmine became inseparable. 'She fell in love with this guy and he with her,' said Enza. 'She was able to open up to him, to speak with him and cry with him.' But Denise was also mindful that Carmine was a member of Carlo's *'ndrina*. She would ask him over and over again what he knew about what had happened to her mother. 'He always said he didn't know and didn't want to know,' said Denise. 'I never had an answer.' Adding to the pressure on Denise, her affair with Carmine was something else she had to keep secret. 'Carmine told me to say absolutely nothing to anyone,' she said. 'If my father knew, he'd be furious. He'd given Carmine the job of accompanying me and controlling me, not dating me. No one could know we were seeing each other. We would meet at midnight in the meadows outside Pagliarelle so that no one would find out.'

Unable to express almost any of her thoughts and on constant guard against letting her true feelings show, Denise took to staying silent for most of the day. 'I couldn't shout [about] what they had done,' she said. 'I couldn't cry out: "You are all killers!"' When the Coscos asked her to write to her father in jail in early March, she agreed, then found she had almost nothing to say.

To Dad
Even if you are away from me, you are still close to me.

I love you,
Denise

PS Don't worry about me.

PPS I could get you some wild boar if you want. As you can see,
like you, I am someone of few words. But what I write here is
what I could never say to you. I just want you to be fine.

On 25 February, in a public demonstration of her loyalty to the family,
Denise signed a formal waiver giving up her right to witness protection. Secretly, however, she re-established contact with Enza and
other activists in Libera, asking if they could hide her if she left
Pagliarelle. On 5 March, she also clandestinely met the *carabinieri* a
second time and gave a further statement. For the officers, Denise's
new evidence filled in most of the remaining gaps in Lea's life, right
up until the last few hours. But for Denise, reliving that night only
increased her stress. She couldn't shake the thought that seemed to be
getting ever louder in her head: that she should run away from
Pagliarelle like her mother.

In early April 2010, when her aunt went away for a few days, Denise
seized her chance. She took the bus to Crotone, then jumped on a
long-distance train to the north. After a day, she arrived at a Libera
safe house near Turin. 'I had to go,' she told her hosts. 'They wouldn't
let me live.' Initially, the Coscos didn't notice Denise was gone. But
when one week became three, there was no hiding it any longer. On
23 April, Vito Cosco drove down from Milan and confronted Marisa
and her husband, demanding to know where Denise had gone.

That afternoon, the surveillance team tapped a series of calls
between Marisa and Denise. 'Vito's been here!' Marisa said. 'Wherever

you are, you have to be here tomorrow! They say they just want to talk to you. Afterwards you can go off wherever you want. Otherwise you're basically telling them to go fuck themselves.'

'I know I have to go back to talk to these assholes,' replied Denise.

'Look, they just want to feel relaxed,' said Marisa. 'They want to know that you know what you have to do.'

'What I have to do?! What I have to do?!' shouted Denise. 'I have to keep quiet! I have to be stopped!'

'So fuck them all!' said Marisa. 'But we're all so sick of this mess here. And I think once they know where you are and what you're doing, they'll calm down. Vito was going to see your father but he didn't go because he didn't know what to tell him. Right now, they're afraid that you're back in the programme.'

'The programme your sister was in!'

'They're just afraid, Denise,' said Marisa. 'Don't over-think this. Don't imagine the worst. They don't care where you are or how you are. They only care about themselves. They only care that no one speaks the truth.'

Denise returned to Pagliarelle the next day. Vito, apparently reassured, flew back to Milan. Denise had to wait a week before visiting her father in jail. The prospect of speaking to Carlo once more terrified her as much as it had the last time. She turned to Carmine once again. 'I have to wait a week,' she texted him. 'I know what you think – that I'm wrong – but I just want to have the chance of a different life.'

'This is the week you can change things,' Carmine wrote back. 'No one's standing in the way of the life you want. Just do things right, and the others will relax.'

The reality, as Enza discovered years later, was precisely the opposite. Carlo's brothers had kept him closely informed of Denise's behaviour. She wasn't getting any better, they told him. When Denise had disappeared, Carlo told his brothers that he had made a decision. If and when she reappeared, she had to die. Carlo added it would be easiest if Carmine did it.

Carmine, ever more in love with Denise, had been half-expecting the call. He had already decided to disobey. But now that it had come, the clock was ticking. The boss had given the order that his only daughter, whom he loved, was to be killed. It wasn't a decision he would have taken lightly. But it was one that, given Denise's erratic behaviour, he would have concluded was unavoidable. Carlo had to protect the 'ndrina and the 'Ndrangheta. He had to enforce the code. Women were the organisation's property and the repository of its honour, to be cherished or disposed of as duty required. Now he had made the decision, he would want his orders carried out as swiftly as possible. As Carmine's betrayal became apparent to Carlo over the next few weeks and months, he knew Carlo would make him pay dearly for it.

XI

Barely a day after Denise returned to Calabria's east coast, Alessandra made her first strike against the Pesces on the west. In the early hours of 26 April 2010, in simultaneous raids in Rosarno, Milan and Bergamo, codenamed Operation All Inside, hundreds of *carabinieri* moved in on the Pesce empire. They arrested a total of thirty people. Ten warrants were issued for *'ndrina* members on the run. Among those accused was clan boss Antonino Pesce, Giuseppina's uncle, who was already in jail. His nephew and protégé, Giuseppina's brother Francesco Pesce, was arrested in Rosarno. Reflecting Alessandra's convictions, seven of the detained were women. They included Giuseppina's mother, sister, cousin, grandmother and great-grandmother, as well as Giuseppina herself.

The charges against the Pesce family included extortion, money laundering, loan sharking, drug smuggling, mafia association and two counts of murder.[1] The range of accusations indicated how, inside their dominion of Gioia Tauro and Rosarno, the Pesces' hegemony was total. 'They completely control their territory and their government,' said Michele Prestipino. 'People who live there accept that to get something they have to knock on the door of the mafia and that there is no future other than what the mafia sees.' The 'Ndrangheta's power in Rosarno was at its peak. In a town of 15,000 people, the authorities had identified 500 'Ndrangheta members and hundreds more associates. That crushing dominance meant a strange kind of peace prevailed. 'There is not much need for a lot of violence,' said Prestipino. 'Everybody knows that if these people want to use violence, they can. They achieve consensus without firing a shot.'

The range of assets seized during Operation All Inside was further evidence of the Pesces' reach. While the prosecutors promised heftier hauls to come, even on this first pass they confiscated vehicles, properties and businesses worth €10 million from one of the poorest areas in Europe. Pesce businesses included a petrol station, a car dealership, a food distribution company and a sugar refinery and chocolate factory whose company documents named Rocco Palaia, Giuseppina's husband, as its owner. A Rosarno radio station, Radio Olimpia, was particularly interesting. Not only was it an asset in its own right, the *carabinieri* had discovered that jailed bosses and *picciotti* were using Olimpia's request show to communicate with each other. Prisoners would ask their family a yes/no question – Is my appeal successful? Were my orders carried out? – and the families would reply by calling in and requesting one of two songs to relay the answer. Giuseppina's fugitive uncle Vincenzo would also call in from time to time and ask the presenter to use his nickname and describe him as a listener 'at large'. In other words: I am still in the area; I am still free.

Giuseppina was charged with mafia association, money laundering, extortion and running messages. She faced more than a decade in jail. That wasn't what troubled her, however. The Calabrian newspapers had reported that she had been detained with a man. Three weeks earlier, she had been warned by her Uncle Vincenzo that her family suspected she was having a relationship with Domenico Costantino. Her cousin Francesco had had her followed day and night. Now that she had been found with Domenico in the middle of the night, their suspicions would be confirmed. The family's punishment would far exceed the state's. 'In my family, those who betray and dishonour the family must be punished by death,' said Giuseppina. 'It is a law.' 'She was going to die and she knew it,' said Alessandra. 'She accepted it.'

What Giuseppina could not accept was the sudden implosion of her three children's future. She had never been apart from Angela, fifteen, Gaetano, nine, and Elisea, five. Now they were with Rocco's family. With Giuseppina headed for a lengthy sentence, or execution, and probably both, one way or another her children were going to be raised by the 'Ndrangheta. Her son Gaetano was a gentle boy especially unsuited for the life now before him. Ahead were years of brutalisation. Giuseppina's father Salvatore used to joke that when a cousin was giving birth, he'd send flowers for a girl and a .38 for a boy. A few years back, when an uncle had asked Gaetano what he wanted to be when he grew up and the boy, in all innocence, had replied 'a policeman', his uncle beat him, then promised to get him a gun to remind him who he was. Giuseppina's fear, she wrote later, was that 'they will put a gun in his hands anyway. When I get out of jail, my son could already be in a juvenile detention centre. And my two daughters will have to marry two 'Ndrangheta men and be forced to follow them around.'

Giuseppina vented her frustration by starting a hunger strike and refusing to talk to prosecutors. But at other times, her spirit seemed broken. She tried to hang herself with a sheet in her cell a few days after she was arrested. Three months later, by which time she had been transferred to San Vittore prison in Milan, she slashed her wrists with a razor. 'There were times when I wanted to die,' she said later in court. 'I couldn't stand the thought of my children without me. I'd never been apart from them. I felt like I was watching the world collapse in on me.'[2]

The prosecutors were largely unsympathetic. If an 'Ndranghetista was feeling guilt or paying some other price for her crimes, then they had done their job. This was war. Prosecutors had begun receiving Kalashnikov rounds in the post and finding gun cartridges leaning up against their windscreens. One bullet sent to Pignatone in May 2010 was accompanied by a note which read simply: 'You're a dead man.' Two of his staff found their cars' engines and brakes had been tampered with. Nor could the prosecutors rely on much public support. The same day as the raids on the Pesce clan, police in Reggio arrested Giovanni Tegano, an 'Ndrangheta boss on the run for seventeen years. As he was led from the city's central police station to a squad car to take him to jail, Tegano was cheered by a crowd of hundreds. 'Giovanni is a man of peace!' shouted one tearful seventy-year-old woman, to which Tegano smiled and waved back.[3]

The threats against them only reconfirmed prosecutors' determination to bring down the 'Ndrangheta. The pace was relentless. Alessandra and Giovanni Musarò had thirty separate investigations under way against the west coast 'Ndrangheta. 'We weren't going to let them breathe,' said Giovanni. 'They were used to enduring one operation, then having a rest. But we just kept on. Someone would be arrested, they would be replaced and then we arrested that person too.'

On 13 July, in a follow-on from Operation All Inside, the *carabinieri* staged more raids across the country. This time they were more ambitious. Operation Infinity involved more than 3,000 officers and resulted in 300 arrests from across the 'Ndrangheta hierarchy. The standout success was the arrest of *capo crimine* Domenico Oppedisano, now eighty, who doffed his trilby to photographers as he was driven through the streets of Rosarno.

If Oppedisano conformed to the traditional image of a southern *mafioso*, other arrests reflected the organisation's more recent sophistication. Around half of the raids took place in and around Milan. Those detained included businessmen, lawyers, bankers, accountants, politicians, policemen and public healthcare managers. Pignatone marvelled at the range of figures now behind bars and what it revealed about the 'Ndrangheta's ability to 'infiltrate such a wide variety of environments'. A new cosmopolitan generation of 'Ndranghetisti was emerging, he said, who understood how globalisation had opened up the world to illicit businesses as much as it had to legitimate ones. 'They are graduates,' he said. 'They can count on a network of professionals, bureaucrats and politicians. They can penetrate any part of Italy and anywhere overseas.'

Pignatone's junior prosecutors were jubilant. Many had prepared for this moment for years. Alessandra had been waiting all her life. Now the 'Ndrangheta was being hit hard, its bosses arrested and its precious secrets exposed. 'That was the moment we revealed that we knew not only that the 'Ndrangheta existed as a hierarchy and a structure but that it could be proved,' said Alessandra. The interior minister, Roberto Maroni, described the raids as a 'blow to the heart of the 'Ndrangheta's organisational and financial structure'. Oppedisano's arrest was greeted with a standing ovation in the Italian Senate.[4] It was going to be a long war. But the prosecutors had finally shown that they could make the world's mightiest mafia bleed.

The 'Ndrangheta was a secret criminal organisation which oppressed people with inhuman violence. If the Italian state was to win its war with it, if the government was to lift the yoke the mafia had imposed on the people, it had to offer them transparency, legality and humanity. But in the heat of battle and with the first flush of victory, the last of those, humanity, was being forgotten.

Giuseppina was useful to Alessandra. She represented further evidence to support her theory about women's influence in the 'Ndrangheta. But when Alessandra heard about Giuseppina's suicide attempts, she felt no compassion for a woman whose predicament was entirely her own fault. 'I didn't believe Giuseppina was sincere,' she said. 'And in fact, she quickly admitted that she wasn't really trying to kill herself but merely trying to persuade us to help her reunite with her children.'[5]

The same cold-bloodedness was on display in the state's indictment of Carlo Cosco and Massimo Sabatino for the murder of Lea Garofalo on 27 May 2010. The charge sheet, confidential at this stage in the

Italian legal process, included a detailed reconstruction of Carlo's movements on the night Lea died. But there was also an extensive account of Lea's relationship with the witness protection programme. To many inside the small group of lawyers and officials allowed to read it, it made for damning reading. Lea had put her faith in the state, and the state had abandoned her. It seemed minded to do the same to Denise. How could Italy expect to beat the mafia if it couldn't even protect those who tried to help it? The state's lack of sympathy had killed Lea almost as surely as Carlo had. Enza Rando, Lea's lawyer, was especially critical. 'Lea had to make her own way,' she said. 'The state just didn't understand how to make witness protection work, especially for a woman. Lea had the strength and weakness of a mother. Brave but at the same time afraid. She never received the help she needed.'[6]

Alessandra bristled at the criticism. She would have preferred a faultless protection programme which led seamlessly to the prosecution and conviction of *mafiosi*. But people died in war. Sometimes *mafiosi*, sometimes *carabinieri* and prosecutors, and sometimes witnesses. Lea's death was no reason to show weakness. It was every reason to show resolve. 'Prosecutors always get blamed,' she said. 'But the facts are that Lea applied for witness protection and didn't have enough information to justify it. Protection costs a lot of money. If your information is not important or deep enough, you don't get it.'[7]

Even if Alessandra was right about the limits on government finances, there was no disputing that the state had failed in one of its primary duties: the protection of its citizens. Lea had crossed the divide to fight on the side of the government, and had lost. As a result, according to the indictment, she had probably been tortured, killed and dissolved in acid. Why? Because the 'Ndrangheta thought she was theirs to keep or discard as they chose – and because, in the end, the state had done the same. Alessandra might be right that this was a war. But if the state was fighting with the same ruthlessness as the 'Ndrangheta, would the people care who won?

It wasn't that Italy's anti-mafia prosecutors had been born peculiarly unfeeling. It was that they were trained to be. From law school through their training to their years on the job, they had been told that emotion had no place in the service. The mafia was heat and blood. Prosecutors were cool focus, discipline and procedure.

But as long as they withheld their hearts from the fight, it was easy to confuse a prosecutor's professional detachment with indifference, or even disdain. The mafia's victims deserved sympathy. Often the best the prosecutors could muster was pity. Cut off from the world, on an endless shuttle between windowless office, bullet-proof car, steel-doored court and secure apartment, it was easy for a prosecutor to forget that war was ultimately played out in flesh and blood, and often won by capturing hearts and minds. Alessandra dismissed Giuseppina's suffering. She marvelled at the emotional decision-making which led Lea Garofalo to her death. 'Lea Garofalo went to Milan where she knew her husband was, even after she had been threatened by him, almost like a form of protest,' she exclaimed. Lea had followed her heart, and that had doomed her. Alessandra's considered response was heartlessness. 'I study women in the 'Ndrangheta,' she said. 'I go to conferences about it. It's a subject I'm very passionate about.' But no one should mistake intellectual interest for personal attachment. 'I don't get involved in these women's lives,' she said. 'I can't.'[8]

XII

The war was heating up. In August, a bundle of industrial dynamite was detonated outside the Reggio home of Calabrian attorney general Salvatore di Landro. In early October, an anti-mafia magistrate in Sicily announced that he had intelligence on a secret summit between the leaders of Cosa Nostra, the Camorra and the 'Ndrangheta at which Italy's three big mafias had drawn up a hit list of assassination targets. On that list was Giuseppe Pignatone. The next week, Pignatone received a phone call at work telling him there was a surprise waiting for him outside. That turned out to be an Eastern European rocket-propelled grenade launcher hidden under a mattress. The Italian press began calling 2010 'the year of bombs and bazookas'.

Pignatone professed he was encouraged by what he viewed as the actions of an organisation in distress. While the threats had to be taken seriously, there was no question of easing off when the crackdown was so clearly being felt. There were more indications that the 'Ndrangheta was being shaken. Ordinary Calabrians were stepping forward to assist the state and that, said Pignatone, 'had never happened before'. When Justice Minister Angelino Alfano prematurely declared the 'Ndrangheta 'fatally wounded', the Calabrian prosecutors winced at his haste. Still, said Pignatone, there was no doubt that 'positive results are giving us even more positive results'.[1] One development was almost unprecedented, he added. Inside jail, an 'Ndranghetista had begun talking.

At the beginning of October 2010, the prosecutor's office in Palmi received a letter from San Vittore jail in the centre of Milan. San Vittore is Italy's most notorious mafia prison. Thousands of *mafiosi* have served time there and most pass through at some stage, including Carlo Cosco, Massimo Sabatino and Salvatore Riina, the Cosa Nostra boss who ordered the executions of Giovanni Falcone and Paolo Borsellino. Even to write to an anti-mafia prosecutor from inside San Vittore and request a meeting was a risk. But to specify that the meeting must take place without a lawyer – indicating that the inmate was considering talking freely, since mafia lawyers worked for the organisation rather than the individual – was so dangerous as to suggest the prisoner was beyond caring. Giuseppina Pesce was already a dead woman walking. Maybe she was thinking of becoming a dead woman talking, too. 'If you can make her talk,' said Pignatone as he handed the letter to Alessandra, 'we'll have done in three years in Calabria what took us thirty years in Palermo.'[2]

Alessandra was doubtful. Still, she agreed with Pignatone that Giuseppina was more likely to open up to another woman. And to Alessandra, even the smallest chance of a woman prosecutor unlocking the 'Ndrangheta through the evidence of a woman *mafiosa* was irresistible.

On 14 October 2010, Alessandra was driven by a security detail through the gates of San Vittore. She was escorted to a meeting room by a prison warden and a marshal. After a few minutes, Giuseppina was led into the room by a prison guard. She walked slowly and hesitantly. Giuseppina had the prison look: wan, with greasy hair, her shoulders hunched like a beaten animal. 'She looked at me with such loathing,' said Alessandra. 'Such pride and resentment and hatred. I represented the state, which was ruining her life.'[3]

After this inauspicious beginning, the atmosphere quickly deteriorated. Giuseppina blurted out that she wanted to be moved to a state
safe house and to see her children. In return, she would help them
catch some 'Ndrangheta bosses on the run. Alessandra dismissed the
offer out of hand. 'She wanted to give us a couple of names in exchange
for her freedom,' she said.[4] It was pathetic, thought Alessandra. And
it wasn't how the prosecutors worked. They didn't negotiate with
gangsters. That was how the mafia drew you in. Alessandra closed her
laptop and made to leave.

Giuseppina looked up at Alessandra with alarm. This wasn't how
the meeting was meant to go. Giuseppina's idea had been to negotiate
with Alessandra the 'Ndrangheta way, which was to say, hard: reveal
little of what you have, affect nonchalance about any deal offered and
eventually extract as much as possible for as little as possible. What's
more, Giuseppina was a Pesce. Her family killed state officials. Her
family was power. She had summoned the state to see her. And yet
here was this woman prosecutor – a woman! – turning everything
upside down and heading for the door.

Alessandra would later admit she was bluffing. Of course she
wanted to know about 'Ndrangheta fugitives. She wanted anything
Giuseppina could give her. But Alessandra was angling for *everything*
Giuseppina could give her. The state had painstakingly built its case
against the Pesces and the 'Ndrangheta. The evidence was good
enough for trial. But it could always be stronger. It was all but inevitable that several *mafiosi*, including a few kingpins, would walk. There
was so much the prosecutors didn't know or couldn't prove. Who ran
what? Who, precisely, moved how much cocaine? Who laundered
whose money? Who, exactly, pulled the triggers? In Giuseppina
Pesce's head was the evidence that could solve hundreds of crimes
stretching back decades. A full confession would split the 'Ndrangheta
wide open, devastating an organisation whose power depended on
secrecy. It would transform the fight against the mafia. Most crucially
to Alessandra, it would also finally prove – to the 'Ndrangheta, the

judiciary and all Italy – that chauvinism was toxic, witless, self-destructive folly.

Alessandra, then, was gambling. But as she reached the door, Giuseppina cleared her throat. 'Everything I testify to now,' she said, 'I do it for my children, I do it to give them a different future.'[5]

Giuseppina would eventually tell Alessandra everything she knew. It took time. Alessandra and Giuseppina talked for an initial three weeks inside San Vittore prison. Once the *carabinieri* retrieved Giuseppina's children from the Palaias, who had been looking after them, and took them to a safe house in Aprilia, south of Rome, where they were reunited with their mother, Giuseppina and Alessandra spoke for several more months. It wasn't just the size and scale of Giuseppina's knowledge. At the beginning, in those first few hours and days, she also delivered it slowly. Giuseppina was still torn between love for her own small family and loyalty to The Family. 'She was desperate to be with her kids,' said Alessandra. 'But it was really hard for her to betray her family.'[6]

But gradually, as Alessandra offered reassurances about her safety and that of her children, the two women established a rapport. 'She *knew* she was going to die,' said Alessandra. 'She *knew* it would be her brother who killed her. I had to explain to her over and over that it's not normal that if you cheat on your husband, then you have to die.'[7] Giuseppina started to relax. There was even a moment on that first day in October when Alessandra saw her eyes shift from terror and confusion to courage and trust. As they talked, Giuseppina became calmer and more confident. Alessandra could feel an almost tangible sense of a beginning, like the first glow of a new era of collaboration opening up right in front of her.

Transcribed, Giuseppina's evidence would eventually run to 1,514 pages. It included diagrams she drew of the 'Ndrangheta hierarchy, descriptions of rituals, evidence of several murders, and detailed accounts of cocaine smuggling rings, extortion rackets, money laundering, credit card fraud and public corruption. 'No stone was left unturned,' said Alessandra. 'Her knowledge went 360 degrees. She told me so many things.'[8] Giuseppina's evidence not only backed up the existing cases, it prompted a raft of new ones. 'The whole character of our investigations changed from that moment,' said Alessandra. 'It was a real turning point.' Based on what Giuseppina told her, over the next year Alessandra would confiscate a total of €260 million in property from the Pesces and the 'Ndrangheta, including forty businesses, four villas, forty-four apartments, 164 cars, sixty plots of land and two football teams. The number of arrests sky-rocketed. Eventually, Alessandra would be able to lay charges against a total of sixty-four 'Ndrangheta men and women from the Pesce *'ndrina*, including two Palaias and fourteen Pesces. Giuseppina revealed the location of three houses in Rosarno under which the Pesces had built bunkers and pinpointed five other underground hideouts. Even when she didn't know a bunker's whereabouts, she offered other help. Her cousin, acting clan head Francesco 'Ciccio' Pesce, she said, 'liked women, a lot of women'. After she gave Alessandra details of one girlfriend, the *carabinieri* followed the woman until she led them to Ciccio's hideout, which he had equipped with sixteen infra-red cameras. Another boss was tracked to a bunker by tailing his friends, whose names were also provided by Giuseppina.

More than the loss of money or personnel, it was the act of Giuseppina's betrayal that shook the 'Ndrangheta. 'Pesce was a name that creates terror in Calabria,' said Alessandra. 'This – breaking the chain, making it possible for women and children to leave the mafia and be free and safe – it was like a bomb.'[9] When news of Giuseppina's betrayal reached Rosarno, their rivals the Belloccos held a party to celebrate the Pesces' shame. In Reggio, Prestipino and Pignatone were equally ecstatic. 'A woman with the name of Pesce, an organic member of this fearsome 'Ndrangheta family, a woman from a place where women don't have the same rights as men, she betrays them and moves to the side of the state,' said Prestipino.[10] 'Immediately, they lose prestige. They lose power. It's devastating. Ordinary people see it's not true that they will always go unpunished. It's not the case that they're invincible. People say: "They're no longer capable of silencing even one of their own members." People start having doubts about them.'

Just as important, 'Ndrangheta members themselves would start to feel the old certainties erode. 'Giuseppina showed everybody that there was an alternative to 'Ndrangheta – that the state could save you and save your family,' said Alessandra. 'She was living proof that you could leave the 'Ndrangheta. That you could survive it. That you could be free.'[11] Prestipino concurred. ''Ndrangheta members start realising that the 'Ndrangheta life is not irreversible. They have an alternative. Giuseppina is proof to all 'Ndrangheta members and women that a mafia member cannot just quit but can organise their life in a different way. Anyone can do it. This undermines and jeopardises the consensus the mafia has built. It's an existential crisis.'[12]

Giuseppina's motivation for her betrayal was rooted in her desire to give her three children a better life. 'I want to change my ways now and take my children with me and try to create a different future for them,' she wrote in a testimonial statement.[13] But there was something else, too. She and Alessandra had made a connection. In one sense, they were two women united against a world of violent men. When Alessandra felt Giuseppina was holding back on a sensitive matter – her marriage, her affair, how the Pesce men were – she would ask the male *carabinieri* officers in the room to leave, so Giuseppina would feel less liable to be judged and able to speak more freely.

Alessandra and Giuseppina were discovering they had more in common than they initially thought. They were two women with a common enemy, living difficult, isolated and sometimes terrifying lives. That made them natural allies. More than that, it ensured that both were starved of friendship. Giuseppina, in particular, had broken faith with her entire family and her whole life. 'I am alone,' she would often tell the prosecutors. Alessandra sensed that Giuseppina needed someone new to rely on. A state that kept its promises. A prosecutor whose word she could believe. A new life, not just security and survival but a full and meaningful existence, even a hope of joy and love.

Perhaps more than Giuseppina knew, Alessandra understood. Almost for the first time in her career, Alessandra began to allow herself to feel something too. This was not just another case, Alessandra told herself. Departing from a creed she had held on to since law school, she began to see Giuseppina not just as a tool for getting the job done but as an individual with discrete strengths, flaws and needs. Alessandra saw to it that Giuseppina was never alone and was always able to phone her or her lawyer, day or night. She began visiting Giuseppina even when they had nothing professional to discuss. She was aware she was breaking her own rules. Her relationship with Giuseppina was evolving into something beyond the technical or the objective. At times, Alessandra saw herself as a gondolier, ferrying Giuseppina from her old life to the new. In other moments, she spoke about how she and this young girl were establishing 'an umbilical cord'.

At the age of forty, in the most unlikely of circumstances, Alessandra was becoming a mother.

XIII

In Pagliarelle, Denise was unaware of the prosecutors' progress in the hunt for her mother's killers.[1] She had no idea that her father, Carlo Cosco, had ordered her own death, nor that Carmine was refusing to obey him. Still, pretending to live as a good 'Ndrangheta girl while secretly seeing Carmine and keeping contact with Libera, Enza Rando and the *carabinieri* was an impossible balancing act. On 28 September 2010, she visited Carlo in jail. The conversation was awkward and stilted. Denise could sense her charade was wearing thin. 'I had no wish to see my father,' she said later. 'I didn't feel sincere about seeing him.'

A few weeks later, on the morning of 18 October 2010, the Milan prosecutor leading the investigation into Lea's disappearance, Giuseppe Gennari, finally released a public indictment for murder against Carlo. Describing Lea's death as an 'execution' planned and ordered by Carlo, Gennari said Carlo had organised a van to transport Lea out of the city, secured a warehouse where she would be interrogated and tortured, procured a gun to kill her and supplied fifty litres of sulphuric acid in which to dissolve her body. Erasing any trace of Lea would allow the conspirators to claim she had run off to Australia, he said. The motive for the killing, Gennari told reporters, was 'the statements Lea made to the prosecutors, none of which, for unexplained reasons, were ever used in a trial'. Specifically, said Gennari, Lea was killed for her testimony about the murder of Antonio Comberiati. Though Carlo never knew what Lea had told prosecutors, Gennari said he had not wanted to take any chances. In any case, he continued, Carlo believed Lea had to be punished for her disloyalty and the shame she had brought on him. From the moment Lea left witness protection in April 2009, Carlo had been working towards the chance to abduct, torture and kill her. Gennari added that Carlo had had five accomplices, whom he named as Massimo Sabatino, Carlo's two brothers Vito and Giuseppe, Rosario Curcio and Carmine Venturino.

The morning of 18 October in Calabria was warm, one of the last days of summer. Denise and Carmine had driven to Crotone to buy supplies for the Cosco family pizzeria, where both of them still worked. Afterwards, they took a ride along the coast to Botricello beach. Their plan was to swim, sunbathe and perhaps grab a bite for lunch. Around midday, as prosecutor Gennari was speaking to reporters in Milan, the couple watched a line of *carabinieri* cars drive up along the seafront and pull to a stop. Several officers got out. They started walking across the sand. Denise and Carmine watched them come. Then Carmine sighed, tugged on his T-shirt and stood with his head bowed, his arms by his side.

As Denise watched the officers surround her boyfriend, cuff him, slap their hands on his shoulders and start to lead him off across the beach, she felt the blood drain from her face. Her relationship with Carmine was still a secret. Something in their manner told Denise the officers knew all about it. But she had a sudden intuition about something else, too. She followed the officers as they walked Carmine to a waiting squad car. One man put his arm around her and led her to a different car, where he opened the door for her. 'This is one of the men who killed your mother,' said the officer. 'This is the guy who dissolved your mother's body in acid.'[2]

XIV

Giuseppina Pesce and her children were reunited at a safe house in Aprilia on 5 November 2010. Days later, her eldest daughter, Angela, received a package from Rosarno. The *carabinieri* had spirited away Angela and her brother and sister, Gaetano and Elisea, with such haste that the children had left with just the clothes they were wearing. Now the Palaias, Guiseppina's in-laws, were forwarding their belongings. The children were delighted. Unpacking her sweatshirts and favourite jeans, Angela found her mobile carefully wrapped up in a T-shirt. She didn't tell her mother.[1]

The calls from Rosarno started almost immediately. Angela's uncles and grandparents would ask her whether she was eating OK. How was she coping without her family? Was she keeping away from those others? For most of the seven months their mother had been in jail, the children had been living with their aunt, Angela Palaia, with whom Angela shared her first and last name. Aunt Angela called almost every day. She would tell her niece that her family missed her. She would promise Angela to buy her this jacket or those trainers once she returned to Rosarno. Sometimes she would say that Giuseppina had made her own decision for her own reasons but hadn't stopped to consider the consequences for her children, who were being ripped away from their family and friends. It was unfair, said Aunt Angela. Unfair, and bad parenting. Witness protection was no life for a teenage girl. Think of everything Angela was missing out on. The Palaias had everything she wanted. What could the state give her that her family could not? 'Tell your mother you want to be with us,' Aunt Angela would say. 'If your mother wants to go on, then she should go on alone. But you come back and stay with us.'

Angela was torn. She loved her mother. But she had also become close to her aunt in the time they had lived together. And while Giuseppina had promised her a better life once they were reunited, Angela found it was nothing like that, nor like any life she'd ever known. She was soon arguing with Giuseppina, calling her mother selfish for taking her, her brother and sister away from their school, friends and family. Angela stopped eating. She refused to get out of bed. Her aunt would tell her that it was her mother who was making her ill. And it was all so unnecessary, said Aunt Angela. She promised the family would forgive Giuseppina. Everyone loved her. Everyone loved Angela, Gaetano and Elisea too. They were family, after all. The men had a lawyer standing by who would deal with whatever statements Giuseppina had made. Life could go back to normal. It would be as if nothing had happened. Why didn't they all come home? 'Angela started calling me her enemy,' said Giuseppina. 'She would tell me how good Aunt Angela was to her, how Aunt Angela loved her.'

The Palaias' aim was true. Realising that Giuseppina had started collaborating for the sake of her children, they guessed correctly that she would stop for them, too. At the time, Alessandra had no idea of the secret phone discussions taking place inside the safe house. When she found out later, she conceded that, with its keen understanding of family, the 'Ndrangheta had found Giuseppina's weak spot. 'Angela was only sixteen and didn't understand her mother's choice,' she said. 'And everyone knew that without her daughter, Giuseppina would not proceed.'

For the 'Ndrangheta, forcing an end to Giuseppina's cooperation was becoming critical. On 23 November 2010, Alessandra staged

Operation All Inside II, a series of further raids aimed at dismantling the Pesce empire, this time guided largely by Giuseppina's information. Twenty-four more Pesce clan members were arrested. They included two policemen, a prison guard and two more women: the twenty-eight-year-old wife of a low-level 'Ndranghetista said to be passing messages between bosses; and Carmelina Capria, forty-seven, wife of clan head Antonino Pesce and, allegedly, the family accountant.

In response, the clan stepped up the pressure on Giuseppina. As 2011 began, the calls to Angela became more frequent. In early March, a second mobile somehow found its way to Giuseppina. She, too, was soon speaking to Aunt Angela. Aunt Angela told Giuseppina that her husband, Rocco Palaia, still loved her, as did the whole family. She tried to reassure her, saying she shouldn't worry about retribution. Everyone made a mistake once in a while. Rocco was prepared to forgive her. What was most important was her children's health. For a sixteen-year-old girl to be apart from her family wasn't natural. It was clearly distressing her. For her daughter's sake, said Aunt Angela, Giuseppina had to stop collaborating, renounce the statements she had made and come back to Rosarno.

Giuseppina said little in these conversations but neither did she hang up. And as March 2011 passed into April and Aunt Angela continued her emotional blackmail, Giuseppina's brother-in-law, Gianluca Palaia, began relaying precise instructions as to how Giuseppina should end her collaboration. Once she left witness protection, Gianluca told her, the family would find her a lawyer, cover her legal fees and rent her a new apartment. He arranged for her to receive €3,000, which he described as a gift from 'a good man'. Like Aunt Angela, Gianluca tried to be reassuring. 'Don't worry,' he said. 'No one's going to do anything to you.' Even Giuseppina's daughter, Angela, tried to persuade her. 'You see? You see?' she would say. 'Now it's up to you.'

Towards the end of March, Giuseppina was granted permission to leave her safe house for a few hours to meet a lawyer. At a *carabinieri* station in Aprilia, she met Giuseppe Madia, a defence lawyer from Rome who had represented *mafiosi* before and had now been retained by the Palaias. Madia asked Giuseppina to read a letter to the prosecutor's office that he had drafted on her behalf. It stated that Giuseppina's health had suffered from her time in prison; that the authorities had taken advantage of her fragile state of mind by forcing her to cooperate; and that her evidence was false and she was withdrawing it. Giuseppina objected to several claims but eventually agreed to sign. She also accepted Madia's proposal that she refuse to sign off on the witness statements she had given Alessandra and exercise her right to silence in any further interviews.

Giuseppina copied into her own handwriting the typewritten letter drafted by Madia, then signed it and dated it 2 April. On 4 April, she consented to a *carabinieri* interview during which she freely answered all questions. She was, she said later, 'caught between two fires'. When Madia told the Palaias that Giuseppina was still cooperating, Aunt Angela, Giuseppina's brother-in-law Gianluca Palaia and a third clan member, Angelo Ietto, simply turned up at her safe house, explaining to the authorities that they were giving their cousin 'emotional support' at this difficult time. Giuseppina realised that, once again, her destiny was being decided for her. 'I had made the choice to make my daughter's life better, but collaborating had ended up hurting my daughter,' she said. Now she had to do what her daughter wanted. The 'Ndrangheta were inside her house, sitting with her children. If she refused to cooperate, they would take them away for ever. 'I couldn't betray my children,' said Giuseppina. 'I couldn't say no.'

On 11 April, Alessandra flew up from Reggio to Rome, then drove down to Aprilia to see Giuseppina. Months of interviews had been leading to this moment. It was 179 days since Giuseppina had begun cooperating and one day before the legal deadline by which Italian prosecutors in any investigation must present their evidence to court. Alessandra was bringing with her close to two thousand printed pages, transcripts of all Giuseppina's interviews over the past six months. Within those pages was the most detailed portrait of the 'Ndrangheta that had ever existed. It was enough to bring down one of Europe's most powerful crime families and blow open a secret, murderous cocaine-smuggling cabal that had terrorised Italy for 150 years. It was also the fullest possible vindication of Alessandra's intuition about 'Ndrangheta women. She found it hard not to feel a moment of triumph as she set the stack of files down on the table in front of her star witness.

Alessandra explained to Giuseppina that her signature was just a legal formality. All she had to do was sign a covering letter, declaring that the statements that followed were her own words and a true representation of the facts as she knew them to be.

Giuseppina looked at the papers. She told Alessandra she couldn't sign.

'Are you refusing to sign because everything you've told us is lies?' asked Alessandra.[2]

Giuseppina, trying not to look Alessandra in the eye, started to cry. Sobbing, she invoked her right to silence. Stunned, Alessandra packed up her files and said she would leave Giuseppina with her lawyer for a few minutes to consider her options. She returned half an hour later.

'Is this really what you want?' she asked.

Giuseppina began to cry again. 'It's not what I want,' she said. 'It's what I must do for my children.' She refused to say any more.

Alessandra tried to carry on as before. On 16 April, she arrested Giuseppina's mother, Angela Ferraro, and her sister, Marina, on charges of extortion and mafia association. The two had been detained a year earlier and released on bail but with the new evidence from Giuseppina, their offences were now serious enough for custody. Their detention brought to seventy-four the number of Pesce clan members that Alessandra had arrested in the year since she launched All Inside.

Lea Garofalo. The picture is undated but seems to
capture Lea in her early twenties, just after she
became a mother. The image became iconic.

Lea, on the left, and Denise captured by CCTV in Milan in their last
minutes together on the evening of 24 November 2009.

Alessandra Cerreti, pictured in her office in Reggio Calabria.

Reggio Calabria, as seen from the hills to the south-east of the city, looking north-west across the Straits to Messina.

San Luca. For decades, the 'Ndrangheta has convened an annual meeting on 2 September in this Aspromonte hill village, using a religious festival as cover.

Carlo Cosco in a police mugshot taken after his arrest in February 2010.

Giuseppina Pesce the day after her arrest in April 2010.

Domenico Oppedisano being driven through the streets
after his arrest in Rosarno in July 2010.

Giuseppina Pesce
in her mugshot
after her arrest.

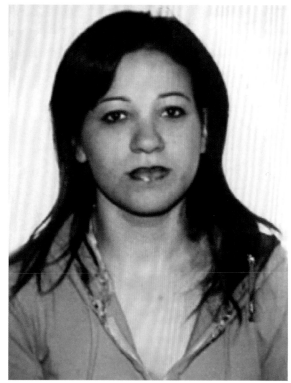

Maria Concetta Cacciola.
Confined to the family home for
weeks at a time, only one other
picture of her has ever surfaced.

The gate of the warehouse in San Fruttuoso, Monza, where Lea's remains were discovered in October 2012, three years after her death.

Breaking a lifetime of *omertà*, Carlo speaks in court on 9 April 2013.

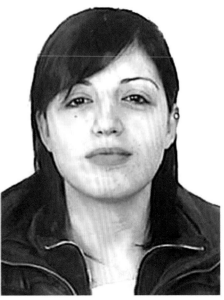

Giuseppina's mother Angela Ferraro and sister Marina Pesce.

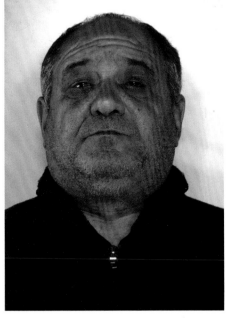

Concetta's mother Anna Rosalba Lazzaro and father Michele Cacciola.

Lea's funeral on 19 October 2013. Thousands from all over Italy turned out for a woman who, four years after her death, united the nation against the mafia under the slogan 'I see, I feel, I speak'.

The next day, however, the Pesces hit back. A report appeared in the *Gazetta del Sud*, the main southern daily, quoting Giuseppe Madia saying Giuseppina had recanted. Alessandra shrugged off the story as typical mafia lies. They just couldn't admit weakness, she thought. The state was winning this war.

On 21 April, Alessandra struck again. Once more acting on Giuseppina's evidence, she launched Operation All Clean, this time aimed at the Pesces' finances. Forty-one companies were seized, most of them based in and around Rosarno, including trucking firms, orange and lemon traders, service stations, a sports complex, a sports fishing operation, a plastics firm and a pizzeria. In addition, the prosecutors confiscated fifty properties – villas, apartments, houses and garages – fifty-four plots of land, fifty-one cars and motorcycles and 102 trucks. The total value was estimated at €190 million. 'Today we can say with satisfaction that Rosarno is truly free,' said Pignatone.

But barely had Alessandra had time to savour her new victory when, on 26 April 2011, she was handed a copy of the Reggio newspaper, *Calabria Ora*. On its front page, the paper had printed what it said was a letter from Giuseppina Pesce to Calabria's attorney general.[3]

Dear Mr Judge,
With this letter I want to withdraw all the allegations I made in my previous statements. I decided to do this not out of fear but out of conscience because I said things that do not correspond to reality. I made those statements at a time when I was seriously ill and suffering from being separated from my children.

The doctors who came to visit me when I was detained witnessed the seriousness of my illness and how severely I was affected by prison to the point where, out of desperation, I put my own life in danger. I was hoping to see my three children, one of whom has serious health problems. But my hopes were in vain and I was sent on to Milan. That was the moment I realised I would die if I did not make the statements I was expected to make.

The magistrate who led the case can detail the genesis of these statements, born of answers to questions loaded with merciless accusations against my close family. The more I accused, the more I was believed. And I was so depressed that I slandered my closest family members with untruth. Fear and illness made me make those statements which now make me feel nothing but shame in my heart. I feel stripped naked, exposed to everyone, with no thought for my dignity or feelings. I feel like they used me. But I also feel better that today I have found the courage to withdraw these allegations, even as I fear the monstrous process that I have helped set in motion. I pray that everyone, even those whom I have hurt unjustly, might spare me a little understanding for what I have been through and continue to live with.

Sincerely,
Giuseppina Pesce

Calabria Ora followed up its scoop by printing a front-page interview two days later with Madia, the lawyer, under the headline: 'Forced to Repent: Pesce said whatever the prosecutors wanted'. The article began with a quote from Madia: 'Do you know how many times I have spoken with my client? Once, in a *carabinieri* station, then nothing. Can you imagine? Today I don't even know where she is.'

Madia alleged that Alessandra had 'extracted' Giuseppina's testimony by using the 'threat' that unless she cooperated, she would never see her children again. 'Read this medical report, read what it says about Mrs Pesce,' he told the *Calabria Ora* journalist, handing him a file which he said was signed by Nicola Pangallo, a psychiatrist who interviewed Giuseppina in prison. 'The prisoner is in a very serious condition which does not allow her continued remand in prison … The service agent reports that the prisoner had attempted suicide by hanging. The patient is completely detached from current reality and obsessed by the idea of leaving prison and seeing her children again. When she spoke to her daughter, her daughter replied: "Is that my mum?" [The patient said]: "I'm afraid my children no longer recognise me."'

Dr Pangallo went on to recommend that Giuseppina receive specialist care in a prison located close to her children, in order to allow more frequent contact. 'And where do the prosecutors think the nearest prison to Reggio is located?' Madia asked the journalist. 'Why, Milan, of course, a thousand kilometres away.' It was after her transfer that Giuseppina had collapsed and begun collaborating, he added. 'It's obvious Mrs Pesce has not told the truth. She only said what the judges wanted her to say. That's why she made these statements.'

In an editorial, *Calabria Ora*'s editor-in-chief, Piero Sansonetti, decried the prosecutors' conduct. 'The fight against the mafia, like all exercises of justice, must be conducted within the rules, strictly within the rules, totally within the rules,' he wrote. 'Otherwise it might land a few blows on the mafia but inflict far greater damage to our legal system and society.' The next day, 29 April, which happened to be Alessandra's forty-first birthday, Sansonetti gave a television interview in which he repeated Madia's allegations, demanded a parliamentary inquiry and accused Alessandra of extortion and blackmail.

It was the start of a year-long campaign by *Calabria Ora* against Alessandra and the other anti-mafia prosecutors. Throughout Giuseppina would be described not as an individual who had made her own choices but as a disturbed and weak woman who had been used by the prosecutors and manipulated into betraying her family. A week later, Sansonetti wrote another editorial in which he appeared to justify breaking the law and to characterise the 'Ndrangheta as victims of oppression. 'To tell the truth, I often don't like laws,' he wrote. 'Respect for the law is not always, in my opinion, deserved. I have never sided with the law. Disobedience is a virtue. I tend to think it's better to stand in defence of the weak whoever they are, good or bad, guilty or innocent.' Over the next few months, *Calabria Ora* published a string of stories castigating the prosecutors. One was an interview from prison with Salvatore Pesce, Giuseppina's father, who criticised the way his daughter had been treated. Giuseppina's uncle, Giuseppe Ferraro, also spoke to *Calabria Ora*, accusing Alessandra of black-mailing his niece by having the *carabinieri* kidnap her children and forcing her to make statements under the influence of psychotropic drugs.

It wasn't clear how much of this the Pesces actually believed. The intended audience seemed to be the citizens of Rosarno as much as Alessandra and the state. Still, the judiciary had to respond. The head of Italy's anti-mafia directorate in Rome first denied any wrong-doing, then summoned Alessandra to the capital, where she was ordered to make out a report and explain her actions. A prosecutor in Catanzaro was even deputed to investigate Alessandra for extortion. 'This slander campaign went on and on,' said Alessandra.

Alessandra knew she was becoming a liability to the judiciary. Even to colleagues who backed her, she was in danger of becoming a cautionary tale: the spectacular rise and fall of the woman prosecutor who flew too high. She had the backing of Pignatone and Prestipino. But no prosecutor could tolerate criticism for ever, least of all one on the front line of a war against the mafia.

Alessandra's only hope was to change Giuseppina's mind again. It seemed improbable. But in the months that followed, Alessandra began to fixate on the last conversation she had had with Giuseppina, going over it in her mind time and again. The letter in *Calabria Ora*, in which Giuseppina withdrew her statements, was clearly written for her. But when Alessandra had challenged Giuseppina to declare that her evidence was lies, Giuseppina had refused to speak. She became convinced Giuseppina was trying to tell her something. Refusing to sign wasn't recanting. Giuseppina might only be refusing to sign her statements *at that moment*. Who knew what kind of pressure the 'Ndrangheta was putting on her?

In early May, Alessandra was passed transcripts of bugged conversations between the Pesces. The contents seemed to support the idea that, contrary to Giuseppina's letter, she was far from reconciled with her family. In one exchange on 5 May, caught on video, between her brother Francesco Pesce and her grandmother Giuseppa Bonarrigo, Francesco reassured the family matriarch that the Pesce family itself had 'nothing to be ashamed of. If she [Giuseppina] screwed up, she did it alone, without anyone else from the family.' Besides, Giuseppina's evidence wasn't all that damning, said Francesco. The family had found experts who would testify that she was mentally ill. 'She's crazy, crazy,' agreed Giuseppina's grandmother. 'She did it for the children. Imagine!' Francesco added that Giuseppina's testimony was, in any case, mostly hearsay. Women weren't like men, he said. They just stayed in the home and listened to men talk. All Giuseppina had been able to pass on was what she had heard. It was a problem made in the home, said Francesco, 'and we'll solve it in the home. We just have to try to get her home by telling her we love her, we forgive her and she's my sister.' At the words 'solve it in the home', Giuseppina's seventy-eight-year-old grandmother nodded and drew her thumb across her throat.

That conversation would stay with Alessandra. Giuseppina's motivation for talking had always been to give her family a better life. That maternal compulsion meant all was not lost. Giuseppina would still want a new life for her children. She hadn't disavowed her statements, merely set them aside. If she was planning to take her children back to Rosarno, it would only be until she thought it was safe to leave again. Over the months they'd worked together, Alessandra had grown to trust Giuseppina, to care for her and to respect her. Giuseppina was resilient and resourceful. The more Alessandra thought about it, the more she was convinced Giuseppina was executing a plan by invoking her right to silence. 'She's being clever,' she told her staff. To the 'Ndrangheta, Giuseppina was trying to appear as though she had been successfully brought to heel. But to Alessandra, Giuseppina was indicating she remained true to the cause. She was still planning to cooperate. She was just biding her time. 'She's telling me that what she had said in all those months of interviews was true,' said Alessandra.

Still, time was not on Giuseppina's side. As her grandmother's gesture indicated, her family would likely kill her as soon as they could. Since Giuseppina had stopped cooperating, the witness protection service would soon eject her, as they had done with Lea Garofalo – and if Lea's fate was any indication, Giuseppina's death would follow swiftly. However Alessandra was planning to save her star witness, she needed to act now.

XV

E ven as she struggled to find a way to rescue Giuseppina, Alessandra found her *pentita*'s example was inspiring another 'Ndrangheta woman to follow suit.[1]

In June 2010, anonymous letters began arriving at the yellow two-storey house in Via Don Gregoria Varrà, Rosarno, that Maria Concetta Cacciola shared with her parents. The letters claimed that Concetta was having an affair with one of her Facebook friends. The accusation was absurd. Her friend had been in Germany all the time that Concetta had known him. But Concetta's father and brother, Michele and Giuseppe, didn't hesitate. Shouting 'You filthy animal!' they grabbed Concetta, punched her to the floor and kicked her until they cracked one of her ribs. Desperate to avoid any public tarnishing of the family name, the two men then refused to let Concetta be treated in hospital. Instead, they arranged private visits to the house by a doctor related to the Pesces. All this happened in front of Concetta's three children, Alfonso, fifteen, Tania, twelve, and Rosi, six.

It was three months before Concetta was well enough to step outside. Even then, one of her cousins followed her wherever she went. Finding herself alone in the house one day, Concetta called a women's refuge on the other side of Calabria but hung up before anyone answered. Then on 11 May 2011, the *carabinieri* summoned her to the station in Rosarno. Alfonso's scooter had been confiscated for a minor driving offence and Concetta needed to pay his fine before it was returned. The twenty-minute walk to the station was the first occasion in eleven months that Concetta had been allowed out of the house on her own.

Concetta entered the *carabinieri* station and asked to speak to an officer. From the moment Officer Carlo Carli led her into an interview room and closed the door, it all just tumbled out of her. Concetta first asked if Carli knew the reputation of the Cacciola family and her husband Salvatore Figliuzzi. When Carli said he did, Concetta told him her family had kept her a virtual prisoner at home for the eight years since Salvatore had gone to jail. The situation had become intolerable in the last eleven months, she said. She told Carli the saga about her Facebook friendship, the poison pen letters and the beating. Her family now never let her out of their sight. As if to underline the point, Concetta's phone soon started ringing. It was her mother, Anna Rosalba Lazzaro, asking where she was. Concetta said she had to leave. At the door of the interview room, she predicted that one day her family would murder her. 'If they find out I'm here saying these things, they'll kill me for sure,' she said.

Officer Carli wanted to know more. Using Alfonso's scooter as an excuse, he summoned Concetta back to the station four days later. This time, she spoke to a female officer and, feeling less inhibited in front of a woman, told the officer she now wanted to escape her family and Rosarno. She had bought tickets to northern Italy several times but never had the nerve to go through with it. She'd even ripped up her ticket once when one of her cousins followed her into the travel agent's. The thing was, Concetta confided to the officer, her family was right. Calling herself 'Nemi', she had begun a second online relationship with 'Prince 484', a Reggio man called Pasquale Improta.[2] Initially, it had been innocent. But now it was starting to evolve into an affair. Pasquale was living a few hours away in Naples. When she'd told him about the beating, he'd urged her to go to the *carabinieri* to ask them to protect her. Concetta wanted to be with Pasquale. She had told her mother she wanted to divorce Salvatore. After all, he had never loved her and had only married her to assist his rise inside the 'Ndrangheta.

Concetta said her father would never let her divorce her husband. But it was her younger brother, thirty-year-old Giuseppe, who really scared her. He had been raised as a true believer, she said, and knew nothing outside the 'Ndrangheta. She had had to warn friends to stay away from her in case Giuseppe suspected they were helping her. The only time she could relax was when Giuseppe went away on business or once when he vanished for a few days immediately after a murder in Rosarno. Even then Giuseppe's wife had taken Concetta aside and whispered to her not to speak freely inside their house because Giuseppe had had the place bugged. 'Giuseppe gets these rages,' said Concetta. 'He could do anything. He could make me disappear. He's just waiting for proof that I'm having an affair. Sooner or later, he'll come to me and say, "Come with me." That's the day I'll vanish.'

On 23 May, Concetta returned to the station and spoke to Officer Carli again. With each successive visit, she seemed to be building up her courage. This time she gave more details about how her father and brother beat her. She added that she was thinking of leaving for Naples. On 25 May, she went to the *carabinieri* station in Gioia Tauro. On this occasion she ended the conversation by saying she was prepared to make a statement about her family in return for witness protection. When she returned to Gioia Tauro station the next day, her fifth visit to the *carabinieri* in two weeks, she found Alessandra and Giovanni Musarò waiting for her.

Concetta told the two prosecutors she could talk for a maximum of ninety minutes. 'It was a complicated interrogation,' said Alessandra. 'We had to know who we had in front of us, why she was talking to us, what she was able to tell us and whether she was lying. And she was very scared. She had told her family that she had to go to the *carabinieri* to pay a fine. That gave her more time than usual away from home. But she was worried. She kept looking at her watch.'[3]

The prosecutors quickly concluded Concetta was credible. Her knowledge of the Rosarno clans was extensive. She told them details about the murder of Palmiro Macri, sixty-two, shot in a clan feud by a gunman using a Kalashnikov in July 2008 as he drove through Rosarno in his Fiat Panda. She described how a boss called Umberto Bellocco had killed Salvatore Messina, his wife's brother, then blamed the murder on Concetta's cousin, Gregorio Bellocco, something which caused a rift between the Belloccos and the Pesces for years. She told the story of how the Belloccos had extended their protection rackets inland to the town of San Ferdinando. She pinpointed the location of at least two bunkers, buried under an old factory in Rosarno, and explained how they were equipped with televisions and refrigerators stocked with food and champagne. The bosses' hypocrisy seemed to outrage Concetta. Hanging on the wall where 'these men without honour shut themselves up like beasts', she said, would be an image of Saint Pio of Petrelcina. 'I'm speaking about murderers,' she added, people who 'butcher wretched people that thought they were friends, men they invited to dinner, not killed for honour or the family's sake but just for money and power'.

The two prosecutors were struck by Concetta's resolve. 'I was very impressed,' said Giovanni. 'Very often, people like her who go through pain and suffering – they are conflicted. Concetta was terrified but she was also very resolute.'[4] When Alessandra asked her whether she would want to take her three children with her into witness protection, Concetta demurred. 'I don't want my children to weaken my resolve like Giusy,' she said. 'I need to find my strength in the choices I make. After I'm in the programme, you can go and find my children, tell them what I've done and why, and they can make their own decision about whether to join me or not.'[5]

But something about Concetta's story bothered the two prosecutors. Giovanni zeroed in on the reason her father and brother had beaten her. He asked her to explain the anonymous letters. They couldn't just have appeared from nowhere. 'Giovanni was pressing her a bit,' said Alessandra. 'He could see she was lying. She was hiding something.'

Concetta said nothing. But when the two prosecutors called a short break, Concetta waited until Giovanni and a male *carabinieri* officer were talking, then approached Alessandra. 'If you wish, I can tell you about my relationship with Pasquale,' she said, 'but I'm too ashamed to talk in front of the men.' Even inside a *carabinieri* station, negotiating her exit from the 'Ndrangheta, 'Concetta was still a victim of the mafia system,' said Alessandra.[6]

Four days later, on the night of 29 May 2011, Concetta stole out of the family home in the middle of the night and ran to a waiting *carabinieri* car. In her room, she had left a letter for her mother.

Dear Mama
I do not know where to start. I can't find the words to justify this action of mine. Mama, you're mama! Only you can understand a daughter. I know the pain that I'm causing you. By explaining everything to you, then at least you can explain to everyone else. I didn't want to leave you without saying anything. How many times have I wanted to talk to you? How much did I want to spare you pain? But I failed. And all this pain, I turned it into aggression, and I took it out on the person who, above all, I love the most.
That's why I'm entrusting my children to you. But one thing I beg of you. Don't make the mistakes that you made with me. Give them a better life than I had. Paired off at thirteen, I thought marriage would give me a little freedom. Instead, I ruined my life. Salvatore never loved me nor me him. You know that. So don't make the same mistakes with the children, I beg you. Give them space. If you shut them away, they'll start to behave badly because they'll feel trapped by everything. That's how you treated me.

I can't write much more. I just wanted to ask you to forgive me, Mother, for the shame I'm bringing you. In the end, I realised that I was alone – alone among everyone. I've never known luxury and I never wanted money. But now I have the peace and love and the satisfaction you feel when you make a sacrifice. This life has given me nothing but pain. The most beautiful thing in my life is my children. I keep them in my heart. Give your strength to them. Don't let their father have them; he's not worthy of them. Take care of Alfonso. He suffered as a boy and that's why he is how he is. He's not strong. You need to watch him closely.

I will live as long as God allows but I have to try to find some peace in my heart. Mama, forgive me. Please pray for forgiveness for all the harm that I'm causing. I'm going to a place where I can find some serenity. Don't look for me or you'll get into trouble. I can't speak to you any more and I can't hug you, I can only write – but I couldn't leave without telling you I was going and wishing you well. I have only you and my children in my mind's eye. I love you, Mama. Hug my children as you always have and don't talk about them to anyone who's not worthy of them. Ma, farewell. And forgive me. Forgive me if you can. I know I'll never see you again. This is how it must be with a family of honour. That's why you have lost your daughter. Goodbye. I will always love you. Forgive me, as I too pray for forgiveness. Goodbye.

On the dashboard of the family car, Concetta also left a brief note for her father and her brother. 'I'm going with my friend Giusy,' she wrote.

Formally admitting a witness to the protection programme took months. But Concetta needed immediate protection. The *carabinieri* took her to a secluded holiday resort, the Colle degli Ulivi, near

Cosenza, in the hills above the coastal town of Sibari, two hours' drive north of Rosarno.

The Colle degli Ulivi was a safe, nondescript place, generally used by northern Italian families on holiday. It had three restaurants, a bar, a solarium, a jacuzzi and a giant pool, and offered its guests horse riding, mountain biking, tennis, archery, karaoke and walks in the hills or down to the beach. At meal times, giant buffets would be laid with fruit, salads and cold meats, or you could order *à la carte*, and there was every type of wine. Concetta's protection officers stayed on site but otherwise let her roam as she wanted.

Concetta loved it. She could walk into town or down to the shore-line whenever she chose. In the hotel, as the temperature rose with the onset of summer, the rooms slowly filled with guests: young families, old couples, foreigners. No one knew her. No one knew the meaning of the name Cacciola. There was no shame and no punishment. And Concetta realised that at thirty-one, for the first time in her life, she was truly free.

Pasquale came to visit for a couple of nights. Staff and guests would later recall how Concetta seemed just as happy striking up conversations with perfect strangers, arriving promptly at meal times in the hope of meeting someone new. She picked up several lone men over the two months she was there. 'In this new environment, she got to know a lot of men,' said Giuseppe Creazzo, the prosecutor who would later investigate her case. 'She made love with a lot of them. It was a way for her to be alive. It was the best way she knew to communicate.'

On 16 June, Alessandra drove up to Sibari and Concetta gave her as much detail as she could on the bunkers. Two days later, Giovanni arrived for a third interview to go over Concetta's earlier evidence. Concetta identified various 'Ndranghetisti from mugshots that Giovanni brought with him and added details of the murders and protection rackets she had described. When Giovanni asked, Concetta reconfirmed in a written statement that she was willing to leave her three children with their grandmother. 'I believe they're in no danger,' she wrote. 'I believe my children don't need the state to protect them.'

Concetta struck Giovanni as 'more serene and at peace' than when he had last seen her. Importantly, 'she was also still determined.' Unprompted, Concetta went into fine detail about how the Bellocco clan ran their loan-sharking operation. Two brothers of a friend of hers, Rita Stefania Secolo, had borrowed €600,000 from the Belloccos. Two years later, their debt was a million euros. 'Stefania told me that the Belloccos had threatened to kill her brothers if the money was not repaid,' said Concetta. 'They told her they would take an apartment building owned by her family as part payment. They even shot up a shop on the ground floor and told Stefania they would have killed somebody if the gun hadn't jammed.' Stefania ended up living on the top floor of the building, above her old apartment, paying rent to the Bellocco extortionists who had moved in below.

Every day Concetta stayed at Colle degli Ulivi was another small adventure. When the formal approval for her witness protection came through in late July, she was moved to Bolzano in the Alps. But when a new man she brought back to her hotel room turned out to be a former convict, her protection officers moved her again, this time to Genoa on Italy's north-west coast.

If leaving gave Concetta a new sense of peace, it created uproar in Rosarno. 'Your escape sparked off hell,' her friend Emanuela Gentile told her, in a call tapped by the *carabinieri*. 'Your father really freaked out. Your mother went around yelling "They ruined us," and was crying and tearing her hair out. Your brother grew a long beard and locked himself far away in a house by the sea out of shame. He never leaves. Now *he* is the prisoner.'

Alessandra and Giovanni couldn't help enjoying the ruckus. 'It was the fact that she was a woman called Cacciola,' said Giovanni. 'That was really unacceptable to them. The 'Ndrangheta's reaction to Giuseppina and Concetta was not proportional to the information they gave us – most of it was hearsay, not a murder confession or anything – but to the 'Ndrangheta it wasn't about the information. It was the symbolic value of them turning state's evidence.'

Alessandra took particular pleasure in reading the transcripts from the Cacciola family. The *carabinieri* had tapped their phones and planted a bug in the family car. You could almost hear the 'Ndrangheta shattering. In one recording, Anna Rosalba Lazzaro, Concetta's mother, railed about the female *carabiniere* in Rosarno with whom Concetta had spoken. 'That officer slut!' shouted Lazzaro. 'She has a thing going with the judges! She's a whore!' Another time, Alessandra listened as Concetta's mother tried to wrap her mind around her daughter's actions. 'She saw nothing in her life,' said Lazzaro. 'But she never saw the whole truth. She's always been like that. She eloped at thirteen! She's never seen anything in her life, poor devil. And they took advantage of that, those unworthy bastards! Bastards! It's so easy just to talk. You just say your brother told you this, your father told you that, your mother's cunt told you something else.' Lazzaro suspected that one day Concetta would send for her children. She found the thought unbearable. 'She wants to tear them away from their roots and take them where? How is she going to provide for them? She can't even sweep the floor! No! She must come back home. The *carabinieri* don't have any actual evidence. In a week nobody in Rosarno will ever speak about these things again.'

Michele Cacciola, Concetta's father, was just as disturbed. At home, he would unleash tirades that could last an hour. 'This unworthy piece of shit!' he shouted in one episode recorded on 11 July 2011. 'I worked twenty years for her!' Michele seemed most upset at his loss of standing. 'I had [such] a family that they [the people of Rosarno] were all jealous of me,' he yelled. 'I enjoyed watching my grandchildren grow. Nobody was happier than me!' Michele saw Concetta's departure not as her bid for a new life but an attack on him by the state. 'These contemptible people, these unworthy bastards, to take a daughter from her father! How is this the law to come at me and take my daughter? Did I start a fight with them? Do they even know who I am? If they have something on me, then arrest me! They are taking daughters away from their fathers!' Not that talking to a mere woman would serve the state's purpose, said Michele. 'They wait for her to disgrace me. But what can she know about me? She knows nothing. What can a *woman* know in my house? You think I told my daughter about my fucking business? She knows nothing!'

These 'Ndrangheta men, thought Alessandra. Treat their women like dirt. But one walks away from them, and they fall all to pieces.

XVI

As soon as Alessandra was sure Concetta was safe, she switched her focus back to Giuseppina. Since she had stopped cooperating with the judiciary, Giuseppina's options had steadily narrowed. The 'Ndrangheta plan to return her to Rosarno was well under way. Her family had rented her an apartment in Vibo Marina, a small seaside town north of Rosarno, and a judicial order transferring Giuseppina's house arrest there was being drawn up. Alessandra suspected the clan would kill her almost as soon as she arrived. Meanwhile, the witness protection service was mulling Giuseppina's ejection from the programme as an uncooperative witness. As May turned to June, Alessandra reckoned she had weeks or even days to save her witness.

The order for Giuseppina's transfer to Vibo Marina was issued on 9 June. Before it could be executed, on the morning of 10 June, Alessandra received a call from the protection officers at Giuseppina's safe house in Aprilia. Giuseppina, her boyfriend Domenico Costantino and her daughter Angela had gone for a day in Lucca in Tuscany, four hours to the north, leaving her younger children, Gaetano and Elisea, with a babysitter. The officers added that Angela had been threatening for a while to sneak out of the house to go and see a friend in Lucca. When Domenico had driven up from Rosarno a few days earlier, Giuseppina had seized the chance to make her daughter happy one final time. 'I was living those days as if they were the last I would ever spend with my children,' she said later.

It was the opportunity Alessandra needed. As a collaborator, even one who had stopped talking, Giuseppina enjoyed a measure of freedom. But she still needed permission to travel long distance. By the letter of the law, a trip to Lucca violated the conditions of her house arrest. Alessandra raced to the *carabinieri* surveillance office in Reggio. En route, she called the Lazio *carabinieri*'s mafia surveillance team. Alessandra told the officer on duty that she needed the *carabinieri* to intercept Giuseppina on the highway from Lucca back to Aprilia. If Giuseppina could be caught in the act of flouting the conditions of her detention, then Alessandra could have her summarily sent back to prison. A jail cell, explained Alessandra, was now the only place Giuseppina could be sure of staying alive. But they had to catch her first.

No problem, the *carabinieri* officer replied. What car were they looking for?

Alessandra said that she didn't know the make of the car, its colour or its licence plate, or the route it was taking.

That wasn't much to go on, replied the officer.

Alessandra said that was precisely why she was asking for a hundred *carabinieri* to set up as many checkpoints as possible along the various routes from Lucca. Somewhere in the four hundred kilometres between Lucca and Aprilia would be a car of some description in which would be three people – Giuseppina, her boyfriend and her fifteen-year-old daughter.

The officer said he would call her back. Minutes later the duty officer in charge of all Lazio's *carabinieri*, a captain, was on the line. 'We wouldn't use a hundred men even for Osama bin Laden,' he said.

Alessandra insisted. This one *pentita* could take down the entire Rosarno 'Ndrangheta, she said. 'And unless we arrest her right now, she's going to be murdered.' Alessandra told the captain she had a trump card: Giuseppina's mobile, whose GPS signal the *carabinieri* could use to track her. According to the screen Alessandra was watching at that moment in Reggio, Giuseppina had just left Lucca and was now heading to Florence. That meant she would likely be taking the main toll road all the way to Aprilia. The journey would take three and a half hours. That was how long the captain had to save the most important witness ever to testify against the 'Ndrangheta.

The captain said he would try. Within minutes, his men were setting up roadblocks and checkpoints. 'We were following her mobile in real time on the screen,' said Alessandra, 'and I was in constant contact with the *carabinieri* captain and his officers on the ground.' But as Alessandra watched, the dot on the screen approached the first roadblock, then sailed through. Half an hour later, it approached a second, then kept on going as before. Alessandra phoned the captain. 'What the fuck is going on?!' she shouted. 'How come they're getting through?'

The captain, unaccustomed to being sworn at by a southerner, and a woman, told Alessandra that his men were doing their best. She had given them almost nothing to go on. But his men would do what they could.

By now Alessandra was also phoning officers at individual checkpoints, asking them to keep the line open so she could listen to what was happening. One by one, they all reported seeing nothing. The dot on the screen kept moving south. As Giuseppina floated through roadblock after roadblock, the *carabinieri* captain's attitude changed from defensiveness to despair. When the screen showed Giuseppina approaching Aprilia, the captain told Alessandra it was over. 'We've lost her,' he said. 'We've lost her.'

'You have to block ALL the traffic on the highway!' shouted Alessandra. 'All of it! Do it right now!'

The captain protested. The screen had Giuseppina at three kilometres away. Only one checkpoint lay between her and the safe house. Alessandra was suggesting that he block one of the main arterial roads in all of Italy when it was already too late. 'She's gone, she's gone,' he said.

'You do NOT give up, Captain!' shouted Alessandra. 'You block the entire highway, you do it right now and you keep this line open! Do it, Captain!'

The officer reluctantly agreed. Alessandra went back to checking the screen. There was a few moments of silence. Then the captain's voice came back on the line.

'HOLD ON!' he shouted.

'Hold on …'

'There's a car …'

'With a WOMAN!'

Alessandra heard sirens, then the sound of tyres braking hard. She guessed several squad cars had encircled the suspect vehicle and brought it to a stop.

'STOP THE CAR!' came a voice on a loud hailer. 'ARMED POLICE! STOP THE ENGINE AND EXIT THE CAR WITH YOUR HANDS IN THE AIR!'

There was a moment of silence.

Then a woman's voice shouted: 'Don't shoot! Don't shoot! My name is Giuseppina Pesce!'[1]

For all that Alessandra felt for Giuseppina, she and Prestipino decided to let her stew in prison for a while. Alessandra had been desperate to save Giuseppina. That didn't mean she was pleased with her. She had put her faith in this 'Ndranghetista and the 'Ndranghetista had reverted to type: shutting down, submitting to The Family, resuming *omertà*. Giuseppina had ground to make up with Alessandra. She needed to know it.

Of course, it was also possible that Giuseppina wouldn't see her rescue as anything of the sort. There was the manner of her capture: men with guns drawn, screaming at her to lie face down on the ground. And since Giuseppina was back in jail, the authorities had had no choice but to separate her from her children once more and send them back to the Palaias in Rosarno. After all the risks she had taken and the torment she had endured, precisely nothing had changed for Giuseppina. She could be forgiven for questioning the point of it all.

Alessandra was counting on the transformation she thought she had discerned in Giuseppina. When she had first arrested Giuseppina in Rosarno a year earlier, the 'Ndranghetista had been defined by the men in her life: daughter to a criminal father, wife to a violent husband, obedient servant to violent and criminal men of honour. Even Giuseppina's identity as a mother had been defined by the men. Though she loved Angela, Gaetano and Elisea, she had also accepted that her role, however repugnant, was to prepare them for the 'Ndrangheta.

But in the last year, Giuseppina had broken with all of that. She had become the director of her own life. She had reclaimed her freedom. She had retrieved her children. She had even chosen her own lover. Above all, she had recovered herself – and there was no giving herself away again. She had not, as the Pesce men told reporters, acted as a sick, weak woman. She had not been used by Alessandra. Just the opposite. The first time she went to prison, she had been cowed and terrified and had tried to kill herself within days. Now, back in a cell and away from her children once more, she was calm and in control. A jail cell had a way of stripping everything away. Being reunited with her children was the only thing that mattered, and Giuseppina knew what she had to do to achieve that. When she heard about her friend Concetta and the note she had left, she wondered whether the two of them might be the start of a movement.

As Alessandra bided her time, she monitored Giuseppina's correspondence. Dispatches arrived every day from Aunt Angela, Giuseppina's mother Angela Ferraro, her sister Marina, her father Salvatore, even her husband Rocco Palaia. Mostly her family congratulated her on ending her cooperation and described the new life that they had prepared for her in Calabria. But by now, Alessandra thought she knew Giuseppina well enough to hope that she wouldn't believe a word. Not that her husband forgave her, not that the Palaias would take good care of her son, not that anything could ever go back to how it was. The likelihood was that the 'Ndrangheta would try to turn her children against her and probably even persuade her son to kill her. Alessandra felt that by insisting on the pretence, the clan was over-playing its hand. Moreover, as Alessandra saw it, by attempting to give Giuseppina no choice, they were offering her no alternative but to reject them. The only way for Giuseppina to save her children was to stay alive and look after them – and the only way to do that was to re-enter witness protection and take her children with her. There was every chance, thought Alessandra, that her family's letters would have the opposite effect to what was intended.

The letters Giuseppina received from Rocco, laced with sarcasm and suppressed fury, were especially useful. 'My dear tourist,' he began in a letter dated 15 June:

> I hope you are in as good health as I. I thought you were allergic to jail but I see I was wrong. I told you many times to stay in your own place, in your own shoes. But you walked off alone for a holiday in Lucca. Who are these relatives in Lucca that I do not know? I'm not angry with you so much, but with that bastard Mimmo [Costantino], who took you there. What was he doing there? Tell me.

Rocco wrote that he feared his children were suffering. He couldn't understand why she was in Lucca when she was meant to be in Vibo Marina. So much of what had happened was confusing to him, he wrote. 'If [only] you were in your place at this time. But you are out.' Still, he had advice for Giuseppina on how to set things right:

> The first thing you need to do is to write to your father and explain the situation. How come you were with Mimmo? I want to know as well. After that, if you leave protection, good. If not, I'll see you on July 12th. We can still return to being a normal

family, as we were before. I hug you and urgently await your
news and explanations. I have forgiven you many times. I hope
this is the last.

On 24 June, Rocco wrote again. 'My dearest love (if I can call you
that); he began. He then described a prison visit from his brother,
Gianluca Palaia, and their daughters Angela ('my princess who fell
from the clouds') and Elisea. He assured Giuseppina that, as a responsible parent, he would make sure the children had money for clothes.
'It doesn't matter that you abandoned me like you did. Let's leave our
arguments until we're both out. Even then, we can pretend it never
happened.'

He added that he had to tell her about her friend Maria Concetta
Cacciola:

Do you remember 'Cetta? Who lives near the mini-market? Her
husband is also in prison and she had an affair, possibly with a
cop – something she should rightly be killed for. Anyway, when
she realised her family had found out, what did she do? She
called the police and entered witness protection – and in the
family car she left a note saying she was 'going with her friend,
Giusy'. They say she's making statements to the authorities now.
She really did it all.

Your situation, of course, is very different. Everyone's forgiven
you for what you did. Me most of all. But, still, I wondered if this
put you in mind of anyone?

'It was typical mafia style, disguising a threat,' said Alessandra after
she read the letter. '"Don't worry. You didn't do what Maria Concetta
Cacciola did, so nothing can happen to you." Which is exactly the
opposite of what he meant.'[2] Alessandra sent the letter on its way.
When she received a letter from Giuseppina dated the same day, she
knew Rocco's letter had hit its mark.

I am writing to tell you a few things that I feel I have to tell you, and I really hope in my heart that you can hear me. After the last time we saw each other, a lot has happened. All that media propaganda, and all the accusations, and everything that came after. I would love to have the opportunity to explain to you everything that happened. Especially to you. I had to stop collaborating for my children's sake. They weren't happy. But this morning I fired the lawyer, Giuseppe Madia, and employed a woman defence advocate, Valeria Maffei. It's my intention, if you are still interested, to resume the path of collaboration. I only hope I can regain your confidence. Sorry, again, for what happened. I hope I have a chance to apologise in person.[3]

The next day, 25 June, Giuseppina wrote again:

I renew an urgent invitation to be heard. I want to resume the collaboration. It was interrupted, for reasons that you already know. But now I am willing to finish what I started. I pray this happens before my transfer hearing on 12 July – for obvious reasons concerning my personal safety. I repeat my apologies for my hesitancy. I am keenly aware that I caused great difficulties and wasted so much time.

The turnaround was amazing, thought Alessandra. The prosecutors had done nothing but let the 'Ndrangheta's internal dynamics play out. The clan's threats alone had been enough to propel Giuseppina back to the state. Alessandra's instinct was to give it longer. But Giuseppina was right to be afraid of the 12 July hearing. After it, she would likely be returned to the general prison population, and that would be all the opportunity the Pesces needed. Alessandra waited a few more days, then sent word that she and Prestipino would see Giuseppina again on 7 July.

At the meeting Alessandra was intially defensive. She adopted the same manner she had affected when she first met Giuseppina nine months before: cold and analytical, betraying little empathy or warmth. After all she had done for Giuseppina, she demanded to know how Giuseppina could accuse her of threatening her children. And how could she say that Alessandra had forced her to collaborate?

Giuseppina explained that her 'retraction', published in *Calabria Ora*, had been written for her by the Palaias' lawyer. 'I was opposed to this letter,' she said. 'But they said this thing had to come out, had to be made public. Everyone had to know that I was not a collaborator and this would be proof that I wasn't working with the authorities any more.'

It sounded convincing, but Alessandra wasn't done. How could the state trust Giuseppina again, she asked. How could it know if she was genuine this time? The interview went on for hours, with Alessandra demanding Giuseppina explain herself and Giuseppina begging for Alessandra to trust her again. In addition to repairing her credibility as a witness, it seemed just as important to Giuseppina that she mend her friendship with Alessandra. 'You have to trust me again,' said Giuseppina.

'You have to earn it,' replied Alessandra.

After several hours of talking, however, Alessandra was satisfied. She'd had to make sure but she was now certain that Giuseppina's intention to collaborate once more was authentic. Trust between *pentita* and prosecutor was restored.

Giuseppe Madia, the Palaias' lawyer, passed word of his dismissal back to Rosarno. To the family, that could only mean one thing: Giuseppina was planning to testify again. Even when the clan had tried to appear gentle and understanding, Alessandra had always felt it straining to contain its crueller instincts. Now it unleashed them. Leading the campaign against Giuseppina was her own mother, Angela Ferraro.

Reading transcripts of bugs placed in the jail where Giuseppina's mother and sister were being held, Alessandra realised Ferraro had stopped referring to her daughter by name. Now Giuseppina was simply 'the collaborator' or 'the traitor' or 'that whore'. Like Concetta's father, Ferraro seemed most infuriated by her loss of prestige among other inmates. She set about revenging herself by trying to turn Giuseppina's children against her. On 13 July, the day after Giuseppina's resumption of cooperation was confirmed in open court, Ferraro and Marina were visited together in jail by Sara, the third daughter in the family, who was mentally disabled, and Giuseppina's two daughters, Angela and Elisea.

Ferraro quickly told Angela to cut all ties with her mother. 'She's dead to the family,' she said. 'If she calls, you don't answer. If you happen to pick up the phone, you have to tell her: "You're dead to me. You don't exist any more. For not doing your time in prison, you are the most contemptible, the most despicable."' Ferraro was working herself into a fury, releasing all her frustration and rage. 'Tell her!' she shouted. 'Tell her that her mother told you to pretend that she had died! That she once had a place in your life but no longer! She doesn't give a fuck about who's now in jail! She doesn't care about anything! When the phone rings, you tell her that her mother says to forget she even has a mother! Her mother is gone!'

Six-year-old Elisea began to cry. 'Don't cry, love, don't cry, beautiful,' said her grandmother, softening and gently kissing her grandchildren. 'This is just how it is. This is the truth.' She produced a letter from Giuseppina and began reading from it. 'Forgive me if I am not the daughter you wanted,' Giuseppina had written. 'I know I've disappointed you. I know my sister is very angry with me.' See? asked Ferraro. Even their mother knew she had done wrong.

Angela said she too had received a letter from Giuseppina, asking for her forgiveness and saying that she wanted her children to join her but that they should 'do what their heart tells them'. Ferraro looked at her granddaughter. 'From now on, it's you, me and the family. Don't think that I'm not suffering in here. But I'm in here because of my love of family. You know what that means, love of family? It means loving you, loving my grandchildren, loving my children. My other daughter does not want to be in my heart. But that was her choice, not mine. I could never do what she did. Such a disappointment. But you should all go to the beach. Have fun. *Mama* is just fine here. It's just that I miss you. I miss you all. I miss my home. Let's all hug. We are a nice family. We love each other, no?'

Sara, by now crying as well, started hitting the table between them with her hand. 'I don't care about any of this,' she said. 'She's still my sister. She's still my sister.'

Marina interrupted angrily. 'You have to think of the rest of the family,' she told Sara. 'We've all cut her off. You have to turn your back on her. You have to be strong. Show me that strength in you that I love so much. Turn away from her.'

Reading the transcripts, Alessandra was astonished by the two women's will. 'They were ferocious. Brutal. The way they gave orders to the two girls. "You must separate from your mother, your sister. You must forget her. She has betrayed the family."' Among the adults, she said, only Giuseppina's disabled sister seemed to have a soul.

Back in Rosarno, the clan began tormenting Giuseppina's children in earnest. Angela, Gaetano and Elisea were forced to break all contact with their mother. Their Aunt Angela threw them out. Forced to live with Giuseppina's father-in-law, Gaetano Palaia, they found that the family that had once offered their mother thousands of euros for lawyers and rent now claimed there was no money to feed them. They often went without. Elisea began to lose weight and developed leg cramps and insomnia. Gaetano regularly beat the grandson named after him with a belt. One day Gaetano took the boy to a games arcade where he was hustled into a back room and set upon by four other older kids as his grandfather watched.

Angela was forced to play a part in torturing her mother. On 18 July, a bundle of letters arrived for Giuseppina. In them her father-in-law accused her of being too cowardly for prison. Her husband Rocco

told her, 'the road you're taking will not be as easy as you think ...'
Aunt Angela wrote that 'after everything we talked about, you were
just lying. How happy we would all be if you'd only known your place.'
Finally, there was a letter from her eldest daughter:

> Hello, dear mother. How are you? I hope you're fine ... I'm sorry
> but I'm angry with you, Mama, for what you're doing. You're
> wrong. You're spitting in the pot you eat from. To make the
> same mistake twice ... It's just not worth it. It doesn't make
> sense. And now you can't change back again. Don't be mad at
> me but I don't want that life again. I would have liked to be with
> you because I love you and because you're my mum but I just
> cannot do it. I don't know what they promised you and I don't
> care. What you're doing is wrong. Let me ask you this: is the
> promise you made to them more important than your family
> and our happiness? If you want our happiness, do everything
> you can to step back. If not, then it means you only think about
> yourself. You'll only be hurting us. I can't take it any more. I'm
> only fifteen and everything is ruined. Life is shit. From now on, I
> won't know my mother. All this had nothing to do with me.
> Please forgive these words. But it is all I think about. I want to
> love you, Mum. But you should know that what you are doing is
> wrong.

The letter nearly broke Giuseppina's heart. It might have shattered it
entirely but for one phrase: 'spitting in the pot you eat from'. That
didn't sound like Angela or any fifteen-year-old Giuseppina knew. It
was too old-fashioned. Too 'Ndrangheta.

The following week, a second letter came from Aunt Angela, urging
Giuseppina to acknowledge that her son, Gaetano, was lost to her.
From now on, he would be brought up by her in-laws. 'He's terrified,'
she said. 'I asked him about visiting you and he says he doesn't want
to. He wants to stay here. I think moving him away again would just

be more trauma. He would suffer even more. Try to think of your boy's happiness.'

Four days later, on 27 July 2011, there was a second, short note from Angela. She was writing in secret, she said. Her mother should forget her earlier letter. The words had been dictated by her uncles.

It was not my doing. It wasn't what was in my heart.
Mum, I want to be with you.
I do not want to live with anyone else.
You're my mum, and without you, I am nothing.
Whatever choice you make, I will follow.

It was what Giuseppina desperately needed to hear. It was all she needed, too.[4]

XVII

Mafia prosecutors are realists, not optimists.[1] Still, there was no doubt that the spring and summer of 2011 were a heady few months for Calabria's Anti-Mafia Directorate. Giuseppina Pesce's testimony had dealt the 'Ndrangheta a devastating blow and, though the clan had fought back, Alessandra's intervention had saved both Giuseppina's life and the case. Hundreds of 'Ndranghetisti were in jail. Hundreds of millions of euros in assets had been confiscated. Giuseppina's example had then inspired a second 'Ndrangheta mother, Maria Concetta Cacciola. The panicked reaction in Rosarno seemed to indicate that the clans feared being undone by an avalanche of feminine assertion.

Moreover, any west coast 'Ndranghetista tempted to dismiss Giuseppina and Concetta as anomalies only had to look over the mountains to the east to see how women were humbling the 'Ndrangheta there as well. After Carmine's arrest, Denise Cosco had left Pagliarelle, moved to a safe house in Turin run by Libera, reunited with Libera lawyer Enza Rando and formally re-entered state witness protection. Initially, said Enza, Denise was 'destroyed' by the knowledge that she had fallen in love with one of her mother's killers. But in protection, Denise slowly began to remake herself. She held on to the memory of what Carmine and she once shared. 'Fake love can still be true love,' she insisted. But a memory was all it would ever be. 'It doesn't matter now,' she said. 'The arrest brought things to an end.'

Denise found new purpose helping prosecutors prepare the case against the Pagliarelle clan. 'I have no pity,' she said of Lea's accused killers in a statement released by Enza on the eve of Carlo Cosco's trial. 'I don't care who is my father or who is my boyfriend. I don't even know what I feel more: hatred or anger. These people should get life. Or maybe just killed in the street. Until I hear in court that these people will pay for what they did, I have no life.'[2] Denise elaborated on her state of mind in an interview with Libera's information service. 'I want to live like any other normal twenty-year-old in the town where I was born, with my friends. I am a young woman and I want to be free to study and get a degree in Oriental languages. I don't want to hide. Only the men and women of the 'Ndrangheta should have to hide away, not justice witnesses. We did our duty. I want to live. I want to love. I want to be free to be happy, for my mother's sake if nothing else.'[3]

Denise's defiance, continuing her mother's fight even after Lea had been murdered by her father, and giving hours of sworn testimony against the man she loved, attracted the attention of the national press. The city of Milan decided to join Denise in a parallel civil action against her father's 'ndrina, symbolically uniting Italy's most progressive city with Italy's women against Italy's mafia. When Carlo, his brothers Giuseppe and Vito, and Massimo Sabatino, Rosario Curcio and Carmine Venturino went on trial in Milan on 6 July 2011, the hearing was attended by hundreds of students. They filled the public gallery and held vigils for Lea in the street outside. In opening remarks that resonated with almost every woman in Italy, Enza described Denise as a 'proud witness', once forced by the men of her family to live in silence, now reclaiming her 'freedom to choose her own life'. The case against her father and the other men of the 'Ndrangheta, said Enza, was the 'start of new hope, and a new life'.

These were giddy times to be an Italian prosecutor, and even an Italian woman. Looking back years later, Alessandra could even remember thinking that they might last.

After her transfer to Bolzano on 22 July 2011, Concetta found herself in another strange town, free but alone. It was seven weeks since she had seen or spoken to her three children. Overwhelmed, suddenly, by an almost physical maternal need, Concetta emailed her twelve-year-old daughter, Tania. 'And of course, the girl tells her grandmother,' said Giuseppe Creazzo, the anti-mafia prosecutor who would later investigate the case. 'And the family use the girl to re-establish contact with Concetta and try to persuade her to come home.'

The *carabinieri* missed the first call between Concetta and her mother, Anna Rosalba Lazzaro. By the time of the second, on 2 August, Concetta was in Genoa, and the Cacciolas' plans were well advanced. Concetta had followed Giuseppina's example when she walked into a *carabinieri* station. The Cacciolas duly decided to copy the Pesces' methods to blackmail her into returning to them.

In that call of 2 August, her mother told Concetta that she and her father, Michele Cacciola, would be arriving in Genoa that evening to pick her up. As a witness, rather than a *pentita*, Concetta was not bound by any restrictions on her movements. Within hours, the *carabinieri* were listening to a conversation inside the family car as the Cacciolas headed south for Calabria with Concetta in the back seat. Like the Pesces, Concetta's parents pursued two avenues of persuasion: promising their daughter everything would return to normal if she came home; and insinuating harm to her children if she did not. Unfortunately, Concetta did not have Giuseppina's steel. Confronted by parental authority, she was soon telling her mother and father everything that she had told the prosecutors.

'You told them about murders?!' exclaimed Lazzaro at one point. 'Oh, the disgrace!'

'The sacrifices I've had to make for you, 'Cetta!' shouted Michele. 'How you have dishonoured me!'

Then Michele seemed to remember the plan. 'Don't worry. I forgive you,' he said, trying to sound calm. 'You can't wrong family. You're blood. You're safe. You'll see. You'll say you know nothing. You'll say everything you said is not true. And in ten days, you'll be safe and quiet in Rosarno and no one will talk about you any more.'

After a lifetime of abuse from her father, Michele's uncharacteristic attempt at paternal understanding spooked Concetta. Then Michele revealed he had somehow obtained her phone records. He said he knew about her calls to her boyfriend, Pasquale Improta. That was even more worrying, thought Concetta. How could he possibly forgive that?

When the Cacciolas broke the journey for the night at Lazzaro's family home in Reggio Emilia, Concetta announced she would go no further and called the *carabinieri*. The following morning a pair of officers arrived to pick her up and drive her back to Genoa. Michele Cacciola and Rosalba Lazzaro continued on to Calabria. But now they had found a way to reach their daughter, they weren't about to give up. En route they kept up the pressure in a series of phone calls.

''Cetta, listen to me!' said her mother. 'You must tell the truth. You must say you knew nothing about what was going on. You have to drop everything.'

Between calls, the *carabinieri* could hear Concetta's mother and father discuss a plan to deliver their daughter to an 'Ndrangheta lawyer who would hand her a prepared statement to sign, as the Pesces had done with Giuseppina. It was her mother who, in another call to Concetta, hit on her daughter's weak spot. 'Tomorrow morning, you call the lawyer,' she said. 'This is how you get what you want. This is how you get me to send you your children.'

Concetta coughed, almost as though she had been punched, and the line went dead. The *carabinieri*, too, were shocked. Whatever her differences with the 'Ndrangheta, Concetta had always respected family. She was a dutiful daughter and a good mother, and it was her faith in the maternal bond that had persuaded her that she could safely entrust her children to her mother. She had paid dearly for her trust over the years. Now her mother was using it against her, in all likelihood to try to send her to her death. What kind of person would do such a thing? What kind of mother?

Concetta called her mother back a few minutes later. She sounded broken.

'Wait, Mum, just let me talk, and then you talk,' she said. After her mother assented, Concetta continued.

'I get it,' she said. 'I get it already. Already I can't do anything else. I just couldn't talk right then because I was near those people who want to arrest you. Understand?'

Concetta's mother moved quickly to reinforce her position. 'I don't care about them,' she replied. '*O cu nui, o cu iddi.*' (You're with us, or you're with them.)

'Yes, I know,' answered Concetta.

'You have to do this, 'Cetta! Tonight, I spoke with the lawyer. You understand? Tomorrow you go to the same lawyer. We've already paid him.'

'I know, I know.'

'Tomorrow! The same lawyer. Vittorio Pisani.'

'OK.'

'Swear to me, 'Cetta! You'll do this tomorrow!'

'Yes, I'll call him. I'll call him tomorrow.'

'If you don't call him tomorrow, you can forget about me, 'Cetta. I'm destroyed here.'

'Stop it, Mother. Enough. Leave me alone.'

'Swear to me! Tomorrow morning! You don't understand, 'Cetta. The ones you are with. You're making the men crazy! You call the lawyer tomorrow morning!'

'All right, Mum. All right. Please stop.'

'If you do everything the lawyer says, then the children will be with you again. You don't want to come home? Fine. You go to your Aunt Angela's or your Aunt Santina's or wherever you want. But you make the choice. Us, or them. And you shut up!'

Three days later, on 6 August, Concetta called her friend Emanuela Gentile. To the surveillance team, the change in Concetta's tone was dramatic. A few days earlier, she had sounded free and confident. Now she was in pieces. 'You know, Emanuela, the one mistake I made was to call home that one time,' she said. 'If I hadn't called, I would have continued on the same path. But I called, and I weakened.'

Concetta told Emanuela about her talk with her mother and father. 'They know everything I've been doing,' she said. 'They even have printouts of my phone calls.'

Emanuela said she'd heard that Concetta's father and brother had visited Pasquale Improta at his home in Reggio. 'Your brother's sick in the head,' she said. 'He's relentless.'

'My father told me he wouldn't let Giuseppe lay a finger on me,' replied Concetta. 'He even started to cry. He told me: "I forgive you." But I'm afraid, Emanuela, I tell you. I'm scared. Even if they're telling me, "Come back, daughter, come back," you know how these families are, especially my family, especially the men. They don't forgive. They don't forgive injuries to their honour. My father has two hearts. One for his daughter and one for his honour.'

Something was sure to happen to her if she went home, Concetta said. It had to, though probably not immediately, she thought. 'They'll wait,' she said. 'If they already have you there, in their place, they don't need to hurry. But does it make sense for me to go home and live just a year, maybe a year and a half?' She couldn't make up her mind. 'In one way, I'm thinking I should just do it, you know? Go home. Take the risk. Because I *have* to go back, Emanuela. I have to. They won't send my children to me.'

'*Mama mia!*' exclaimed Emanuela. 'They're keeping your children from you?'

'I asked for them but they haven't sent them. And they won't. Because they know that if they send my children to me, their daughter is lost to them for ever.'

In another call, to Pasquale Improta, Concetta tried to prepare her boyfriend for what lay ahead. 'If I go home, I'm finished,' she said. 'I understand that. I know how it will end. They don't forgive offences to honour or dignity – and I injured both.'

'Concetta,' Pasquale replied, 'can I tell you something? You're too good. Too good.'

'Too stupid,' joked Concetta.

'Too good. They broke your ribs. Other women wouldn't even call them.'

'It scares me to go home, I tell you.'

'If it scares you, Concetta, then don't go. If you go, you'll pay.'

'Well, that's for sure.'

Maybe because he wasn't 'Ndrangheta himself, or maybe because he wasn't a father, Pasquale didn't seem to get it. He imagined Concetta still had choices. Concetta couldn't make him understand. Before she hung up, however, she made sure to take time over her goodbyes. 'Pa,' she said, 'until my last breath, I will love you. Goodnight, my love. Goodnight. I love you.'

On 8 August, Concetta wrote a note to her protection officers, saying that she had spoken to her mother, who was on her way to Genoa with her uncle Gregorio and her eldest daughter Tania. Concetta explained that she couldn't bear not to see Tania.

In fact, Concetta had initially tried to resist. Her surveillance officers heard her on the phone trying to stall Lazzaro, saying she needed to check with the *carabinieri* before she agreed to meet. 'Who do you need to call, 'Cetta?' her mother shouted back. 'Why do you need to ask anyone? Do you hear your daughter?'

On the line came the sound of a small child crying and screaming. Lazzaro was holding the phone towards Concetta's youngest daughter,

Rosalba, seven, named after her grandmother. The girl was in tears. 'She's dying without you, 'Cetta!' she said.

'Tell her not to worry,' said Concetta, softly.

'Tell her to be quiet?' replied Lazzaro. ''Cetta, she's dying here.'

'OK, OK. Tell her I'm close by. Tell her I'm coming.'

'You meet us on the other side of town!' ordered Lazzaro, and hung up.

The following morning, when Concetta's protection officers went to her hotel room, they found the door open with the keys in the lock. Inside, her suitcase was gone.

The surveillance team wouldn't hear Concetta's voice again for more than a week. That wasn't because she hadn't been talking, however. Three days after arriving back in Rosarno, Concetta secretly recorded a statement at the Cacciola family lawyer's office in town. The recording, including one brief interruption, lasted eleven minutes and seven seconds.

My name is Maria Concetta Cacciola, today is 12 August 2011, and I want to clarify what happened to me this May.

During a visit to the carabinieri *barracks, I told them I had some problems with my family. My family had received some anonymous letters. At the time, I was in a bad way. I was jealous. My husband was in prison. Then these letters came and I held up my hands to what they said, and my family shut me in my home, telling me I couldn't go out or have friends. I was angry at my family. I wanted to make them pay. So I told the* carabinieri: *'Maybe I can help you. I have problems with my parents and my family. I'm afraid that my father and my brother are going to do something to me.'*

Initially, they did not take me away. But a few days later, they told me that I should talk to their superiors and the carabinieri *commander came to see me. And that's how it happened. I said* whatever I needed to say in order to get away from home. I was confused. But my reasoning was to make them pay. I was so angry.

Two days later, they told me they had agreed to take me into custody and they met me again at the barracks. There was a car ready and two magistrates were there to talk to me. At first, I was confused. But then, because I wanted to leave, I said things that weren't true and which hadn't happened. Because I just wanted to go away and make them pay for my suffering. Finally, one magistrate said to me: 'It's Friday. Get ready to leave here on Monday.'

In fact, they came to get me on Saturday. They took me to Cosenza. Three days later, the two magistrates came back and began pressuring me about my family. And I, because I was still furious with them, I again accused my father and my brother.

I was a month and a half in Cosenza. From there they took me to Bolzano. But by the time I got to Bolzano, I wanted to retract because I realised that out of anger I had said things that weren't true. It was all just things that I had read in newspapers or heard people talking about and just because I was so enraged I accused my father and brother of being involved even when they were not. I realised I was in the wrong. I realised that because I was so angry, I was accusing people who had nothing to do with anything. It wasn't right. I wanted a lawyer. But they told me I couldn't have one because witnesses weren't allowed lawyers under the law. I told them I wanted to return to my family. But they told me: 'Don't go back to your family. We are your family now. Your family won't forgive you if you go back now. If you thought they wanted to kill you before, imagine what they'll do now they think you have a relationship with us.' And I was afraid, knowing what I had done and how gross an injury I had inflicted.

In Bolzano, I talked to my daughter by email. After that, I spoke to my mother. I wanted to know what my mother thought *of what I had done. In Bolzano, I also met people who might have recognised me. At that point, I was moved immediately to Genoa. They told me: 'You can't have any contact with people you know.'*

From Genoa, I called my mother again and told her I missed her and wanted to see her. I spoke to my mother and my father too. And now I really knew what I had done! My mother came to Genoa but the state told me I couldn't have any contact with my family. When I got into the car with my dad, however, I realised he had already forgiven me for the mistakes I had made. We reached Reggio Emilia. I was scared of going back to Calabria, though not of my father, and of my own free will I left again with the carabinieri *for Genoa. They asked me: 'Are you sure you haven't told your family that you're staying in Genoa?' I said I hadn't, even though I had told my mother.*

I had also told my mother that I wanted to talk to a lawyer. From Genoa I called a lawyer, Vittorio Pisani, telling him I was confused because the state had told me that if I hadn't been represented already in the process then I couldn't start now. Anyway, the state told me to stop calling the lawyer, and added that I was stubborn, that I shouldn't call my family, that I should turn off my phone and everything else. I didn't agree. And I called my mother again, asked her to come back up to Genoa, and she came with her brother and my daughter and I left Genoa of my own free will. Now I have decided to appoint the lawyers Gregorio Cacciola and Vittorio Pisani to represent me …

At that point the recording cut, then resumed:

I've now been back at home for three days with my father, my mother, my brother and my children. Finally, I have found the peace …

'... that I have been looking for,' prompted a female voice in the background.

> ... that I have been looking for. I should add that I have written
> a letter to go with this recording. In the future, I hope to be left
> alone, out of contact with anyone and with no one contacting
> me.[4]

On 13 and 14 August, Concetta's surveillance officers picked up two text messages she sent to Pasquale Improta using a phone she had managed to hide from her family. In them, she told a different story. She said she was a prisoner of her family in the yellow house on Via Don Gregorio Varrà once more. This time, however, 'they brought lawyers to make me retract,' she wrote. 'They made me say that I was using drugs, that I was angry. My brother won't speak to me. Their coldness is terrifying. I don't want to stay here, Pa. I don't see how any good will come of this.'

Concetta asked Pasquale to pass a message to Chief Marshal Salvatore Esposito at the *carabinieri* headquarters in Reggio Calabria. She wanted to return to witness protection, she said. This time, she had to take her children with her. 'I feel caged here,' she wrote. 'What can I do?'

Pasquale passed on the message. On 17 August, Concetta spoke to the *carabinieri* several times to confirm she wanted to re-enter witness protection. Just before 11 p.m. she called Marshal Esposito in Reggio. After confirming for himself that Concetta wanted to return to the programme, Esposito asked how best to extract her and her three children. 'Can you leave the house?' he asked. 'Even later tonight?'

Concetta said no. She asked if Esposito could send officers to arrest her to make it look as though she was being taken against her will. 'It's so difficult here, with my father and my brother,' she said. Even outside the family, she explained, 'there are also those around them, people know what happened. Word that I've been speaking to the *carabinieri* is spreading.'

'Are you afraid of moving or of the repercussions?' asked Esposito.

'Both!' replied Concetta.

Eventually, Esposito and Concetta agreed that she would call when the time felt right – that night or the following morning – and that Esposito would dispatch a car immediately. It would be with her fifteen minutes after her call, Esposito said. 'Call any time,' he added. 'We'll be waiting.'

In Reggio's Palace of Justice, Alessandra was also waiting. It was August, the daytime temperature was breaching 40 °C and the entire country was on holiday. Pignatone, Prestipino and Giovanni Musarò were all away. Only Alessandra remained. 'The situation appeared to be calm with Cacciola,' said Giovanni later. 'There was a wiretap of her talking to a friend in which she said that she knew she would be killed – but not soon. She was talking about a year, a year and a half, because it would be stupid to kill her immediately. And anyway, Concetta was going to be back in protection soon. So we felt safe.'

The next day, 18 August, in a conversation recorded by a bug inside the Cacciola car, Concetta told her mother she had spoken to Chief Marshal Esposito. She added she intended to return to witness protection.

''Cetta, no!' screamed Lazzaro. 'No! Absolutely not!'

'You told me everything would be different!' shouted Concetta.

'I was resigned to you leaving us,' replied Lazzaro. 'But now I'm not. No! I won't accept this!'

'Mum, I have to finish what I started,' said Concetta.

Half an hour later, Concetta phoned the *carabinieri* once more and told them she was in a dilemma. It was impossible to leave the house without being accompanied by her mother. On the other hand, if she left with her and her mother returned home without her, then her mother would face dire consequences. Eventually Concetta agreed with the *carabinieri* that the solution was to wait for everyone in the

Cacciola house to fall asleep that night, then usher her children out into the street and into a waiting *carabinieri* car. They would do it around 1.30 a.m. Four hours later, Concetta called back to say her youngest, Rosalba, had a fever and everything had to be put off for a day or so.

Reading the transcripts, Alessandra was exasperated. 'We were all waiting for her call to come and pick her up. She had called and said: "I want to come back." The barracks were all ready for her and her children. I'd even asked the *carabinieri* to come back from their holidays. So we were just waiting. And then this back and forth. Honestly, at that point, we thought that she was playing with us. We discovered that the part about her daughter being sick was a lie. Her children were at the beach. Concetta just did not have a clear mind. She was changing it constantly. Some days she reached out to us. Some days she didn't. There was such indecision. We really wanted her to make up her mind and make a final decision, a choice. But we thought that at least she had the situation under control. And I think perhaps she herself thought she had more time.'

The next day, 19 August, Alessandra and the *carabinieri* waited by the phone in case Concetta changed her mind once again. No call came.

On 20 August, Alessandra and the *carabinieri* gathered again to resume their vigil. 'The whole team was there on alert, waiting for her to give the word and we'd go in and get her. But we couldn't do anything until she gave us the go-ahead. By law, since she was a witness, we weren't allowed to charge in and break down the door. She had to open the door for us. And she just couldn't open that door.'[5]

At 6.40 p.m. on 20 August 2011, Concetta's father, Michele, arrived at Santa Maria Hospital in the town of Polistena, twenty minutes from Rosarno. Concetta was lying on the back seat of the family Mercedes. She was wearing figure-hugging jeans and a white blouse unbuttoned to show her bosom, and her hair had been recently cut and styled. A red and white foam was spilling from Concetta's mouth, smudging her dark purple lipstick.

In emergency admissions, Dr Fortunato Lucia confirmed Concetta had no pulse. As staff at the hospital called the police, Dr Lucia attempted to resuscitate her using CPR. The paramedics handed the doctor a red plastic bottle of hydrochloric acid which they said Concetta's family had found next to her in the family basement. Dr Lucia tried to put Concetta on an intravenous drip but without a pulse, it wouldn't take. By the time a police patrol arrived at 7 p.m., Dr Lucia had pronounced Concetta dead.

ACT THREE

ITALY AWAKES

XVIII

Maria Concetta Cacciola's death certificate identified her as having been born three decades earlier, a few miles south of the hospital in which she died.[1] It listed her as living ten miles to the west in Rosarno. Born in Calabria. Lived in Calabria. Died in Calabria. As her family had promised her, it was as though the past four months had never happened.

Word of Concetta's death reached Alessandra and the *carabinieri* in a call in the early evening from the local police. The officer said the indications were that Concetta had drunk a litre of hydrochloric acid in the basement of the Cacciola family home. For the second time that year, Alessandra found herself momentarily overwhelmed. 'It was terrible for everyone,' she said. 'No one had imagined it would end so finally, so completely. We were all ready to pick her up. It was very hard to come to terms with.'[2]

Giovanni took Alessandra's call on holiday. He was speechless. Years later, he would say: 'You can't let the work become personal. But the story of Maria Concetta Cacciola was terrible, really hard to bear. She hadn't even been arrested and had no convictions. She was just a witness.'[3] It was the tragedy of Concetta's death, the way it seemed almost mythically pre-destined, that most disturbed Giovanni. 'Maria Concetta Cacciola was a character from a Greek play,' he said. 'She went back even though she was aware she would be murdered. She went back out of love for her children. This almost symbiotic relationship that she had with her mother, the love letter she wrote to her – there is something beautiful about it. Beautiful, and unacceptable.'

Giovanni and Alessandra knew only too well the effect Concetta's story would have on the small towns and hill villages of Calabria. 'It was what had to happen,' said Concetta's father, Michele, in an aside recorded by the *carabinieri* two days later – and the prosecutors knew every Calabrian would be thinking the same. Lea Garofalo was dead. Giuseppina Pesce had been forced to retract in public. Now Maria Concetta Cacciola was gone too. This was what happened to women who betrayed the 'Ndrangheta. There was no escaping fate. The 'Ndrangheta *was* invincible. 'If this phenomenon of women testifying had gathered momentum with Giuseppina, it was going to come to a sudden stop with Maria Concetta Cacciola's death,' said Alessandra. 'By contrast with Giuseppina, Concetta was a symbol that the 'Ndrangheta *could* get to you.'

The evening Concetta died, the *carabinieri* sealed off the basement at 26 Via Don Gregorio Varrà in Rosarno where she was found. They seized mobile phones, a computer, Concetta's diary and several letters addressed to her husband, Salvatore. When they questioned Michele, he told them he had returned home after 5.30 p.m. and had called for Concetta but couldn't find her. He eventually discovered her lying on the floor of a bathroom in the basement. Next to her body was a plastic bottle. Asked why his daughter might have killed herself, Michele exploded and refused to answer. Concetta's mother, Anna Rosalba Lazzaro, was more forthcoming. Concetta, she said, had taken her own life out of shame. 'She felt bad. She said things that she had no knowledge of. She couldn't face those she had accused.' Concetta's family had 'fully supported her' after she returned home, added Lazzaro. They knew she had been unwell. After all, she had a history of it. She had pined for her absent husband for many years. She had also taken diet drugs obsessively. These things had affected her mind.

Giovanni dismissed Lazzaro's interview out of hand. 'It was clear that something had happened that we didn't know about,' he said. The prosecutors knew Concetta was at long-term risk from her family. Like Concetta, they had calculated the family wouldn't harm her so quickly after her return since suspicion would immediately fall on them. On the other hand, they also knew Concetta had told her mother that she would shortly be returning to the protection programme. Maybe the family decided they had kill her while they could.

Because there was no doubt that Concetta had been murdered. Every gastroenterologist said drinking a litre of hydrochloric acid was impossible to do voluntarily. The human reflex was to choke and vomit after just a sip. The pain was unbearable. The acid would eat through the stomach wall. Unconsciousness would be swift. The coroner would later report that Concetta had died of a heart attack and respiratory failure but only after the acid had burned her throat, stomach, pancreas and lungs. 'It's simply not something you can do by yourself,' said Giovanni.

The method of Concetta's death also had the 'Ndrangheta written all over it. Acid was a favourite 'Ndrangheta tool for traitors. They used it on the dead, to erase every shameful trace of a collaborator's body, and they used it on the living. In December 2010, Reggio council's budget manager, Orsola Fallara, had given a press conference in a downtown restaurant at which she admitted making suspicious payments and keeping irregular accounts – and, hours later, was found dying in her car after drinking acid.[4] In March 2011, another 'Ndrangheta wife, thirty-eight-year-old Tita Buccafusca, had run into a police station near Rosarno clutching her young son and offering to testify – and a month later her husband, an 'Ndrangheta boss called Pantaleone Mancuso, reported that she had committed suicide by drinking acid.[5] Mouths which spoke out of turn were rubbed out. Concetta's death was part of a pattern.

For the prosecutors, there was one anomaly in the case, however. Concetta had told them that her family never left her alone, especially since her return to Rosarno. But on the day she died, her father, mother and brother had all been out of the house. 'That seemed quite strange,' said Giovanni. It suggested not just careful planning but also the involvement of a third party.

On 23 August, three days after Concetta died, the Cacciola family delivered a formal written complaint to the prosecutor's office in Palmi. Following the script established by the Pesces, Concetta's parents accused Alessandra and Giovanni of taking advantage of a woman in a frail mental state. Concetta had walked into the *carabinieri* station in May 2010 'depressed' and in 'pathological distress', they said. The *carabinieri* had seen her weakness as an opportunity. They had promised her a new life 'which turned out to be a living hell, taking her away from her family'.

By this view, Concetta, like her friend Giuseppina before her, was a pathetic creature. The complaint claimed that none of what she had done was by conscious choice. She had not elected to create a new life for herself and her children. She had not rejected her family and the 'Ndrangheta. She had not, above all, asserted her free will and reclaimed her independence from her parents and her husband. Rather, according to the Cacciolas, she had been pitiably weak and easily led. This daughter, this woman, had been dazzled by the state's perfidious offers of a better life. In return, her feeble mind had conjured up the kinds of stories about her family's criminality that she imagined the prosecutors wanted to hear. Concetta had soon come to her senses, realised her mistake, made contact with her family again and eventually succeeded in escaping the authorities' clutches. Once back in the bosom of her 'loving and attentive' family, she had confessed to everything, especially the 'invented allegations' she had made against her kin to 'ingratiate herself with the prosecutors'. Happily, she had finally found the peace of mind that she had sought in her family's loving forgiveness and acceptance. Understandably, however, the shame had proved too much. The whole sorry saga could be heard in Concetta's own words by listening to the attached tape cassette or reading the attached transcript. The Cacciolas expected a reply forthwith from the prosecutors and the *carabinieri*, explaining their disgraceful conduct.

Even then, the Cacciolas weren't done. The same day they filed their complaint, Anna Rosalba Lazzaro wrote a letter to the *Gazzetta del Sud*, the main southern Italian newspaper, complaining that in their report on Concetta's death, the *Gazzetta* journalists had described her as having grown up in 'an environment pregnant with the negative values of the 'Ndrangheta'. 'That's simply not true,' wrote Lazzaro. 'On this particular issue, I challenge anyone to show that my house has ever held discussions about criminal matters that have affected or involved the members of my family. I want to add that my husband and I dedicated our lives to giving our children the best civic education possible.'[6] The next day, *Calabria Ora* splashed on an exclusive interview with Lazzaro, which it headlined: 'You drove my daughter to suicide!'[7] On its inside pages, *Calabria Ora* hammered home the message that Concetta's death was inevitable. 'Chronicle of a suicide foretold' was the paper's banner headline.

It was unbelievable, thought Alessandra. The Cacciolas had blackmailed their daughter into returning to them, then stood by as she was executed. Now they were painting her killing as a tragedy for which the state was to blame, while using her death to mend their criminal reputation. At no point had they expressed sorrow or love or any feeling other than outrage at the wrongs done to them. They hadn't even buried Concetta. Had there ever been a family so unspeakable as the Cacciolas of Rosarno?

XIX

The 'Ndrangheta had reasserted itself in spectacular fashion.[1] Once more their challengers were dead or in disgrace. Just as Alessandra and Giovanni had been required to answer questions about the Giuseppina Pesce case, now they had to account for their handling of Maria Concetta Cacciola. The editor of *Calabria Ora*, Piero Sansonetti, celebrated the state's humiliation in a series of editorials. 'The season of cooperation is over,' he wrote.

In Milan, the six defendants on trial for the murder of Lea Garofalo seemed emboldened by events to the south. Their lawyers argued that the case against their clients should be dismissed outright. No body, no murder. Lea, they said, was actually living by the beach in Australia. 'I hope she gets tired of Australia and does us the honour of appearing in this court,' said one.[2] Their clients were innocent not just of killing Lea, they claimed, but of any criminality. Carlo's brother Giuseppe said he was a shoemaker. Vito said he was a builder. Rosario Curcio said he ran a solarium. Carmine Venturino asked to be excused answering questions in court because he only spoke Grecanico, not Italian. Carlo had somehow managed to convince the legal aid authorities that his income was a mere €10,000 a year, thereby qualifying for state assistance. He said he was mystified by the entire process. 'It's not fair that I'm sitting here,' he said. 'I'm an honest person. My mother taught me to respect and love the family. My daughter wrote me letters in prison saying she loved me and missed me and wanted to be with me again. I had nothing to do with Lea's disappearance. I, too, want to know the truth about what happened.'[3]

The defence paraded a succession of villagers from Pagliarelle through court to testify to Carlo's decency. Most claimed to have barely known Lea. When one prosecution witness, a friend of Carlo's and resident at Viale Montello, repeatedly failed to show up at court, the defendants laughed and whooped. 'Maybe he's in the attic,' came one shouted suggestion. A lawyer for Giuseppe further muddied the waters by declaring that his client had not spoken to his brother Vito in years, making a nonsense of any conspiracy between them.

There were, however, signs of tension between the defendants. From the start, Massimo Sabatino sat apart from the other men in the caged dock. 'Shame on you!' Venturino hissed at him one day as they were being led away for the night. 'Shame on me?!' Sabatino yelled back. 'It's your fault I'm doing six years! If I get my hands on you, I'll rip your head off, you piece of shit!'

The defendants also seemed to lose some of their initial confidence as the weeks progressed and prosecutor Marcello Tatangelo painstakingly took apart their denials. Traces from their phones showed all of them had been busy moving around Milan and its outskirts and in each other's company for the three hours after 6.30 p.m. when Lea Garofalo was last seen alive. The *carabinieri* had unearthed a friend of Carlo's who said he had lent Carlo the keys to his grandmother's apartment. It was here, said Tatangelo, that Lea had been taken to be tortured, then shot with a bullet to the neck, before her body was disposed of outside the city. When Salvatore Cortese, Carlo's old cellmate, testified about Carlo's burning desire for revenge on Lea, Carlo couldn't contain himself. 'What are you saying?!' he shouted. 'What's this about getting permission from the bosses to kill Lea? He's making it up! I had nothing to do with anything!' When Sabatino's confession to his cellmate, Salvatore Sorrentino, was read out, it was Sabatino's turn to shout. 'I never said those things about Carlo!' he said. 'It's not true that I said they were bastards and I wanted to kill them! You're making it up! I agree with everything these men say.'

Finally, Denise was called on to testify. A screen was erected in court so her father could not see her. Denise wore a hooded top to further conceal her face. Sensing his daughter a few yards away, Carlo stood, walked to the front of his cage and placed his arms through the bars. In a clear voice and without hesitation, and in testimony that lasted two full days – 20 September and 13 October 2011 – Denise told the story of her mother's early life and their years on the run and in the protection programme. 'We were like sisters,' she said. 'It was almost like we grew up together. We swapped clothes. We liked the same music.' For seven years, she added, she had no contact with Carlo.

'That's a fact,' said Carlo audibly.

Denise frowned. 'Can you request that person to keep quiet?' she coolly asked the judge. 'It's disturbing.'

Denise went on to recount her mother's attempts to make peace with Carlo. She described the attack in Campobasso in May 2009, prompting Sabatino to stand and pace up and down inside the cage. Only once did Denise break down. When one lawyer rebuked her for accusing the defendants of murder when there was no body and no murder weapon, she cried: 'She can't be allowed to say that! It's been two years since I saw my mother!'

In the face of such raw emotion, the defence lawyers tried to conjure up some sympathy for the defendants. 'I know in my heart that my client is innocent,' said Maira Cacucci, Carlo's lawyer. 'Just one look in his eyes and you'll understand.' Francesco Garofalo, a Calabrian lawyer representing Carmine Venturino and Vito Cosco, fell back on a familiar defence: the unstable nature of women. 'Why all these attempts to sanctify Lea, who was born and raised by the 'Ndrangheta?' he asked. 'She was a crazy woman, as her own daughter has described. Lea Garofalo wanted to go to Australia. What better time than after leaving her daughter with her father? That is what happened here!'

Nevertheless, the defence's histrionics did little to deflect what was starting to feel increasingly certain: that all six men would eventually be found guilty of murder. But as the trial wound towards its conclusion, on 23 November, the eve of the second anniversary of Lea's disappearance, disaster struck. Out of the blue, the presiding judge, Filippo Grisolia, was appointed chief of staff at the Ministry of Justice. The trial would have to be abandoned, then restarted. What was more, the statutory limit on detention in custody meant any new trial would have to finish by 28 July 2012, eight months away. The trial had already taken five months. It wouldn't be hard for the defence to spin out a new trial past the deadline. At that point, Carlo and his entire *'ndrina* would walk free.

XX

The 'Ndrangheta had always relied on fictions.[1] One of the biggest was that it could not be challenged, and never by a woman. Lea Garofalo, Giuseppina Pesce, Maria Concetta Cacciola and now Denise Cosco had all exposed that lie. The 'Ndrangheta's response was uncompromising. The women had to die. And their stories had to be rewritten.

Alessandra and Giovanni were now confronting the possibility that, after their early triumphs, the clans were succeeding, at least in public perception. The Lea Garofalo investigation might have revived several old cases and injected new life into the fight against the east coast 'Ndrangheta, but there was no resuscitating Lea. Likewise, despite Giuseppina's decision to start cooperating again, the last public memory of her was that she had recanted. As for Concetta, she had died and then, in a mafia masterstroke, had retracted from beyond the grave. Now, with the very public collapse of the trial against Carlo Cosco and his men, it seemed the clans had got lucky with Denise, too. 'The truth is that there is no more important or fundamental investigative tool than the *pentiti*,' said Giovanni Musarò. The prosecutors had had four women *pentiti*. None had emerged unscathed. The 'Ndrangheta had used Concetta's death, in particular, as a warning. 'When the Cacciolas wrote their denunciation of the prosecutors, they weren't thinking of their daughter,' said Giovanni. 'They were ensuring that this never happened again. It went beyond Cacciola. It was a message to all Calabria. So, yes, at that time, you can say things were not in our favour.'

On reflection, however, it was possible to view the 'Ndrangheta's vehement crushing of any opposition as a sign of weakness. In particular, its absolutist intolerance of freedom seemed to stem from an appreciation of how, once released, it was almost impossible to contain again. Moreover, despite the clans' efforts, Giuseppina and Denise were still breathing. Both also seemed strengthened by the resolve they had discovered in the gale of the 'Ndrangheta's oppression. In Milan, Denise had already faced her father once in court and was telling prosecutors she could do it again. As for Giuseppina, the death of her friend appeared to have had the exact opposite effect to that intended. Giuseppina told Alessandra she had no doubt that the 'Ndrangheta had forced Concetta to drink acid. Her friend's killing made her realise how close she had come to the same fate herself: she had been mere hours from her own return to Calabria when Alessandra arrested her. 'You saved my life,' she told Alessandra. 'If you hadn't stopped me, my children would now be taking flowers to the cemetery, like 'Cetta's.'

The realisation seemed to release Giuseppina of any last doubts. On 23 August, three days after Concetta's death, a letter from Giuseppina arrived at the Palace of Justice in Reggio Calabria, addressed to Alessandra, Pignatone and Roberto di Bella, head of Reggio's juvenile court. 'I know you already know my story,' Giuseppina wrote, 'but here I wish to start from the beginning.'

After six months of imprisonment, on 14 October 2010, I expressed my desire to the prosecutor Dr Cerreti to pursue a new path, driven by my love as a mother and my desire to lead a better life, away from where I was born and lived. I never thought about reductions to my sentence. It was also never my intention to tease anyone. I only did this because I was, and remain, convinced that this is the right choice, not least because the choices my friends and relatives made in life have always been coloured by cowardice and have always led to suffering. Each and every one of us should have the ability to choose between right and wrong.

Maybe I should have managed this earlier, before being dragged into all this mess. But my hope is that we still have time. I want to act so my children can have a better life – a life of principle and of freedom and of choice. I also hope that many people like me who are in situations like mine will find the courage to rebel. I have finally found the strength to take this decision and defy a fearsome, powerful and unforgiving family, in the full knowledge of the risk to me and those I love. Finally, I am doing it.

There were times when I thought I had rushed my choice and not properly thought it through. The courage that I had back on 14 October 2010 deserted me. Angela told me she wouldn't come to see me any more. My husband Rocco wrote me threatening letters. I found out my husband's family were mistreating my children. They weren't feeding them properly, saying they'd given all their money to my lawyer. My son Gaetano was beaten by his grandfather with a belt.

So I gave up. I was confused by my children's relationship with their family. I began to think I had no right to deprive them of their father. I told myself none of us could escape the life we were born into. It all weighed heavily on me. And even though my partner disagreed, I decided to send my children back to Calabria. My plan was to employ a good lawyer to fight for me and, in the meantime, give my children a little freedom of their own, away from me. But I was dying inside. It wasn't what I wanted. It was just what I imagined was right for them.

And, of course, there were the newspapers. What was written, day after day, made me look like a victim instead of someone in command of their own decisions. They sent a letter to the judge and that made me feel even worse: all those lies, this impression of me that was created which was not me. I had to swallow that as well, not because anyone was forcing me to but because I felt that, like in the movies, there was a way of going about things that I had to respect – and that if I wasn't going to be a collaborator any more but was one day going to be returning to Calabria, then maybe those stories would serve to protect my children and myself from the prejudices of my family and my people. The statements I made about being forced to cooperate – those were purely a defensive technique. Everything I stated before 11 April 2011 was the truth.

You know, getting back into the car with Domenico in Lucca and setting off, I suddenly understood the importance of motivation – who I'm doing this for. This is about my children's future. This is about the love of a man who loves me for who I am and not for my last name. Today, while I may have lost credibility as a collaborator, all these experiences have strengthened me as a woman. Just as important, they have restored my confidence in myself. I feel now that maybe I wasn't so selfish, after all. Perhaps if I had been more courageous, today I would already be at the beach with Domenico and my children. What I'm left with is the freedom to choose. And I have always prioritised my love for my children, their health and well-being, and my love for Domenico. These are those who I really love because, however many times I change my mind, they are there for me, thank God.

That's why I believe my collaboration will make a real change, for many people. Please tell Dr Cerreti I'm not crazy, like they said. I tell you all these things so you can tell her about the real person in whom she placed her confidence. I never told any lies. I just had a moment of confusion. I patiently await your reply, sir, humbly aware of my mistakes.[2]

As her staff and colleagues read the letter, Alessandra was pleased to note that they lingered, silently reading every line. Man or woman, they were moved. Though she'd never show it, Alessandra was too. In a world of deception, here was clarity. Instead of hate, here was love. Gone was fear. Here was strength.

After Giuseppina's letter, events moved fast. In early September, she gave Alessandra a comprehensive account of how her former lawyer, Giuseppe Madia, and the editor of *Calabria Ora*, Piero Sansonetti, had coordinated the drafting and release of her retraction letter. (Madia told Giuseppina he had had to approach Sansonetti because the editor of Calabria's small, local daily 'was the only one willing to publish it and adopt our cause'.)

On 15 September, Giuseppina received another letter from her husband Rocco. At first, he admonished her. 'I know you've started making *coccòdeo*,' he said, using the Italian for 'cock-a-doodle-do'. 'I do wonder why you've ruined all our lives, including your own, just to be with the children?' Perhaps sensing Giuseppina's renewed determination, however, he soon switched to a plaintive tone. 'Please, don't make me look bad,' he wrote. 'I don't think I'm asking for the moon. There is no morning that I don't wake up and think of you. Sadly, this is how things have turned out. My family is broken. But I leave you with an embrace, and the hope that God will enlighten you.'[3] A year earlier, Rocco's meekness might have swayed Giuseppina. Now it merely confirmed that she had emerged from their marriage the steelier of the two, and further hardened her purpose.

She was unmoved, too, five days later on 20 September when the first trial to result from Operation All Inside concluded in the sentencing of eleven members of the Pesce *'ndrina*. Giuseppina's uncle Vincenzo and her cousin Francesco Pesce, who had been found hiding in a bunker on 9 August, received the heaviest sentences: twenty years each for mafia association and other crimes; and a total fine of €70 million, of which €50 million was to compensate the citizens of

Rosarno for decades of murderous oppression and €10 million each was to go to the Ministry of Interior and Calabria's regional authority.[4]

The sentencing began a bewildering few days of public humiliation for the Pesces. The next day, 21 September, the *carabinieri* took Angela, now sixteen, Gaetano, ten, and Elisea, six, from their grandparents' home and delivered them to the protective custody of the juvenile court.[5] On 22 September, Alessandra formally announced in court that Giuseppina was once more cooperating with the authorities.[6] On 23 September, at her own request, Giuseppina appeared in court in Palmi by video link to hear charges put to clan head Antonino, her husband Rocco, her mother Angela Ferraro and her sister Marina.[7] On 27 September, Giuseppa Bonarrigo, the family grandmother, chained herself to the gates of Rosarno town hall, where she was photographed by journalists protesting the innocence of her sons.

The public dishonouring of the Pesces was far from over. On 4 October, Giuseppina's in-laws, Gaetano, Gianluca and Giovanni Palaia, were arrested, quickly followed by Aunt Angela Palaia and Angela Ietto. On 13 October, Alessandra seized another eight Rosarno companies worth a further €18 million, bringing the total value of confiscations from the Pesce empire to €228 million.[8] A week later, on 21 October, Alessandra announced that besides Giuseppina, she had a second 'Ndrangheta woman ready to testify: Rosa Ferraro, a cousin from Genoa taken in by the Pesces as a domestic helper after she was thrown out by her husband.[9] The following day, 110 'Ndranghetisti who had been arrested during the mass raids of July 2010 were sentenced to terms of between two and sixteen years.[10]

The climactic disgrace came on 25 November, the day the Pesce clan maxi-trial formally opened. Sixty-three *'ndrina* members were accused. More than fifty were present in court, including several Pesces, Palaias and Ferraros, along with fifty defence lawyers. Those already serving sentences in jail, like clan head Antonino and

Giuseppina's husband Rocco, attended by video link. A handful of Pesces remained on the run. They would be tried in their absence.

Procedure demanded that Alessandra read out the charges to the accused and submit the evidence gathered from years of investigation, including Operations All Inside, All Inside II, All Clean and Crimine. The evidence ran to 65,000 words, the length of a book. Running through it all would take several weeks, and a full trial was not expected to start until May 2012.

That first day did not go as expected, however. The defendants already knew they were being tried by a woman prosecutor on a woman's evidence. The news that Giuseppina would be joined by a second woman from the Pesce household had come as a shock. As they were led in, the men were surprised to see that, in addition, an unusually large proportion of the court officials, *carabinieri* and even lawyers and reporters on duty that day were also women. When the judges entered, one president and two assistants, the 'Ndranghetisti were astonished to see three more women: Maria Laura Ciollaro, Antonella Create and, taking the President's seat, Concettina Epifanio.

To the 'Ndrangheta men, it must have felt like a conspiracy. 'No! no!' they shouted. Pointing at Alessandra and taking the name of another male prosecutor in the case, they yelled: 'We want di Palma! We want di Palma! Not that! Not *that!*'

State and court officials would later insist there was no plot to unsettle the Pesces. The selection of staff and judges was a matter of neutral procedure. In particular, the three women judges had presided over the case since its inception. Nor was there any question that Alessandra had to lead the prosecution in court since she had led the investigation that preceded it. That didn't mean that the officials couldn't enjoy the defendants' discomfort. 'When they saw us all in the court, they began screaming and shouting at me and my colleagues,' smiled Alessandra. 'They were humiliated to be in front of so many women – to be judged by women, to them something less than a man.' To Alessandra and Giuseppina, listening by video link, there was something in the men's outraged reaction that suggested they knew, perhaps for the first time, that the tables were being turned. Alessandra described their shouts of indignation as something close to music. 'A symphony of women's liberation!' she laughed. 'Divine justice for these men!' Prestipino, who also denied any hand in the unusual number of women in court, was similarly jubilant. 'Think of how many women in Calabria live the same lives as Giuseppina Pesce and Maria Concetta Cacciola,' he said. 'Now they have something, an example, some symbolism, to hold on to.' Alessandra noted how across court Giuseppina's mother and sister, Angela Ferraro and Marina Pesce, remained seated and silent throughout. There was perhaps no better representation of the injustice in their own lives than watching their men howl at the sight of an assembly of modern, professional women sitting in judgement over them.[11]

XXI

Giuseppina Pesce wasn't the only one spurred to action by the death of Maria Concetta Cacciola.[1]

In Reggio Calabria, the youth courts had long been the poor cousin of their adult equivalents. The juvenile justice chief, Roberto di Bella, felt that was short-sighted. Like Alessandra, di Bella reasoned that the 'Ndrangheta was, above all, a family operation. 'Since World War II, the same families have controlled the territory,' he said. 'Whether it's smuggling heroin or cocaine or business or politics, this culture, this phenomenon, is born of family and goes from father to son. It's hereditary. It's dynastic.' Somehow, the Italian judiciary had contrived to focus on the fathers but forget their wives – and their children. This was despite di Bella's own experience in Calabria. In two decades in Reggio, he had dealt with more than a hundred serious crimes committed by 'Ndrangheta children. 'We had extortion, robbery, kidnapping and more than fifty cases of homicide or assisted homicide!' he said. 'Kids who used Kalashnikovs. Kids who took part in clan feuds. Kids who were assassins. Kids who killed *carabinieri*.'

Di Bella's experience also taught him that sending 'Ndrangheta children to detention mostly confirmed them on a path to more crime and incarceration. Once inside, they were fated to become killers and bosses, and before long wind up back in jail or dead. 'These children start to breathe this 'Ndrangheta culture from the moment they are born,' he said. The brainwashing was constant, and effective. By the age of twelve, an 'Ndrangheta child would spit whenever they saw a policeman. As teenagers, they would learn to exercise power 'not just over children but over adults, too'. By eighteen, they were beyond rescue. Sometimes hatred for the state was literally ingrained in them. Di Bella had found some children with tattoos of individual *carabinieri* officers on their feet 'so they can tread on them twenty-four hours a day'.

Di Bella had a gentle manner and his neatly parted dark hair and gold-framed glasses suggested a small-town doctor or provincial academic or even a priest. And his work, it was clear, was a calling. One case in particular had stayed with him. In 2002, a sixteen-year-old scion of a Calabrian clan had been detained for possessing a gun and resisting arrest. 'The serial numbers had been filed off the gun and there was a bullet in it,' said di Bella. He surmised that the boy was preparing for his first murder. He knew the family well. The boy's father had been murdered when he was eleven. Di Bella had already sent three of his older brothers to jail. They were, he said, 'one of the most violent and bloody 'Ndrangheta clans'.

Throughout his trial, the boy made a show of appearing tough, said di Bella. 'His eyes were like steel. He did not betray his emotions.' In the end, di Bella felt he had no option but to send him to join his brothers for several years in juvenile detention. Several months into the boy's sentence, however, di Bella received a phone call from the director of the youth prison. The boy was unwell. 'He was suffering from sleeplessness,' said di Bella. 'He had stomach disorders that were stress related. He needed to speak to a male role model but he had none.'

Di Bella had the boy brought back to court for reassessment. He found him a shadow of his former self. 'He no longer had eyes like ice,' he said. 'He was bewildered. He had a lot of fear. He was distressed – strongly distressed – because of the murders and the mafia wars and the people he had lost, including his father.' Di Bella realised the boy's defences were down and he could talk to him directly. 'So I told him clearly that he had to leave his 'Ndrangheta family. I said he would be murdered or be put in prison, like his father and brothers. And this boy said to me, for the first time: "I want to leave." He did not hide that his family was 'Ndrangheta. He asked me to help him leave them at the end of his sentence.'

Di Bella promised that he would do what he could. A few months later, however, he was transferred away from Calabria. Several years after that, the court registrar in Reggio got in touch to tell him that the boy, now out of prison, had come looking for him at the court in Reggio. 'He had been waiting for me for over a year until someone told him I was no longer there,' said di Bella. The magistrate was consumed by guilt. There was no question that he and the state had failed this boy, a child after all, with the simple misfortune to be born into circumstances beyond his control but who, from the depths of his turmoil, had reached out for their help.

When di Bella returned to Calabria in 2011, he discovered the boy, now a man, was back in prison, convicted of mafia association. 'He sent me a greeting from the psychological clinic where he was being treated,' he said. 'A few months later, I heard his elder brother had been arrested once again. This all sat with me.'

On his return to Calabria, however, di Bella was heartened to discover that the fight against the 'Ndrangheta had been transformed. Pignatone, Prestipino, Alessandra and the other prosecutors had brought new energy and new ideas to the struggle. They had forged a new consensus that, in Alessandra's words, 'the 'Ndrangheta is a very complicated phenomenon that defies a single solution. We need to take action on several different levels at the same time.' Alessandra, particularly, had been instrumental in refocusing minds on the internal family dynamics of the 'Ndrangheta. That, too, made sense to di Bella. The youth courts, he felt, had much to contribute to this new direction.

If di Bella had any remaining doubts about the need for change in his own court, they vanished when, one day in Reggio, he found himself judging the children of the children he had judged a generation earlier. Here was undeniable proof that the 'Ndrangheta and the justice system were locked in never-ending conflict. The 'Ndrangheta would keep thieving, maiming and killing. The *carabinieri* and the judges would keep throwing them in jail. It was systemic, perpetual failure. 'We were all *inheriting* the 'Ndrangheta,' said di Bella. And if targeting an 'Ndranghetista when he was young was one of the ways to end this eternal battle, and all the blood and prison and death it wrought, then di Bella felt it was his duty to seize the moment.

When he read the files on Maria Concetta Cacciola's death in August 2011, di Bella sensed his chance had arrived. 'Concetta's children were used as a tool to make her come back and retract,' he said. 'Her parents made Concetta listen to her six-year-old crying "I miss Mummy" on the phone.' It was an unambiguous case of child abuse in the service of criminality. A few weeks later, di Bella read the transcripts of a bugged conversation between Concetta's sixteen-year-old son, Alfonso, and his father, Salvatore Figliuzzi. In the transcripts, Alfonso accused his grandparents – Concetta's parents – of treating his mother so badly that 'they practically killed her. You lost a wife. I lost a mother. Nothing would have fucking happened if it hadn't been for Grandpa and his jealous rage.' Here was another 'Ndrangheta boy crying out to be rescued from his family. One way or another, the state had failed Concetta. Di Bella couldn't allow it to fail her children. 'After Concetta's death, we decided to try a very different approach,' he said.

Di Bella's first move was to have the *carabinieri* remove Giuseppina's and Concetta's children from their grandparents. This twin seizure from two of the most prominent 'Ndrangheta families in Rosarno sparked immediate fury. Di Bella received threatening letters. The Calabrian newspapers ran interviews with fathers and mothers from Rosarno accusing him of breaking up families and stealing children out of sheer vindictiveness. Apparently in all seriousness, some accused him of trying to brainwash their children in the same way the Nazis abducted and indoctrinated their enemies' children during World War II.

Di Bella was unmoved. He had found legal justification for the seizures in international law, particularly the United Nations Convention on the Rights of the Child. 'It says that a child's family has to respect their freedom, their rights and their peace,' he said. 'None of that is respected by the mafia.' The convention became di Bella's basis for a new policy for handling the children of *pentiti* so they could no longer be used to blackmail their mothers. 'Now, whenever there is a woman who collaborates, the officers inform the court about the children so we can intervene and get the children to the woman. This avoids the dangerous vacancy of authority over the children which the 'Ndrangheta tries to exploit.'

Di Bella realised the convention had far wider applications, too. What he had been fighting all these years was not, as his colleagues sometimes excused it, the simple bad luck of being born into a southern mafia family or even some traditional version of *patria potestas*, the customary power of a father. The convention was unequivocal. What was happening inside almost every 'Ndrangheta family was illegal child abuse. 'When we are talking about a child of twelve and his father is taking him to the beach to learn how to shoot a gun, the convention says it's our duty to intervene,' said di Bella. 'A father under house arrest teaching his twelve-year-old how to strip a gun or move a Kalashnikov from one house to another – we have an obligation to intervene there too. A man who is a fugitive for twenty years with his children, forcing them to miss their education – we have the same obligation. All the cases where crimes are committed by children or parents relying on children, or if we have children extorting on behalf of their parents, or when a child is taken somewhere to shoot traffickers and witness a drug fight, or when they use their children as killers during clan feuds – in all these cases, when there is tangible and concrete detriment to the child, the convention says we have an obligation.'

The same duty of care applied to 'Ndrangheta mothers schooling their children in mafia life, the very life force of the 'Ndrangheta. The convention recognised a parent's right to educate their child. But that was subordinate to the child's right to be protected from prejudice and abuse, physical or psychological; and to its right to a responsible education aimed at preparing the child for a tolerant, peaceful, legal life. 'Ndrangheta children didn't have any of that. They didn't have much of a childhood full stop. 'You take a seventeen-year-old 'Ndrangheta boy and ask him what music he listens to and he'll reply "the *Tarantella*", said di Bella. 'He doesn't know Lady Gaga or Madonna. It's such a strict, narrow upbringing. They can't see further than their own family and their own little town.'

Di Bella began to believe that the greatest problem with an 'Ndrangheta upbringing was the way it stunted a child emotionally. At an early age, children learned to hide and control their feelings, lest they betray themselves or others. They internalised the code, which forbade almost any individual expression or identity. And while they formed almost no relationships outside the 'Ndrangheta, inside it, as their friends and relatives were steadily murdered or put in prison or went on the run, they became ever more lonely. 'There is no one to tell the child the right road to take and no individual will to choose a different road,' said di Bella. 'The young man doesn't even contemplate it because he doesn't know a different reality exists. For children growing up in these little mafia towns, the cult of the 'Ndrangheta oppresses everything and everyone.' No surprise, said di Bella, that court reports on 'Ndrangheta children showed psychological devastation. 'Their symptoms are similar to Vietnam veterans,' he said. 'They are inhibited. They all have this strong sense of anguish and anxiety. Their dreams are full of nightmares. And they are alone.'

Taken together, di Bella concluded, the 'mafia family system' was itself 'prejudiced against the welfare of children'. 'A mafia education, mafia indoctrination by the parents, the perpetration of crimes by the child, the physical danger to children,' said di Bella, 'all these are detrimental to the mental and physical integrity of the children and contravene the fundamental rights, liberties and principles of the UN charter. The primary victims of the 'Ndrangheta are their own children.'

The Family had always been an immoral perversion of blood relations. Now it seemed it was illegal, too.

Di Bella was proposing deprogramming 'Ndrangheta children, a matter in which the judiciary had no expertise. When he raised the subject with social workers and psychologists, they recommended not just taking the children away from their parents but trying to offer them a normal adolescence. Growing up was, at heart, about discovering freedom. Freedom was what the 'Ndrangheta denied its children and that was why they turned out the way they did. If the state wanted to change them, said the psychologists, it should place younger children with families far outside Calabria who would let them attend school and hang out with friends and make the conventional choices of any child growing up. Once they were old enough, the children could stay in a hostel where they would be required to attend school. They should be allowed contact with their parents but, crucially, the power to direct their lives should rest with the children themselves. The advice made sense to di Bella. 'These children come from small worlds where everything is 'Ndrangheta,' he said. 'Their inexorable destiny is to be killed or end up in jail. A desire to choose a different path is never contemplated because they don't know the alternatives. You can't desire another world if you don't know it exists.'

The hope, said di Bella, was that if children were allowed to experience a conventional upbringing, a new idea would take hold in their minds: self-determination. 'Our idea was to let them know there is a better world out there with different rules,' he said. This was 'a place where you can be free. Where there is love and affection. Where there is no need for violence or killing in order to let other people under-stand what you're thinking. Where there are equal rights for men and women. Where prison is not a medal you get on your chest. And where you can try out your personality free from the surname you have?' What the authorities would be attempting, said di Bella, was a kind of 'cultural infiltration'. They would insert the children into everyday Italian life and let it gently subvert them. 'The 'Ndrangheta infiltrated us,' he said. 'Now we were going to infiltrate them right back.'

In court, instead of custodial sentences, di Bella began ordering 'Ndrangheta children to be separated from their families in another fashion. He sent many of the older teenagers across the Straits, to a hostel attached to a church high up in the hills above Messina. The programme was run by a young Sicilian psychologist, Enrico Interdonato, who had made a speciality of the mafia. Interdonato would take his charges out for pizza and to night clubs. When he took one boy to a bookshop, he was astonished to learn it was the first time the boy had ever visited one.

Initial results were mixed. One boy, Francesco, arrived with a propensity for violence and a set of rock-hard prejudices against women, immigrants, the police and the state, which were only slightly softened by the time he left. But another boy, Riccardo Cordì, from the 'Ndrangheta stronghold of Locri, was transformed. Riccardo's father, an 'Ndranghetista, had been killed when he was a boy. His brothers were all in jail. Riccardo himself had been headed the same way, appearing in di Bella's court after being arrested for stealing a police car, and then again for fighting.

After a year at the hostel in Messina, that destiny no longer appeared certain. After he turned eighteen and left the hostel, Riccardo wrote a letter which was published in several newspapers.

Dear Editor,

I am a boy of Calabria, I come from Locri and my name is Riccardo Cordì. On 7 March 2011, I was arrested by the police in Locri for the theft and damage to a car owned by the railway police. In July 2011, I was charged with another instance of assault. But the court in Reggio decided to send me away from Locri to see if I could leave behind these experiences. It was the start of my journey.

When I arrived in Sicily, at first it was not easy to be alone and away from home. But everything changed when I began to see a psychologist in Messina who guided me towards the discovery of a new life. I did things, met people and visited Rome, Milan and other places that I had never seen. One morning, I went to see the sea with the psychologist. We could see Calabria, my land. But for the first time, I could see it from another perspective.

I decided then and there that my life would be different. I want to return to Locri but I do not want any more problems with the law. Not because I can't handle it but because I want to live in peace. I want to be clean. Before this experience, I believed the state did not care about the people. The state was just this thing that took you away from home, without you ever knowing when or if you would return. But in recent months, I have met a different state. This state didn't seem to want me to change. Rather, it tried to understand who I was.

And who am I, really? A boy of eighteen. A boy like any other. I was very small when my father was killed and I saw my brothers go to jail. I want a different future for myself. That doesn't mean that I renounce my family. My brothers will always be my brothers and Calabria will always be my land. But now a new road lies before me and I choose it for myself with my own free will. The state has given me this chance. I can choose what I do when I grow up. I can choose what job I do to get by in the city. I can stand tall. I have no idea if I'll succeed but I'm going to try – because something has changed for me. I changed. And I can change further. Others too. There are so many guys like me who need the state to support them as it supported me. Right now, they don't believe this state exists. But I know, and I write this letter so that others can know, too. The road is still steep. But a happy ending, I now know, is not just a dream. It can be real life.[2]

Interdonato, Riccardo's psychologist, said even Riccardo's family, who were 'Ndrangheta through and through, seemed to accept that the state wasn't harming their boy and might even be opening up some new horizons to him. Interdonato and Riccardo still talked every day months after Riccardo had left the hostel. One morning, Interdonato turned on his phone to find Riccardo had sent a picture of himself with a small baby. 'He married his girlfriend this year and they had a son,' said Enrico. 'Family is at the centre of Italy's history. The mafia took those values and *extremised* them until it became a kind of psychological abuse. But Riccardo is beginning a new family. He's writing a new history.'

XXII

Alessandra and Giovanni were still haunted by their inability to prove that Maria Concetta Cacciola's death was murder.

They had plenty of circumstantial evidence. For one, Concetta had never seemed suicidal. On the contrary, said Giovanni, 'Concetta was organising to leave her family again. She had her love affair. The wiretaps showed she and her lover were planning their future together.'

There was also the physical impossibility of drinking a litre of hydrochloric acid by choice. Though initial forensics suggested Concetta had killed herself, a pathologist later found bruises on her neck and other marks on her arms consistent with someone holding her down while a second person held her mouth open, possibly with a funnel, and poured acid down her throat. In addition, the autopsy revealed Concetta had taken no sedatives to dull the pain. She'd felt everything. Presumably, surmised the prosecutors, because she was meant to.

Alessandra and Giovanni were also sure Concetta's family was behind her killing. That was the 'Ndrangheta code. Every family cleaned up its own mess. Alessandra still thought Concetta's indecision, and her belief that it would be months before the family acted, had given the Cacciolas the opportunity they needed. 'This lack of determination, taking too much time,' she said. 'Maybe this was fatal to her.'

There was a further possibility, however. Maybe the Cacciolas *had* planned to wait but had stepped up their plans after Concetta told her mother she was returning to the protection programme. In that scenario, Concetta's mother, Anna Rosalba Lazzaro, would have been key. 'Maria Concetta Cacciola still felt love for her mother,' said Giovanni. 'That's why she told her she was going back into witness protection. But Lazzaro was a classic mafia woman, tasked with preserving the clan. She was the one who said: "You're either with us, or with them".'

Precisely who killed Concetta, however, remained a mystery. 'We can say she was murdered,' said Giovanni. 'The question remains: by who? Her mother and father left the house that afternoon. It wasn't them. Something else happened but we still don't know what.'

If the two prosecutors couldn't say who killed Concetta, they couldn't charge anyone with her murder. They decided that even as they would continue trying to prove a case of homicide, they would prosecute the Cacciolas on a lesser charge. Article 110 of the Italian criminal code specified that 'when more than one person participates in the same offence, each shall be subject to the penalty prescribed for such offence.'[1] Article 580 made it illegal to help or instigate suicide, an offence punishable by between five and twelve years in prison.

Charging the family with pressuring Concetta into suicide would still show that in twenty-first-century Italy no one could expect to assist their daughter's death, to conspire in it, and get away with it. And it was a case Alessandra and Giovanni could readily prove. Concetta had told them how the family had beaten and threatened her. From wiretaps, they had the Cacciola family on tape discussing how to force Concetta to retract. They also had them using her children to blackmail her into returning to Rosarno. In the recording of her retraction, a second woman's voice could be heard coaching her. Two months after Concetta's murder, they had her sixteen-year-old son, Alfonso, blaming Concetta's parents for his mother's death. Finally, the Cacciolas themselves were saying that their daughter had died of shame. There was some poetic justice here, thought Alessandra. The Cacciolas were so blinded by the cult of the 'Ndrangheta and their loyalty to the code that they hadn't realised they were effectively admitting an offence. Concetta had felt no shame on her own. Whether she had killed herself or been murdered, it was the shame poured on her by the family that had made her death inevitable.

During the last few months of 2011, Alessandra and Giovanni steadily built their case against the Cacciolas. By 9 February 2012, they were ready. That morning, as the prosecutors released their indictment to the public, the *carabinieri* arrested Concetta's parents, Michele Cacciola and Anna Rosalba Lazzaro, in Rosarno and issued a warrant for Concetta's brother Giuseppe, who was detained two months later in Milan. All three were charged with conspiracy to force Concetta to perjure herself and to commit suicide. The *carabinieri* called the arrests *Operazione Onta*, or Operation Shame.

The arrests made the press the next day. 'Driven to suicide by her own family' read a front-page headline in *Il Quotidiano della Calabria*, the province's main paper.[2] What caught Alessandra's eye, however, was a lengthy accompanying editorial by the paper's editor, Matteo Cosenza. For the first time in an Italian newspaper, Cosenza linked the cases of Concetta, Lea and Giuseppina as elements of the same essential story. 'Giuseppina Pesce, Maria Concetta Cacciola and Lea Garofalo had the misfortune to be born into a terrible world,' he wrote. 'Despite tremendous suffering, these women decided to break with their families and to choose the path of legality and justice.' All three women had paid dearly for their courage, wrote Cosenza. All had plunged their lives and the lives of their children into dark turmoil. Two of the women had died. Cosenza continued:

Some say we exaggerate when we talk about the 'Ndrangheta and its penetration of Calabria's society and institutions. They say it doesn't exist. These cases remind us of the truth. All honest Calabrians must follow these women's example in their daily lives and stand up to the 'Ndrangheta. Do it for yourself! Do it for the young, who deserve a different future in this wonderful land! It's almost impossible to imagine how someone can make a change after being born into an 'Ndrangheta family – someone who sucks arrogance and lawlessness from their mother's breast and who can't even conceive of a world of civil coexistence, tolerance, respect and happiness. That's why we must bow before Giuseppina, Concetta and Lea. Despite everything, they were able to grasp that they were living among evil and find the courage to say: 'Enough! Stop! We and our children must live in peace, not in perpetual war!'

They paid a high price. They will pay a higher one if we forget them. Calabrians, don't turn away! Let's become the beautiful, strong Calabria we all want! We know the evil among us. Step by step, we will rid Calabria of this great malevolence and redeem ourselves in the eyes of our children, and of the world.

Alessandra could scarcely believe what she was reading. Her big idea had always been to crush the 'Ndrangheta by freeing its women. For years, it had been a private obsession. Over the last two years, month by month, man by man, she had slowly persuaded her colleagues. With each successive case – first Lea, then Giuseppina, then Concetta – the strength of her argument had grown. Concetta's death, in particular, had given Giuseppina renewed determination and spurred Roberto di Bella to rethink everything he was doing at Reggio's juvenile court.

But Alessandra could never have predicted a newspaper campaign against the 'Ndrangheta, calling on all Calabrians to take the three women as their standard bearers. Two years earlier, crowds had blocked the road in Reggio to cheer 'Ndrangheta boss Giovanni Tegano as he was led away to jail. Only a year earlier, *Calabria Ora* had launched its campaign against Alessandra. Now, suddenly, here was everything she had been working towards, all her intuition from growing up during *la mattanza* in Sicily, the summation of her years of study and research, the mountain of evidence she had amassed detailing how 'Ndrangheta women were oppressed and how a tiny few had fought back – all of it, on a newspaper front page, in an article calling for something close to revolution. It felt miraculous. '*Il Quotidiano* created, for the first time, a public debate about the women in the 'Ndrangheta,' she said. 'And suddenly people all around us were talking about how the 'Ndrangheta had been corrupting our lives all these years. It was a real, immediate change.'

It occurred to Alessandra that what she had resisted for so many years – sentiment, empathy, emotion – was precisely what *Il Quotidiano* was using to stir up its readers. To a prosecutor, the 'Ndrangheta's women were a technical tool with which to unlock Europe's biggest criminal conspiracy. To a newspaper editor, the story of the three good mothers was an epic tragedy to rouse a people. And *Il Quotidiano*'s reporters had been industrious. Across the inside pages, they laid out every element of the story for their fellow Calabrians to read. A report on the arrest of Concetta's parents was accompanied by articles on the Pesce investigation ('Pesce clan hit with 11 more arrests') and the Garofalo case ('Garofalo trial: one defendant threatened'). The letter Concetta left for her mother when she went into witness protection was reprinted in full, as was her recorded 'retraction'. There were backgrounders on the clans of Rosarno and eulogies to the two dead women from members of parliament. There were even descriptions of the three bunkers about which Concetta had testified.

The common thread that ran through the coverage was the heroism of Lea, Giuseppina and Concetta and the imperative for all Calabrians to follow their example. At heart, wrote Cosenza, this was a tale about three mothers who had understood their families were a curse on Calabria and who had defied centuries of violent misogyny – whether *mafioso*, Calabrian or Italian – to save their children and their homeland. This was about sacrifice and pain, abuse and terror, blood and acid – and a dream of a new future. And now, said Cosenza, it had to be about the millions of Calabrians, men and women, who would join the rebellion the women had started. Cosenza even set a date for Calabria's revolt: 8 March, the Festa della Donna, International Women's Day. On that day, he demanded that all true Calabrians celebrate Lea, Giuseppina and Concetta. By doing so, he wrote, they would finally reclaim their freedom.

By coincidence, 8 March 2012 was a date already looming large on Alessandra's calendar.

That spring Thursday was sentencing day in the last of the maxi-trials resulting from the 2010 raids against the 'Ndrangheta. More than two hundred men and women from across Italy had already been convicted and sentenced to a total of several thousand years in jail. Hundreds of millions of euros in property and assets had been seized. Entire crime families had been taken down and whole criminal empires dismantled. Now, in a caged dock inside a bullet-proof and bomb-proof court in Reggio Calabria, a final 127 'Ndranghetisti would be judged and sentenced, among them bosses from every significant *'ndrina* as well as Domenico Oppedisano, the *capo crimine*.

Alessandra knew that whatever happened, the 'Ndrangheta would endure. Despite the convictions and confiscations, the organisation retained thousands of men in its employ and hundreds of billions of euros in assets. The bosses could still rule their businesses from jail, even commanding clan feuds and overseeing international expansion. Every prosecutor knew that however hard they worked to bring the 'Ndrangheta to account, tens of thousands of crimes, including hundreds of murders, would remain unsolved.

But there was no doubt that Calabria's prosecutors had shaken the 'Ndrangheta in an historic manner. The organisation's most precious weapon, its secrecy, had been shattered. The century-old myth about a band of southern Italian Robin Hoods was in pieces. No longer would anyone nurse the illusion that the Calabrian mafia was a bunch of brigands with blunderbusses and trousers held up by baling twine who rustled goats and kidnapped provincial grocers. At last, the 'Ndrangheta had been exposed for what it was: a violent, unified, modern criminal conspiracy based in Calabria that threatened every country in the world.

This day had been decades coming, since long before Falcone and Borsellino or *The Godfather* or the night in July 1973 that the sixteen-year-old grandson of a billionaire stayed out late in Rome. The investigation that led to the maxi-trials had taken years and involved tens of thousands of policemen, *carabinieri*, prosecutors and judges. It had necessitated the biggest surveillance operation ever mounted in Italy, amounting to a total of 25,000 hours of tapped phone calls and 83,000 hours of video and audio. The result of all this work was a prosecutors' picture of the 'Ndrangheta that was comprehensive and, to most of Italy, Europe and the rest of the world, nothing less than dumbfounding. Whether measured by the hundreds of billions of euros it earned every year, or the grip it exerted over the illicit global markets for narcotics and weapons, or the political corruption it fomented from Melbourne to Montreal, or even the way it subverted financial markets and national sovereignty around the globe, Calabria's prosecutors had exposed the 'Ndrangheta as the world's most powerful and dangerous mafia.

What especially pleased Alessandra was that the greatest injury to the 'Ndrangheta had been performed by the investigations into Lea, Giuseppina and Concetta. Their cases revealed the organisation not as some fairy tale about wandering knights and righteous honour but a grotesque, illiterate, make-believe murder cult which practised merciless and bloody cruelty, twisted family in the service of greed and delighted in crushing freedom, love and hope. 'More than just the arrests, it was the loss of image and the injury to their legend,' said Alessandra. 'It really wounded them.'

Each morning from 10 February until 8 March, *Il Quotidiano* ran a front-page banner featuring pictures of Lea, Giuseppina and Concetta. Each day, it sent reporters to cover how ordinary Calabrians were joining the fight against the 'Ndrangheta. The prosecutors and women's groups were among the first to pledge support. They were followed by companies and trade unions, school children and university students, political parties and town mayors. After that came youth groups and pensioners' associations, *trattoria* owners and farmers' cooperatives, the Rotary Club, the swimmers' club, ferry operators, fishing captains, theatre companies, artists' collectives, social workers, olive farmers, *gelato* sellers, wine makers, dock workers, folk singers and long-distance truckers. By the time 8 March arrived, even the northern-focused national press had begin to take notice of the scores of anti-'Ndrangheta marches involving tens of thousands of people taking place across Calabria.[3] The story of Lea, Giuseppina and Concetta was becoming big news. A slogan had emerged: 'La Calabria Non Ci Sta!!!' ('Calabria Won't Take It Any More!!!') And as the women's stories were repeated over and over, their faces printed and reprinted on placards and posters, T-shirts and banners, and broadcast on television and in international magazines, Alessandra realised that, slowly but steadily, Lea, Giuseppina and Concetta were becoming the new legends of the 'Ndrangheta.

To the clans, this was catastrophic. Their invincibility was cracking. 'These women had rebelled against the 'Ndrangheta's machismo and that act, and the stories of what happened to them, had cost the 'Ndrangheta their control and their system of consensus,' said Alessandra. 'That was the 'Ndrangheta's whole foundation and its whole essence. This was a huge crisis for them.'

On the morning of 8 March, it took a full hour in Reggio Calabria's main court to assemble all 127 'Ndranghetisti and their lawyers, as well as the prosecutors, officials, reporters and three judges. It took another two hours for the presiding judge to read the list of convictions. By the time he had finished, ninety-three 'Ndranghetisti had been convicted. Sentences ranged from eight months to fourteen years. *Capo crimine* Domenico Oppedisano got ten years, probably enough to ensure he would die in prison.

Most importantly to the prosecutors, in its judgment the court formally acknowledged the 'Ndrangheta as a cohesive global entity with a presence in 120 locations around the world. Once and for all, the true nature of the world's biggest mafia had been established in irrefutable case law. 'Today's ruling recognises the accuracy of our reconstruction of the structure of the 'Ndrangheta as a unified organisation, arranged in a complex hierarchy, governed by a top council, rooted in Calabria with branches overseas,' Pignatone told reporters. 'This represents a crucial step in fighting the 'Ndrangheta in Calabria and wherever it has taken root.'

As Pignatone and his team congratulated each other quietly inside the Palace of Justice, Calabrians were dancing in the streets outside. As *Il Quotidiano* had demanded, almost every town in Calabria was holding an anti-mafia parade. In Reggio itself, there were conferences, plays, rallies, workshops, exhibitions and speeches. As a show of public defiance, it was unique in Calabrian history. The icons of this new movement were Lea, Giuseppina and Concetta, their faces almost ubiquitous.

None of the women could be present to see their triumph. That morning, however, Alessandra had arranged for a letter from the students of Mattia Preti girls' high school in Reggio Calabria to be delivered to Giuseppina in prison. The girls' words, thought Alessandra, would at least give Giuseppina a flavour of what was happening. 'Dear Giusy,' it began,

We wouldn't have had the strength. We wouldn't have had the strength and courage as women. We wouldn't have had the strength and courage as daughters or sisters. We wouldn't have had the strength and courage in this city and in this country, where so often everything is silenced by fear and shame. But when someone finds the strength and courage to speak, especially as a mother, that fear disappears, and we want to redeem ourselves and remain silent no more.

We listened to your story in silence. And these seemingly distant events suddenly became real. You opened our eyes. You opened the eyes of so many young men and women who will not forget your strength and courage. With everything you've gone through, and are still enduring, with these words we wanted to give you back a little of the strength you've given us. You're a beacon for women's emancipation. Your freedom makes possible our own. Your freedom makes possible the freedom of this land.[4]

Giuseppina was overjoyed. Once, she had dreamed she and Concetta might be the start of something. Now it was happening. Everywhere, it seemed, people were hailing Lea and Giuseppina and Concetta and coming out against the 'Ndrangheta.

In Reggio, Alessandra was equally touched by *Il Quotidiano*'s front page. Above a child's drawing of the three women, the paper had printed a headline that encapsulated what, for more years than Alessandra cared to remember, had been her personal creed: 'With women, we will all break free.' Below it, editor Matteo Cosenza had written an open letter to Denise Cosco:

Dear Denise,
I do not know you but you should know the affection and admiration I have for you. I don't know if you'll be able to read these thoughts in the secret place where, at this time of liberty and warmth and celebration, you are forced to live. Your choice,

to testify twice against your father about the death of your mother, Lea Garofalo, reflects how your mother lived. You had to choose between your living father and your dead mother and you chose the triumph of truth, legality and justice. You've even had to testify against a man who was your partner.

You should know that your mother is proud. She made her sacrifice for your future, which she dared to imagine as one of dignity and free of the oppression she was born into. It would be so easy to give in to hatred. But nothing can be built on hate. Nobody, either, is born a criminal. These people are part of our family, our neighbourhoods, our schools, our traditions and our homeland. Many 'Ndrangheta men did not decide to be as they are. They never had a choice. Our collective action, if it is serious and profound, can prick their consciences. It can make new men of them.

My dear Denise, this disease has spread so wide that as long as the fever doesn't heal, it will continue to infect us. We must remember the example of the women who broke this so-called code of honour to proclaim their own right to freedom, respect and dignity. The road ahead is long and hard. We know this struggle will take more than a little festival. But we have your example. Your testimony gives us confidence that even in the darkest night, even amid the torment that you, your mother and the other women have experienced, there is light ahead. We must build a different future. Nothing about the present suffering and violence is either natural or inevitable. This task will take all our commitment. We will have won when you are once again free to stroll the streets of Calabria, enjoying the sun and the sea breeze in peace. It is your right. It will be our failure if you are denied it.[5]

XXIII

The maxi-trials, the marches, *Il Quotidiano* – something was stirring in Calabria. Alessandra and the other prosecutors sensed a moment of possibility, even hope. It was exhilarating, but also disquieting. The state had fought for generations to change Sicily and that war still wasn't won. The campaign against the Calabrian mafia now had its first convictions but, really, had just begun. Even the cases against the Coscos, the Cacciolas and the Pesces had years to run through the various appeals and procedural tiers of the Italian justice system. Lea, Giuseppina and Concetta might be the icons of this new movement, but if Carlo Cosco or the Pesces or the Cacciolas somehow walked free, then the spring of 2012 would be remembered as a brief, bright instant which vanished as quickly as it appeared.

By now, Alessandra knew that the best way to ensure a result in the Pesce case was to end all contact between the family and Giuseppina. Roberto di Bella's juvenile court had already taken care of the children, Angela, Gaetano and Elisea. Now Alessandra had Giuseppina moved to Paliano prison outside Rome, a penitentiary set aside for mafia collaborators.

Housed in an old fifteenth-century palace on a natural rock fortress with idyllic views of the town and the Apennine mountains, Paliano housed around fifty *pentiti*, men and women. Prison facilities included a library, a theatre, a church, a sports field, three workshops, four kitchens, four laboratories, five gyms and a playroom for children. Inmates were taught primary and secondary education in its five classrooms. For the better educated, there were courses in accounting and business studies as well as vocational training. All the inmates were encouraged to work: in the prison pizzeria, growing tomatoes and cherries and cavolo nero in the organic garden, making clothes or embroidering cushions. There was a choir. There was internet. There were private bathrooms with bidets.

The idea, said Paliano's head warden Nadia Cersosimo, was to show how life in the mafia was a pale, negative image of reality. Inside a clan, respect was synonymous with fear, and family with crime. Paliano taught its prisoners that true respect was about voluntary admiration, not involuntary deference, and true family was about love, not mutual defence. Mafia families coached their children to despise the law and hate the state. Cersosimo said her own parents had taught her respect for the law and loyalty to the state – and at Paliano, she attempted to raise her inmates afresh as she herself had been brought up. It didn't always work. But when it did, it could change lives. One prisoner gained a degree in economics. Two inmates, a man and a woman, married in the prison chapel. 'We all share in these new paths,' said Cersosimo. 'It's a family.' Alessandra was among many prosecutors who were impressed. 'She runs that prison as if it were her home,' she said.

At Paliano, Giuseppina was allowed regular visits from her children. She watched the Lea Garofalo trial and the Cacciola arrests on television. She followed the proceedings against her own family in Palmi by video link from an underground security bunker set up for the purpose at Rebibbia prison in Rome. When she turned thirty-two on 24 September 2011, she was allowed a small party.

As Giuseppina and Alessandra resumed their collaboration, they also revived their friendship. Between trial days during late 2011 and early 2012, Alessandra would fly up to meet Giuseppina at Rebibbia and finesse her testimony. Sometimes during the hour-long drive from Paliano, Giuseppina's protection officers would report being shadowed by cars with blacked-out windows. But Alessandra had insisted on a new team of bodyguards for Giuseppina and their evident professionalism convinced Giuseppina she was in no danger. Alessandra was pleased to note the tight bond of trust that was quickly developing between Giuseppina and her protection squad. When, in December 2011, Giuseppina began giving detailed evidence for the first time against her father and brother – the two 'Ndrangheta men to whom she was most loyal – Alessandra credited the confidence she now felt able to place in the state.

Giuseppina's main concern remained the happiness of her children. A year earlier, it had been Angela's despondency that had derailed Giuseppina's cooperation. Now Angela seemed resolved to support her mother. Gaetano and Elisea, too, appeared happy in the care of Roberto di Bella's youth programme. Still, abandoning family and everything you'd been taught from birth was never going to be easy.

In December 2011, realising that the three children would be apart from Giuseppina for Christmas, Alessandra decided to make sure all three received presents. Out shopping, she spotted a cuddly toy that inspired her to try an experiment with the youngest, six-year-old Elisea. 'When these children think of *carabinieri*, they think of hooded people in black balaclavas who seize their father or uncle in the middle of the night,' said Alessandra. Alessandra decided to give Elisea a bear dressed in a *carabinieri* uniform. 'I thought she could see this bear as a more friendly figure and, through my gift, the girl could get used to the idea of the state.'

When Alessandra saw Giuseppina in January 2012, she asked if Elisea had liked her present.

'Yes, yes, she liked it,' replied Giuseppina. But Alessandra could see she was embarrassed. 'I'm afraid she took the *carabinieri* uniform off,' said Giuseppina eventually.

Alessandra told Giuseppina not to worry. 'Slowly, slowly,' she said. 'Let's see if things change.'

And slowly, slowly, they did. Each time they met, Alessandra would ask Giuseppina for an update on the bear. In February, Giuseppina smiled and said the bear was now wearing its shoes. 'Then she told me it was wearing its trousers,' said Alessandra. 'Then it was wearing its hat. Very gradually the bear began to wear more and more of its uniform. It took from January to September. But, finally, the bear was completely dressed and Elisea placed it right by the front door. She told her mother it was "so that the *carabinieri* can protect us".'

Alessandra saw the bear's transformation as an extraordinary metaphor for how, with their mother's encouragement, Giuseppina's children were altering their outlook on the world. 'It was something amazing, what Giuseppina was managing to do,' she said. 'Slowly and progressively, she was setting out with her very fragile young children on a new path to something else. It was small steps on a long path. But slowly and surely, she was making them understand that the state can help them.'

All Alessandra's efforts with Giuseppina were to prepare her for the trial ahead. The first hurdle came on New Year's Eve 2011, when a new 180-day deadline for Giuseppina to sign her witness statements fell due. The day before, Alessandra flew in to see Giuseppina, bringing with her several thousand pages of documentation. Eight months earlier, Giuseppina had refused to sign. Now, even on the phone, Alessandra could tell she was nervous again. The prosecutor arrived at Rebibbia fearing a repeat performance. She relaxed when she realised that what she had understood as anxiety was actually excitement. Giuseppina signed then slumped in her chair. She had now officially replaced her family with the state.

A bigger ordeal for Giuseppina would be facing her family in court. The hearings in Palmi weren't scheduled to begin until May 2012, giving Giuseppina and Alessandra months to ready themselves. Once proceedings were under way, however, they would be a marathon. The trial was expected to last a year. Giuseppina's evidence was so detailed that her testimony and cross-examination alone would take a week, Monday to Friday, eight to ten hours a day.

Alessandra arranged for Giuseppina to speak via video link from Rebibbia. When a number of Pesce relatives were given permission to attend the trial in Rebibbia, Alessandra requested a screen in court to block their view. But Alessandra knew her star witness and her family would still be aware of each other's presence, and would be feeling each other out, testing each other's will. She decided to train Giuseppina like an athlete. She stressed physical fitness, encouraging Giuseppina to exercise for her stamina and advising her to take chocolate and fruit juice into the hearings to sustain herself. She told her to ask for a break any time she needed it. To prepare Giuseppina's mind, Michele Prestipino began joining Alessandra on her visits to Rebibbia. The prosecutors would put Giuseppina through her paces, spending days going over questions and evidence and likely questions from the defence, so that Giuseppina knew the case and the judicial procedure back to front.

Alessandra had also long understood that if Giuseppina was to betray her family, she would need a substitute to hold on to. Alessandra had given up the habit of a lifetime to become something approaching a mother to her. As Giuseppina's day in court drew nearer, Alessandra was heartened to see their relationship deepening. Once they finished the formal work of taking statements and verifying evidence, the two women found that what remained was warmth and closeness, an acceptance and appreciation of each other. One day, when Alessandra was setting up her tape recorder in their usual room at Rebibbia, Giuseppina entered carrying a gift. Alessandra unwrapped it to find a small hand-embroidered cushion. On it, Giuseppina had stitched the words: 'Thank you for everything. With love, Giusy'. 'I was touched,' said Alessandra. 'After all, I was the one who had arrested her. Twice. In prison, she couldn't make much but she had done what she could.

And the care she took in making this cushion! The tiny stitching. She'd scented it with a flowery fragrance and the smell filled my apartment for a week. It was a symbol, a token of her gratitude that she was still alive, thanks to my stubbornness. And a very feminine one, which seemed to indicate a particular warmth and regard for me.'

When the first day of Giuseppina's testimony finally arrived on 22 May, Alessandra judged that she and Michele Prestipino had done all they could.[1] Giuseppina was determined and confident. In a remarkable reversal of roles, she even tried to soothe Alessandra's nerves. A year earlier, when Giuseppina had suspended her cooperation, Alessandra had told her in parting that she would hold on to the dream that Giuseppina would one day restart her collaboration and face her family in court. Now Giuseppina winked at Alessandra. 'Don't worry,' she said. 'Dreams can come true.'

Still, as Alessandra stood in Palmi's main court, watching the video monitor as Giuseppina took her seat in Rebibbia, she was tense. Bringing a collaborator to testify against the mafia in court was a high point in any Italian prosecutor's career. Bringing Giuseppina to testify against her family, perhaps the only time that such a knowledgeable witness would give evidence against so powerful a clan, was the judicial event of the decade. The next few days would be a procedural and bloodless war, but a war nonetheless. On one side, truth and justice. On the other, murderous criminality and intense blackmail. Alessandra found herself simultaneously in thrall to the proceedings and terrified by them. How would Giuseppina cope?

Alessandra began by asking Giuseppina to describe her life as a *mafiosa*. Giuseppina explained her duties, which included passing messages between the men and managing the Pesce extortion rackets. She gave an overview of the other businesses: trucking, drugs, weapons and corruption. She laid out the organisation's structure, specifying which of her uncles and cousins were its bosses and lieutenants, and the line of succession. She spoke about how the men maintained a legal fund for family members on trial or in jail. She explained how her grandmother Giuseppa Bonarrigo's house served as a meeting place where the men believed they could talk without fear of being bugged.

Giuseppina spoke in detail about the men's fear of surveillance, and how they used detectors to find listening devices in their cars or under the paving at her grandmother's house, even the secret cameras hidden in the walls of a nearby school and hospital. She described how her father, Salvatore Pesce, had lived in a bunker under her grandmother's house, linked to the surface by a passage hidden inside a barrel, before he was arrested in 2005. She talked about the family's links to judges, *carabinieri* and government officials. She told the story of how her cousin, Francesco, would stay outside the polling station on election day, telling voters: 'Vote for so-and-so, he's a friend.' She ran through Rosarno's history of killings and clan wars, especially between the Pesces and their rivals, the Belloccos. The rules were straightforward, she said. 'You killed one of ours, we killed one of yours.' The same went for traitors. When a cousin, Rosa Ferraro, discovered that Salvatore had put the Pesce family supermarket in her name, and was using it to launder money and defraud a salami maker, Ferraro had denounced him in the street. To the Pesces, said Giuseppina, such disgrace could only be answered with death. Rosa's imminent murder had only been narrowly avoided by her surrender to the authorities.

Alessandra then led Giuseppina through her own decision to testify against her family. Giuseppina began by saying that her marriage to Rocco Palaia had been loveless. 'He never worked and he was never at home if one of the babies was ill,' she said. 'He wasn't home for a Sunday walk with his family. He didn't even give me money for medicine.' She cried when she talked about her new boyfriend, Domenico Costantino. 'The only man who ever loved my children,' she sobbed. 'The only one who respected me as a woman.' Still, once her affair was discovered, Giuseppina knew she was dead. 'She who betrays and dishonours the family must pay with their life,' said Giuseppina. 'That's the law.' Asked who would administer her punishment, Giuseppina replied that her husband, Rocco, had told her that the family had 'a pit ready for me' but that it would be her brother, Francesco, who would pull the trigger. 'It has to be the eldest son in the family,' she said.

This attachment to primogeniture typified the backwardness of mafia life, said Giuseppina. So did the violent misogyny. It had been standard mafia behaviour for her family to blackmail her into signing a retraction by holding her children hostage. So was beating and starving her children when she defied the clan and resumed her cooperation. Giuseppina had been able to give the culture of the mafia some thought during her months at Paliano. She now delivered her conclusions to the court. 'In a sense, whatever problems we have as a family, it came from that, the whole environment in which we were living,' she said. '*That's* the evil I see. That's the reason I'm in jail today. That's why my sister, mother and family are all in jail – because the men carry on this thing. They fill us, the women, with their evil. They make us complicit, ensure we never break the chain and make us continue their criminality by running dutifully to prison to see them. That's the evil of the mafia. That's what I always tried to protect my children from. That's why I couldn't stand the idea of my children without me and why I made this choice: so my children might avoid my fate and have a better life, where they are their own masters and can choose what they want to do. That's also why I cut all contact with my brother. Because as a man, he'll never accept my choice.'

As she spoke, Giuseppina could hear coughing from the defendants' dock. It happened whenever she mentioned her brother. Even from hundreds of miles away down a video line, she recognised the voice and understood the message. 'Her brother was saying: "I hear you," said Alessandra. "'I hear what you're saying about me.'" To Alessandra's relief, Giuseppina was unperturbed. Turning to

Alessandra during a break, she joked, 'Does my brother have a sore throat?'

It was the first of several attempts by the Pesces to throw Giuseppina off balance during the trial. Her mother still refused to use her daughter's name, referring to her only as 'the collaborator'. Through a prison guard, her sister Marina sent her a photograph of the two of them together with their children. 'That was very destabilising for Giuseppina,' said Alessandra. 'She loved her sister a lot. That was very strong pressure on her, and she just had to find a way to handle it.'

Giuseppina found the presence of her father, Salvatore, hardest to bear. She had often told Alessandra that among her family, she was closest to her father. She would cry when she spoke of him, saying he was the only one who ever understood her and that if he hadn't been in jail, he would have protected her from Rocco.

In court, as Giuseppina finished her final day of evidence, her father asked to make a statement. Alessandra sat motionless. As Salvatore walked from the dock to the witness stand, Giuseppina could see him for the first time. He was wearing a white shirt with blue stripes. 'Giuseppina started crying as soon as she saw him,' said Alessandra. 'The shirt was the last present she had ever given him. It was her father's way of reminding her of her blood ties, of telling her who she was. On the screen, I could see Giuseppina's tears streaming down her cheeks.'

Quickly and quietly, Alessandra suggested Giuseppina take a break. With Giuseppina safely out of earshot, Salvatore Pesce then began to speak. Initially, he turned his anger on Alessandra, accusing her of abusing her office and forcing Giuseppina to lie by threatening to take her children away and giving her drugs. He said Alessandra had exceeded her powers by arresting Giuseppina's mother and sister, Angela Ferraro and Marina Pesce, in Milan. 'You have acted unlawfully,' he shouted at Alessandra. 'And why? You want to die?'

Alessandra interrupted to request the court transcript be forwarded to the director of public prosecutions in Rome to decide whether Salvatore's threat to her constituted an offence. Salvatore was then allowed to continue. 'I want to tell my daughter that everybody loves her,' he said. 'After this is all over, when all the lights have been turned out and all these careers have been improved and when you're all by yourself, you will find us here waiting for you. We'll be here.'

Alessandra marvelled at how, in open court, Giuseppina's father could tug at his daughter's heart while threatening her in the same breath. Was there no end to these men's malice?

Weighing herself during the week of Giuseppina's testimony, Alessandra calculated that she lost two or three kilograms a day. She was surprised to see Giuseppina coping far better. 'She carried on through the trial – with great pain and suffering but also with great strength,' said Alessandra.

Alessandra knew Giuseppina drew most of her courage from the same source that had always inspired her: her children. A few days before Giuseppina testified, her eldest daughter, Angela, had given her a necklace with a silver cross on it. 'That was another message,' said Alessandra. 'Angela was telling her: "If you feel afraid, if you feel scared, touch the necklace and think of us." During the trial, she had a moment or two when I thought she was collapsing. But she immediately recovered, and I know her strength came from thinking about her children and how she was doing this for them. That gave her all the strength she needed.'

Alessandra pondered the maternal affection she felt for Giuseppina, once again characterising their connection as 'umbilical'. She wondered how it compared with the bond that still existed between Giuseppina and her family. The trial hearings would continue for the rest of 2012 and sentencing wasn't expected until May 2013. Few sights were more likely to rekindle a daughter's love for her parents than the spectacle of them in a cage. The day the case concluded, however, would likely be the last Giuseppina would ever see her parents and her family. Giuseppina needed to come to terms with their inevitable separation.

After the stress of testifying, Alessandra and Michele Prestipino left Giuseppina alone for a few weeks. At Paliano, it was summer and the tomatoes and aubergines were ripening in the penitentiary garden, ready for the *pentiti* to pick in the early evening to make giant trays of *parmigiana* in the kitchens. One hot July day, when they judged enough time had passed, Alessandra and Prestipino flew up to Rome and took the drive east out into Lazio and to Paliano. The two prosecutors arrived in the early afternoon. In their honour, warden Nadia Cersosimo had organised a surprise supper, attended by all the staff and inmates, cooked using vegetables and herbs from the garden. The guests ate and chatted amiably with the *pentiti*. Afterwards, Giuseppina presented Alessandra and Prestipino with pickles and jams whose lids she had decorated with embroidered doilies: a simple design of cherries and apricots next to the initials of Paliano district. Regarding Giuseppina, it struck Alessandra that her witness had changed once more. For the first time, she wrote, 'I had the distinct impression that I had replaced her family in her emotions.' That family loyalty, that unquestioning bond – it was gone.

If anything, Alessandra began to realise, it was now she who was becoming too attached to Giuseppina. In quieter moments, she would admonish herself for imagining that their bond could ever be more than temporary. She would have to move on to other cases. Giuseppina would need to live her own life. Still, Alessandra's staff were incredulous when, a few weeks after her visit to Paliano and hours before she left with Paolo on her annual August holiday, she took a call from Giuseppina on her office line, a number which an 'Ndranghetista should never have possessed. 'It's her kids' custody,' Alessandra explained to her secretary, her hand over the receiver. 'Some bureaucrat is mucking her around. She might be upset.'

Like any good mother, Alessandra never stopped worrying.

XXIV

When the Lea Garofalo trial collapsed in November 2011, it had seemed like a disaster. Within a week, however, a new judge, Anna Introini, was appointed and immediately added new urgency to the proceedings.

Introini was one of the most senior women in the Italian judiciary. A fifty-nine-year-old veteran of several mafia cases, as well as attempts to prosecute Silvio Berlusconi, her experience had left her with little patience for defence gymnastics or procedural delays, let alone mafia misogyny. Mindful that Carlo's term of custody expired on 28 July 2012, Introini ruled, over the defence's objections, that no previous hearings need be repeated and that Denise's damning testimony still stood. She also instituted an accelerated timetable of two court days a week.

When hearings resumed in December 2011, the weight of testimony against Carlo and his 'ndrina quickly mounted. A fellow prisoner at San Vittore in Milan testified – over Massimo Sabatino's shouted denunciations – that he had heard Sabatino describe how Carlo had asked him in May 2009 to dress as a washing machine repair man and kidnap Lea in Campobasso.[1] A number of Carlo's acquaintances spoke of their fear of him. Others had such trouble with their memories that they unwittingly gave the same impression.

Proceedings were further accelerated by Carlo's refusal to take the stand. One day, sending a message to the 'Ndrangheta that he was observing *omertà*, he cupped his hands over his ears. 'The message was: "There's no problem, don't worry, feel safe, I'm not going to talk", said Alessandra. Still, by not testifying, Carlo couldn't help but speed up his trial. By the time Matteo Cosenza wrote his letter to Denise in *Il Quotidiano* on 8 March, Judge Introini had said she would announce a verdict and sentence on 30 March 2012.

When the day came, Introini passed word that she would deliver judgment at 8.30 p.m. Outside court, the hall was packed. On one side, relatives of the defendants whispered with their lawyers. On the other, student activists huddled around Enza Rando, passing her letters of support for Denise. Journalists hovered. In the caged dock Carlo, his brothers Giuseppe and Vito, Massimo Sabatino, Rosario Curcio and Carmine Venturino greeted their relatives through the bars.

Just after 8 p.m., a court official announced proceedings were about to start. As the reporters squeezed into the press seats, Carlo chatted quietly with his *'ndrina*. When Judge Introini entered, the court fell silent. Introini took her seat. 'In the name of the Italian people,' she said, 'the Court of Assizes condemns Carlo Cosco, Giuseppe Cosco, Vito Cosco, Rosario Curcio, Massimo Sabatino and Carmine Venturino ...' Judge Introini ruled that all six men had taken part in Lea's murder. She convicted all six of helping to dispose of Lea's body by dissolving it in acid and of pretending that Lea was alive and well and living in Australia. Introini gave life sentences to all. She specified that Carlo and Vito should serve their first two years in solitary, while the other four should serve one. All six men were also ordered to pay a total of €200,000 to Denise, €50,000 each to Lea's sister Marisa and her mother, and €25,000 to the city of Milan.

It was hard to imagine a tougher set of sentences. Alessandra was delighted. The 'Ndrangheta seemed shocked. In the public gallery, Carmine Venturino's mother and sister began to cry. Other relatives screamed in despair. 'Are you happy now?' yelled one woman at the activists.

Outside court, Enza read a prepared statement. 'The most important part of today is that a young girl of a murdered mother has had the courage to bear witness for justice,' she said. 'She broke through the fear and silence and made her contribution to justice and truth.' Libera's founder, the priest Don Luigi Ciotti, added: 'This sentence will go down in history. We must bow before this young girl who found the nerve to break *omertà* and restore dignity, truth and justice to her mother.'[2]

Denise had testified against a father who had murdered her mother and ordered her own death. By staying true to Lea, she had broken not just with *omertà* but with her upbringing, her family and all Calabria. What her mother had started, she had finished. She was only twenty years old. She deserved the widest possible admiration.

When Alessandra considered it over the next few months, however, Carlo's conviction felt anticlimactic. Going to jail, even for life, was something an 'Ndrangheta boss like Carlo Cosco accepted as the price of power. Even if the state had punished him, he had punished Lea for her disloyalty. The journalists writing about the case might focus on his sentence but their stories couldn't help send the message that if you crossed the 'Ndrangheta or Carlo Cosco, you died.

And, of course, the way the 'Ndrangheta worked, Carlo might be in prison, but his stature inside the organisation had risen. In the 'Ndrangheta's view, he had done the righteous and honourable thing by killing his unfaithful turncoat wife. He and his *'ndrina* had shown discipline in court. They hadn't talked. They'd barely recognised the court's authority. They even managed to torture Denise further by refusing to say how and where Lea had died or what they had done with her body. Carlo had been tested over and again and he had remained steadfast. In the 'Ndrangheta's eyes, he was already a *santista*, literally sanctified. Now he would be recognised as one of the biggest bosses in Italy, free to expand his empire from prison and plan for the day when he settled his score with Denise, just as he had done with her mother. Carlo was unshaken. The 'Ndrangheta endured.

Barely three months after Carlo's conviction, however, came news that his organisation had been smashed. At 9 a.m. on 21 June 2012, seventy policemen in riot gear descended on *il fortino delle cosche* at No. 6 Viale Montello. Breaking down doors, they evicted two hundred residents, including several 'Ndrangheta families and more than fifty Chinese and African immigrant families. In two hours, the mafia's forty-year occupation of one of Milan's most historic buildings was over. Carlo's base of operations was destroyed.[3]

Behind closed doors, other cracks were appearing in Carlo's empire. During their investigation of Lea's death, the *carabinieri* had discovered a secret diary that Lea had kept throughout her early years with Carlo. 'I didn't know it existed,' said Denise. 'She kept it when she was pregnant with me. Reading it, I learned she was very much in love with my father.' Her mother's words gave Denise a new perspective. 'Our family's is a story about courage,' she said, 'but more than that it's about love. Everything began with the love my mother had for my father.' To Denise, the way her mother wrote about her father, Carlo must have returned that love. 'He had other motives for marrying her,' she said. 'But I think he did love her.'[4]

Facing up to life in prison, Carlo's *'ndrina* was experiencing similarly mixed emotions. In July 2012, the prosecutor in the case, Marcello Tatangelo, received a letter from Carmine Venturino. 'I want to confess what I know about the murder of Lea Garofalo,' wrote Carmine. He went on to state that he had assisted in Lea's murder and lied about it afterwards. He added that while under Carlo's command, he had had to obey 'the law that exists in Calabria, which is different to the one that governs the rest of the world'. His lawyers had assured him he would be acquitted since without a body, there could be no murder.

That had turned out to be incorrect. As a result, Carmine was now following his own counsel. The trial had taught him, he wrote, that 'I am not a mobster. I am not a monster.' He wasn't immune to suffering, like Carlo and the other men. Rather, 'the pain of losing Denise leaves me no choice,' he wrote. 'It's a very delicate thing. But I think everyone would like to know the facts of Lea's disappearance, especially Denise. I do this out of love for Denise. She was brave. She is an example to me. I have to tell you the facts of what really happened.'[5]

Carmine Venturino was thirty-three when he was sentenced to life. He had been born in November 1978 in Crotone, on the plain below Pagliarelle. He told Tatangelo in a series of interviews over the summer and autumn of 2012 that one of his earliest memories was of how his family's attention, and love, was focused on his brother, who was born disabled.[6] Carmine didn't blame them. He described his family as 'poor but honest'. Like most Calabrians, however, he said his parents would never have thought of crossing the 'Ndrangheta.

When Carmine fell in with a crowd from Pagliarelle and began smoking hash, heroin and cocaine, his family let it happen. They made no objection either when in September 2006, aged twenty-seven, he moved to Viale Montello in Milan. At first, Carmine was a user. Soon he was dealing for one of Carlo's cousins. Within a year, he was working for Carlo, who had moved back into Viale Montello on his release from prison. With the money he was earning, Carmine rented his own apartment. One day in 2008 Carlo showed up at his door with a blanket and a pillow, asking if he could stay. 'He never left,' said Carmine. His rapid promotion from drug user to lieutenant in Europe's biggest drug mafia was, said Carmine, 'sweetness, followed by bitterness'.

Carmine had heard about Lea Garofalo in Pagliarelle. 'Everyone was talking about it,' he said. 'We all knew that Carlo had had to go away because of her and that that was why he wanted to kill her.' In their apartment, Carlo told Carmine that Lea was trying to take

Denise away from him. He was frustrated that Denise didn't try to fight her mother more. He didn't articulate, yet, what his plans were for Lea. Then again, said Carmine, he didn't have to.

Carlo's chances of exacting his revenge increased significantly in spring 2009 when Lea left witness protection for the second time. She sent a message via her sister Marisa, asking Carlo if she and Denise could return to Calabria. Carlo had every reason to agree. Lea was playing into his hands. One day in April, said Carmine, 'Vito Cosco came to me in Milan and told me that Carlo wanted to buy four sets of camouflage military gear, four balaclavas and four sets of boots and gave me a note with a set of measurements on it. I asked what they were for and Vito replied we would need the stuff to kidnap and kill Lea.' Carmine added that he already knew where to buy the gear because he had bought ski masks there for another murder.

Carlo told his 'ndrina that since he was already suspected of trying to kill his wife, he couldn't risk direct involvement in this new attempt. Instead, he wanted Vito, Carmine and Rosario Curcio to murder Lea. Carmine duly bought the clothes with cash and loaded them into a stolen red Fiat van, together with an Uzi sub-machine gun equipped with a silencer and two magazines that he picked up from Viale Montello, all ready for the drive down to Calabria. But the plan was foiled when Carlo, having arrived in Pagliarelle to scout the attack, found that Lea had installed a new steel door on the house where she was staying, and that the police had stationed a car outside.

Carlo returned to Milan with a new plan. He'd spoken to Denise, and she'd told him she wanted to finish school in Campobasso. Carlo had rented her and Lea an apartment there. 'That was where we were going to kill Lea,' said Carmine. Carlo set 5 May as the date for Lea's murder. He recruited another 'Ndranghetista, Massimo Sabatino, to pretend to be a washing-machine repair man and gain access to the flat. Sabatino was to kidnap Lea. The other men, waiting outside, would then drive her to an isolated spot in Bari in the south, where they would kill her and get rid of her body. But on 3 May, Carmine had a car accident. 'I was drunk and high,' he said. 'I was so scared.' With two stitches in his head, Carmine told Carlo he wasn't well enough to take part. Rosario Curcio, too, pulled out at the last minute, saying he couldn't leave his business unattended. 'Stay well out of this,' he advised Carmine. When Carmine told Vito he couldn't come, Vito slapped him across the face, knocking him to the ground. In the end, Carlo dispatched Giuseppe, Vito and Massimo, only for Massimo to screw up the kidnapping. Carlo was incandescent. 'You're all useless!' he shouted at Vito. 'Do I have to do everything myself?!'

Evidently, Carlo decided he did. When Lea and Denise moved back to Pagliarelle for the summer holidays, staying with Lea's grandmother, he and Carmine drove down from Milan. Carlo began seeing Denise regularly. One night, he and Carmine took Denise out to a nightclub. They stayed out until 5 a.m. Denise's phone had run out of charge and she couldn't call her mother to tell her she would be home late. 'When we dropped Denise back at her grandmother's house, Lea slapped Denise because she'd been so worried,' said Carmine. 'When we left, Carlo turned to me and said: "That was totally uncalled for. That bitch has to die."'

The next day, Carlo called Vito, Carmine and Rosario Curcio together. He said they were going to kill Lea right away, as soon as possible, and he had a new plan for how to do it. Carmine would watch Lea's grandmother's apartment. As soon as Lea left to fetch water from the square, Carmine would call Carlo on a new burner phone that Vito had given him. Carlo would then arrive on the back of a motorcycle driven by Rosario and shoot Lea dead as they drove past; then he and Rosario would head immediately for the coast, dump the gun and wash off any powder residue in the sea. In the event, Carmine did as he was told but Lea turned out to be buying cigarettes from the village shop. She was back in her apartment before Carlo and Rosario arrived.

Carlo just couldn't seem to kill Lea. He had tried and failed three times in five months. By now, his obsession was all-consuming.

Enough people inside the 'Ndrangheta knew what he was planning that if he didn't pull it off, he risked losing status. But as August turned to September, Carmine was surprised to observe a new calmness in Carlo. The reason, Carlo confided to him one day, was that he had finally figured out how to murder his wife.

Lea was beginning to trust him again, Carlo said. She was calling him and texting him all the time. 'Carlo showed me text messages from Lea in which she had written that Nini – her nickname for Denise – wanted a little brother,' said Carmine. 'They were messages of love. I was amazed. Later they even went out for *gelato* together.' Carlo calculated that if he could take his wife on a late-night date to Botricello, he could take all the time he wanted. The longer he waited, the more comfortable Lea felt, the easier it would be. 'Carlo was very happy with himself,' said Carmine. 'He said now it would be so simple to kill her. He told me Lea was trapped.'

In November 2009, Lea and Denise left for Florence to attend court. Initially Carlo thought he would try to kill Lea there. Then he told Carmine he had a better idea. He had convinced Lea and Denise to spend a few days with him in Milan. Carlo said they would kill Lea in the city where she had first betrayed him. There was a symmetry to the plan that pleased Carlo. He wanted all his men in on it.

Once Lea and Denise arrived in Milan, said Carmine, 'we followed Lea day and night, all the time.' The plan, as in Campobasso, was to wait for the right moment, then kidnap Lea, try to find out what she had told the *carabinieri* in 1996 and 2002, then kill her and dispose of the body to make out that she had disappeared to Australia.

For four days, the gang played cat and mouse with Lea around Milan's streets. On one occasion, Carmine watched Lea enter a laundry and pulled over ready to snatch her when she emerged before deciding there were too many security cameras and the street was too busy. Another time, Carlo took Lea out to dinner and told his men to take her when she stepped outside for a cigarette, but it was a cold night and Lea stayed put. The following night, Carlo took Lea to dinner again and told Carmine, Vito and Rosario to wait for the two of them in a quiet street near an underpass, ready to intercept the two of them and kill her on the spot when Carlo drove past. On the way over, however, Carlo ran a red light and was stopped by a *carabiniere* so Carlo called it off. That was also the night that Carmine met Lea for the first time. A few hours after he was meant to have killed her, he found himself driving over to Lea's hotel at Carlo's request and giving her a small block of hash.

Carmine and Rosario began to think Carlo was about to be thwarted one more time. Rosario, for one, still believed that Lea was Carlo's private concern and not something with which the *'ndrina* should be involved. Maybe Carlo would kill her this time. Maybe not. Right now it looked like he was dating her. Every 'Ndranghetista knew the clan had its hot and impetuous side, its machismo. But its activities were also based on cold calculation, especially when it came to matters like the murder of a clan daughter. Carlo's planning was all over the place. He affected calmness but you could tell he was in turmoil. This was the kind of thing that could sink them all, said Rosario. He and Carmine should play no part in it.

But Carlo was insistent. The gang would have their last chance on 24 November. Lea and Denise were due to take the 11.30 p.m. train back to Calabria. Carlo told his men he had come up with yet another plan. He had asked his friend Massimiliano Floreale if he could borrow the keys to Floreale's grandmother's apartment on Via San Vittore, on the edge of Milan's historic centre. He had also arranged for Denise to have dinner with her cousins so that Lea and he would be alone again. Shortly after 6 p.m., Carlo picked up Denise at the Arch of Peace, near Sempione Park, and dropped her off at her cousins'. Then he set off to fetch Lea.

Around the same time, Carmine drove Vito to the apartment on San Vittore in a Volkswagen Passat he had stolen that day. When the pair arrived, Vito entered the apartment. Carmine's job was to stay outside. If anything was wrong, he was to signal by turning on his hazard lights. While waiting, Carmine called Rosario to arrange a time and a place to pick him up. But when Rosario answered, he said he couldn't come. He was with his girlfriend and she was in one of her moods. Rosario said he couldn't shake her. It was clear he was lying. 'You should stay out of it too,' he told Carmine.

Just after 6.30 p.m., Carlo picked up Lea from Sempione Park. After she climbed into the Chrysler, he told her he had to drop in briefly at an apartment a few streets away. Shortly before 7 p.m., Carmine saw Carlo and Lea pull up on San Vittore in the Chrysler. The pair parked and got out. Carlo rang the bell to the apartment. Vito buzzed him in. Lea entered, then Carlo.

Fifteen minutes later, around 7.15 p.m., Carmine saw Carlo exit the apartment, walk quickly to the Chrysler and leave. 'He didn't say a word,' said Carmine. Vito left the apartment seconds later and climbed into Carmine's Passat.

'We did it,' said Vito, breathing heavily.

Vito gave Carmine a mobile. It was Lea's, he said. 'Get rid of it right away before anyone calls,' Vito instructed. Vito then left on foot.

Carlo and Vito now had to construct their alibis. Carlo also had to try to persuade Denise that Lea had just upped and left. That left it to Carmine and Rosario to get rid of Lea's body.

Carmine exited the car, ripped the SIM card out of Lea's phone and threw it into a drain, followed by the phone battery. He threw the rest of the phone in a bin. He got back into the Passat and phoned Rosario. Carlo had evidently called Rosario in the meantime. Rosario now said he would help after all, and Carmine drove over to pick him up.

Looking for somewhere to dispose of the body, the two men spent more than an hour trying to locate the keys to a warehouse owned by a friend in San Fruttuoso on the outskirts of Monza, about half an hour away by car. Unsuccessful, they drove back to San Vittore and ascended the stairs to the apartment. Carmine opened the door, turned on the light 'and there was Lea Garofalo's body on the ground,' he said. 'She had a sofa over her.'

Carmine wrenched back the sofa. He scarcely recognised Lea. 'She had bruises all over her face. Her mouth was bloody, like it had been crushed. There was blood all over her nose and neck and a pool of blood on the floor. The clothes across her chest were ripped. There was a green cord around her neck with which she had been strangled and which had cut into her neck so deeply that it had disappeared. I knew the cord. It was from the curtains in my apartment.'

Whatever doubts Carmine and Rosario had once harboured, the ferocity of Lea's killing erased them. They trussed the body with a sheet, just in case Lea was merely unconscious. Then they lifted it into a large cardboard box they had brought along. They scrubbed the floor with hot water and rags. Then they threw the rags into the box, used duct tape to seal it and heaved it downstairs to the ground floor. Carmine waited in the hallway with the box while Rosario went to fetch the Passat. Then the two men lifted the box out through the apartment block's front door, down the street and into the back of the car.

With nowhere to dump the body, Carmine and Rosario drove to the home of Floreale's parents. They dropped off the keys to the apartment, left the Passat locked in the street and went home to change clothes. A few hours later, by which time it was nearly midnight, Carmine called Floreale and asked to meet him at the apartment on San Vittore. Once both men had arrived, Carmine apologised to Floreale that the floor of his grandmother's apartment might be a little dirty. Spotting a piece of the green cord on the floor, Carmine immediately burned it in an ashtray. He then noticed a spot of blood on the sofa and told Floreale that the two of them should dump the couch in the street, which they did, next to some rubbish bins. Floreale asked no questions.

Around 1.30 a.m., Carmine went to see Carlo at the Green Dragon. Carlo said Denise was asleep at Viale Montello. Carmine updated Carlo on the clean-up. Carlo said he now had the warehouse keys and that Carmine and Rosario should take Lea's body there the next morning. Carlo and Carmine then went back to Carmine's apartment. Before they turned in, Carlo asked if he could borrow some antiseptic cream for a cut on his finger. He showed Carmine the mark.

'Lea,' he smiled.

The next morning, 25 November 2009, Vito and Rosario drove Lea's body in the Passat to the warehouse outside Monza. Carmine went in a separate van. By the time he arrived, Vito had left to clock in for work at a construction site. Rosario and Carmine took Carmine's van to fill up a ten-litre jerry-can with petrol. Then they drove back and lifted the box containing Lea's body out of the Passat and into the warehouse. 'We took a large metal trunk that was in the warehouse,' said Carmine. 'We opened the box with the body in it and shoved the body into the metal trunk. You could just see her shoes sticking out. We shook some of the petrol on the body and lit it. We threw the cardboard box on top.'

Carmine said he and Rosario watched Lea's body smoulder for an hour. 'It didn't burn well,' he said. 'At one point, Rosario said that maybe it wasn't working because there wasn't enough air getting in. So I took an axe and knocked several holes in the bottom of the trunk. But even with the new holes, the body burned very slowly.' Carmine left Rosario and went to find Vito to ask him for advice. Unsuccessful, he returned to find that Rosario had moved the body out of the trunk with a section of scaffolding and dropped it on top of some wooden pallets, placed more wood on top, then, after adding more petrol, set light to everything again. 'The body was much more destroyed now,' said Carmine. 'The head was almost gone. There was a lot of smoke and a strong smell of burned meat. Next door, there were some gypsies burning leaves and at some point one of them, a woman, came up to the fence and asked if we could give her a pallet for their fire. I passed them one through a hole in the fence. She couldn't have failed to notice the smell of cooking meat. She didn't ask any questions.'

Neither Carmine nor Rosario had slept more than a few minutes the night before and by 1 p.m. exhaustion was setting in. 'Before leaving, we put what was left of the corpse in a small pit that had already been dug in the warehouse grounds. Only a part of her chest and her legs were left. But there were many bone fragments, which we collected with a shovel and dumped in the trunk. Finally, I chopped up what was left of the body into small pieces with the axe. It was all blackened bones and flesh. Then we covered it with earth and a metal sheet.'

Carmine and Rosario left to sleep for a few hours. They returned that afternoon with Vito, who sent Carmine to buy five more litres of petrol. The three men then shovelled what remained of Lea's body back into the metal trunk, loaded some extra wood on it, doused it in petrol once more and set light to it a final time. They watched it burn down to the embers, broke what remained into shards by beating it with the back of the shovel, and left.

That night, Carmine caught up with Carlo in the Green Dragon. He was with Denise. Carmine told Carlo Lea's body was nearly gone. Carlo told Carmine about Denise's five-hour interview with the *carabinieri*. That was another headache they would have to deal with, he said.

The next morning, Carmine and Vito returned to the warehouse one last time. They scooped the ash and burnt embers into a wheelbarrow, washed and scrubbed the metal trunk and threw all the remains they could find into a nearby manhole. The following day, 27 November, Carmine met the friend who owned the warehouse to return the keys to him. 'Finished?' asked the friend. 'All done,' confirmed Carmine.

Carmine never spoke again to Carlo or any of the other men about those three days. The only time Carlo brought up the matter was in March 2010 when he heard that Denise had spoken to the *carabinieri* and accused him of murdering Lea. If that was true, said Carlo, 'then we all know what we have to do.'

*

Carmine offered to show the warehouse to Tatangelo and the *carabinieri* forensics team. It was October 2012, almost three years since Lea had died. The forensics officers took fragments of dust from the warehouse and, using a bulldozer, dug into the soil and excavated the manhole. Over several days, they were able to gather more than three kilos of material, which they transported to their laboratory in Milan. Processing the samples took several more days. But by early November, they were able to confirm the presence of 2,812 bone fragments, as well as a dental screw with which Lea had been fitted in 2007, and microscopic parts of the necklace and braided white and yellow gold bracelet that Carlo had given Lea when they first met.

Denise had initially been distraught at the knowledge that she had fallen in love with the man who had disposed of her mother's body. Now she found comfort in his contrition. When Tatangelo brought Carmine and the other defendants back to court in April 2013, Denise listened to his testimony throughout. Carmine didn't spare her feelings with his descriptions of what he had done to her mother's body. But it was clear he felt compelled by devotion to her. 'I want to say that this is a very difficult day for me,' he said. Carmine said that in prison he had learned that family was nothing without love, and that love conquered any other allegiance. 'I am not accusing ordinary people or strangers but people with whom I shared three years of my life, some of them from the same family. I made this choice out of love for Denise. Her father does not love her. Her family does not love her. But she owns my heart. It sickens me to think that I am contributing to her pain but it is also thanks to her example that I am here today.' Carmine said he was aware he was signing his own death warrant by speaking. 'I know I'm cannon fodder now,' he said. 'Sooner or later, Carlo will kill me.' Still, he added, he had no choice. 'I am really in love,' he said.

Carmine's confession was striking as much for the reasons why he had spoken out as what he said. The code stressed discipline and the suffocation of feeling. Hardening their hearts was how 'Ndranghetisti won. By out-killing and out-terrorising, they could outlast their rivals. And yet here was Carmine, a drug dealer working for one of the 'Ndrangheta's hardest men, speaking out because he couldn't contain his tenderness. Even in the 'Ndrangheta's darkest depths, a faint light still shone.

When Lea's former lawyer Annalisa Pisano read about Carmine's testimony in the newspapers, she found herself reeling for different reasons. For three years, she had dreamed about Lea calling out her name, surrounded by flames in a warehouse. 'I thought I had to be wrong,' she said. 'I'm not the kind of person who believes in that sort of thing. But when I heard this was how it ended for her, in the worst possible way, of course I remembered my dream right away.'

Initially, Annalisa was horrified by what her nightmare might mean. Had she deserted Lea? Had Lea died calling for her help? In time, however, she came to think of it differently. According to Carmine's evidence, Lea had died long before the flames consumed her. If there was any truth to her dream, Annalisa began to think it was as a testament to the bond between her and her client. 'I began thinking that, in a way, this was some sort of consolation,' she said. 'If her last moments really were spent thinking about me, then maybe she knew that I loved her.'

XXV

Giuseppina's evidence had led to the arrest and trial of sixty-four members of the Pesce *'ndrina*. So detailed was it, and so numerous the charges to which it led, that the trial lasted for a further year after she testified. But shortly after 6 p.m. on 3 May 2013, after seventeen days of deliberation, the three judges filed back into court in Palmi to deliver their verdict.

Twenty-two of the accused were acquitted. Forty-two were convicted. Three-quarters of the sentences were for more than ten years. The most severe went to Giuseppina's immediate family. Her uncle, clan head Antonino Pesce, was sentenced to twenty-eight years. Giuseppina's father Salvatore received twenty-seven years and seven months. Her husband Rocco Palaia was given twenty-one years and two months; her mother Angela Ferraro thirteen years and five months; her sister Marina Pesce twelve years and ten months; and her brother Francesco twenty-five years and eight months. Ten more Pesces, two more Ferraros and one other Palaia were convicted. Even Giuseppina's eighty-year-old grandmother, Giuseppa Bonarrigo, was sentenced to a year and eight months for receiving stolen goods. The only clemency shown was to Giuseppina, sentenced to four years and four months for mafia association, most of which she had already served.[1] 'The Pesces were destroyed,' said

Giovanni Musarò. 'There was barely a single one left walking around Rosarno.'[2]

While most of the family absorbed their ruin in silence, a few Pesces found the humiliation too much. Giuseppina's younger sister Marina, whom Alessandra described as blessed with 'the face of an angel', began howling and screaming and tearing her hair when the sentences were read out. 'She completely freaked out,' said Alessandra. Outside court, grandmother Bonarrigo – one of the few Pesces allowed bail – growled to reporters that real Pesce women went with their men to the grave. Not long afterwards, Alessandra arrived at work at the Palace of Justice in Reggio to find a group of 'Ndrangheta wives from Rosarno staging a protest outside. 'It was surreal,' she said. 'They had signs which read "Shame on you", "The sentences are unjust" and "The innocent are in jail". Some had even chained themselves to the gates.' In all seriousness, apparently, Europe's biggest mafia was presenting itself as a victim of the state. Alessandra assumed the demonstration was also designed to send a message. 'The idea was to show that real Calabrian women were still with the 'Ndrangheta. But I saw it as a sign of desperation, of weakness. You really need to prove something that you shouldn't need to? You really need to demonstrate something that, a few years ago, everyone would have taken for granted?'

The Pesces were broken and their rule of Rosarno was over. Two weeks after the verdicts, Giuseppe Pesce, the last *'ndrina* boss still on the run, turned himself in to begin his sentence of twelve years and six months. 'Enough,' he said as he walked into the Rosarno *carabinieri* station. 'I'm sick of running. Let's finish it here and now.'

Still, the people of Rosarno took longer to digest their new reality. The Pesces had ruled the town for decades, and most of the bosses were still alive and still sending their boys to collect *pizzo* from shopkeepers and restaurant owners. But people noticed that the price of extortion was falling. A violent reaction from the Pesces was inevitable but when it came, it was pathetic: a grenade which slightly injured the brother of Giuseppina's boyfriend, Domenico Costantino, when he opened a farm gate to which it was strapped. Maybe the Pesces *were* finished. It was hard to believe. But then so was the sight, little more than a year after the end of the maxi-trial, of a bulldozer driving through the front door of Giuseppina's grandmother's old house, the family's former meeting place. The authorities had confiscated the house in 2011 but had struggled for years to find a contractor willing to do the work. Now Gaetano Saffioti, a builder from Palmi, told reporters he was delighted to raze the Pesces' palace to the ground. So happy, in fact, he had done it for free. 'The fight for legality is won with deeds, not words,' he said.[3]

Watching as one of Europe's most powerful crime syndicates was pulled apart brick by brick, Alessandra found herself wondering whether it was the Pesces' obsession with honour that had ultimately doomed them. It was almost as if the family had died of shame. 'If a woman betrays her family, it has a huge resonance,' she said. 'It means the family is unable to control its women.' To an 'Ndrangheta crime family, it seemed there was nothing worse.

Less than a month after the Pesce convictions came new verdicts in the Lea Garofalo case. Carmine's confession had exposed Carlo's lie that Lea was still alive. When proceedings reopened in Milan on 9 April 2013, Carlo made a desperate attempt to regain the initiative, announcing from the dock at the end of the first day: 'President, I wish to speak!'

His lawyer, Daniel Sussman Steinberg, appeared stunned. Carlo had been clutching a piece of paper all day. Now it was clear why: he, Carlo Cosco, was breaking *omertà*. After a brief consultation between Carlo and Steinberg, the lawyer announced that Carlo would like to make a 'spontaneous statement' and Carlo was escorted to the witness box.

Speaking in halting Italian, he read: 'Madam President, and gentlemen of the court, I accept full responsibility for the murder of Lea Garofalo.'

In the courtroom, nothing moved.

'I wanted to do so during the original trial but circumstances prevented me,' Carlo continued. 'My daughter hates me and deservedly so, because I killed her mother. But I cannot endure the shame of the accusation that I want to kill her. For me, it is inconceivable that my daughter is under anyone else's protection. From whom? I would give my life for her. Woe betide anyone who touches my daughter!'

It was an astonishing outburst. There was, after all, no reason for it. Carlo had already been convicted of Lea's murder. Legally, his confession changed nothing. But psychologically, it changed everything. Carlo, it seemed, had cracked. The hardest of the 'Ndrangheta's hard men had let his feelings show. He was an 'Ndranghetista, a *capo*, a *santista*. He was a drug smuggler, an extortionist and a murderer. But first and foremost, it now appeared, he was a father. 'I hope one day that my daughter will forgive me,' said Carlo. 'I live in hope of her pardon.'

Others, however, perceived an altogether different message. When Carlo began reading his letter, he had scratched his ear. Then he scratched his eye. A little while later, he touched his finger to his lips. To those able to read the signals, Carlo was sending another message to the 'Ndrangheta. 'Listen to me,' he was saying. 'Watch me. You'll hear and see that I will say nothing.' Carlo wasn't confessing. He was offering reassurance and proposing a bargain. *I am responsible for all this*, he was saying. *Whatever the price, I will pay it. But I will not collaborate. And in return, nobody touches my daughter.*[4]

Now that Carlo had finally opened his mouth, however, he seemed to find it difficult to close. Over the next few weeks, he spoke expansively about his early married life with Lea. He explained the attack in Campobasso by saying he had asked Sabatino to beat Lea to 'teach her a lesson' after she threatened his mother. He described meeting his daughter again after seven years. '*This* became my obsession,' he said. 'To be with my daughter, to know where she was. Not to kill her mother. I never intended that.'

Carlo's testimony was all about love. Carlo loved his daughter. Carlo loved his mother. When Lea hurt Carlo's mother, Carlo had only asked Sabatino to slap Lea around a little because, really, Carlo said, he loved Lea too.

It was the same when Carlo killed her. 'I really didn't mean to,' he said. 'That morning, 24 November 2009, I went to get Denise and her mother in the hotel. When I saw them, I had an idea to surprise Denise. She had told me she wanted to live in Milan. So I thought I'll ask my friends for a key to their apartment to give to Denise as somewhere where she could come and go.'

A few hours later, Carlo took Lea to show her the apartment on Via San Vittore where their daughter could stay. But Lea had misunderstood. 'When she saw the apartment, she was angry,' said Carlo. 'She told me I was a liar because I told her I had nothing, no money, and actually I had an apartment. The truth was that it wasn't mine. I lived with Venturino. But Lea told me that I was an asshole and that I would never see Denise again.'

Carlo caught his breath.

'I had a fit of rage, Madam President,' he said. 'I punched her. Twice. She fell and hit her head on the couch. I grabbed her by the shoulders and this time she fell and hit her head on the floor. Even before I saw the blood, I knew she was dead.'

It was all just a terrible accident, Carlo was saying. One of those things that happened when a big-hearted husband and father was overcome by emotion. 'All this happened because I loved Lea,' said Carlo. 'If I hadn't loved her, nothing like this would ever have happened. But when she threatened me with never seeing my daughter again, I couldn't see my love for her any more. Because I love Denise above all else. For me that's the greatest torment. Denise must know that I care for her. She must know the truth.' Trying to rationalise his client's intervention, Steinberg, the lawyer, described Carlo as split by a 'lacerating internal struggle' which prompted him to lash out at Lea but acquitted him of premeditated murder.

Prosecutor Marcello Tatangelo was unconvinced. 'You're only talking now because Lea Garofalo's body has been found,' he said. Carlo hadn't shown remorse at the time, he added. Quite the opposite. Days after Lea's murder, Carlo had hosted a party in Pagliarelle to toast her death under the guise of an eighteenth birthday party for Denise. But Tatangelo was curious nonetheless. 'Why speak up now?' he asked.

'Eh,' shrugged Carlo. 'People said things that weren't right. You mentioned acid. You said I hated my daughter's mother. How could I let that go?'

Unmoved by Carlo's protestations of love, on 29 May 2013, appeals judge Anna Conforti, another of the most senior women in Italy's judiciary, confirmed life sentences against Carlo and his brother Vito, Rosario Curcio and Massimo Sabatino.[5] Carmine's sentence was reduced to twenty-five years. Giuseppe Cosco was acquitted but remained in prison since by now he was also serving an unrelated ten-year sentence for drug trafficking. Five months later, using evidence given by Lea seventeen years earlier, seventeen 'Ndranghetisti were arrested in Pagliarelle, Petilia Policastro and Crotone, charged with seven murders, possessing illegal weapons and drug dealing – charges which related to the clan feud that had raged in the Calabrian hills between 1989 and 2007.[6]

Outside court on the day Carlo's life sentence was confirmed, Enza told a crowd of supporters, 'Denise thanks you all. That you are all here gives her strength.' Denise could now finally bury her mother, added Enza, and the funeral would be in Milan. 'This is the city where she was killed,' said Enza. 'But it's also the place where everyone finally mobilised to fight the mafia.'

Only Maria Concetta Cacciola's case remained unresolved.

Partial closure came in Palmi in early July 2013, in the same courtroom where the Pesces had been humbled. Giuseppina testified in Concetta's case, breaking down when asked to describe her friend and recalling how 'terrified' Concetta was of her brother Giuseppe. 'She told me if you knew him, then you knew he could kill her,' she said. 'She was forbidden to leave the house, to go out or to have friends. She never went to a party. She was never allowed to have fun.'

On 13 July 2013, Concetta's father, mother and brother were found guilty of provoking her suicide. Michele Cacciola was given six years, Giuseppe five and her mother, Anna Rosalba Lazzaro, two.

If Alessandra and Giovanni were unhappy with the lightness of the sentences, the judge was too. 'The court had started doubting that Concetta's death was suicide,' said prosecutor Giuseppe Creazzo. The judge indicated he had been dissatisfied at being unable to impose the kind of sentence that a conviction for murder would allow. 'So he sent the case back to the prosecutors for them to investigate further if it was murder.'

Salvatore Dolce, who had interviewed Lea Garofalo in 2002 and was now assistant prosecutor in Palmi, was ordered to investigate the Cacciolas' two lawyers, Gregorio Cacciola and Vittorio Pisani. After seizing their computer terminals, he found proof that Concetta's statement had been through various drafts on their computers before she even returned to Rosarno – proof of a conspiracy to force her to retract. In February 2014, the two lawyers were arrested. On 8 September, Vittorio Pisani sent word that he wanted to confess. Alessandra and Giovanni had him moved to the *pentiti* prison at Paliano. They spoke to him a few days later.

Pisani told the two prosecutors that he had started working for the Cacciolas in June 2011, a few months before Concetta died. He said the family had initially approached him because they suspected Concetta was having an affair with a policeman. They wanted him to use his contacts on the force to investigate. 'It was an abnormal request,' said Pisani, 'but I took it because I had money troubles and I didn't want to lose the chance of working for a family like the Cacciolas.'

Later that month the *carabinieri* discovered one of the Cacciolas' bunkers, then a second. The Cacciolas and Belloccos were convinced the information had come from Concetta. The Belloccos insisted that she be made to return to Rosarno and retract. By this time, the Cacciolas, impatient for a result, had begun threatening Pisani. When Concetta returned to Rosarno, Pisani was under no illusion that she too was being coerced. On 12 August, he witnessed Concetta record her retraction. When she died eight days later, he knew the family was responsible. For a year and a half, Pisani had tried to bury his conscience. The Cacciolas and the Belloccos were unimpressed, however, and Pisani became convinced he was in danger. 'I was scared,' he told the prosecutors. 'And I needed to be able to look myself in the mirror again.'

'Tell us, why was so much attention paid to this one woman?' asked Giovanni.

'As a warning,' replied Pisani. 'It was to say: "Enough now."'

The identity of Concetta's killer remained a mystery. But the case was still open and the prosecutors were inching closer. On 30 July 2015, the Court of Appeal in Reggio Calabria increased Michele's sentence to eight years and eight months, Giuseppe's to seven years and four months and Anna Rosalba Lazzaro's to five years and six months.

XXVI

In October 2014, Alessandra and Paolo packed up their tiny apartment in the roof of the *carabinieri* barracks in Reggio and moved back to Milan. Alessandra had been promoted to deputy public prosecutor in Italy's financial capital. Most of the rest of the anti-mafia team had already left Calabria. Giuseppe Pignatone, Michele Prestipino, Giovanni Musarò and Renato Cortese, the flying squad chief, were all taking up more senior positions in Rome.

The reassignments made sense. Some of the biggest 'Ndrangheta clans had been smashed, especially on the stronghold of the Gioia Tauro plain. The cost to the prosecutors of their success was an increased threat to their lives. Alessandra, who like Pignatone and Prestipino had lived inside close protection for years, knew she had added new names to the list of those who wanted to kill her. Of those she knew about, there was Giuseppina's father, Salvatore, who had threatened her in court, and Concetta's mother, Anna Rosalba Lazzaro, who had been bugged cursing Alessandra as 'that bitch, that bastard bitch. I want her dead!'

Giovanni Musarò was another prosecutor now forced to make peace with the idea that he was fighting for a nation in which he no longer really lived. In 2010, in an unrelated case, Giovanni had ordered the arrest of the entire Gallico *'ndrina* in Palmi, a total of thirty-two

'Ndranghetisti including an eighty-four-year-old grandmother. Subsequently, clan head Domenico Gallico suffered the humiliation of watching his 'ndrina turn their backs to him in court. In October 2012, Gallico asked to meet Giovanni in his cell in Viterbo prison, north of Rome. Giovanni was mystified, but agreed nonetheless. 'It was a very strange situation,' he told a parliamentary inquiry later. 'I was shown to a very small room. When Gallico entered, he was alone without an escort and uncuffed. He came around to my side of the desk and said: "*Dottore*, what a pleasure that we can finally meet face to face. May I have the honour of shaking your hand?"'

When Giovanni extended his right hand, Gallico pretended to do the same, then with his left hit Giovanni across the face, breaking his nose. 'I fell from the chair,' said Giovanni. 'As I lay there up against the wall, he kicked and punched me maybe fifty or sixty times.' During the attack, Giovanni remembered thinking: 'If I don't block his punches, he's going to break my neck. He's going to kill me.' After thirty seconds, several guards pulled Gallico off, kicking and screaming. 'Are you crazy?' asked one, pinning him to the floor. Gallico pointed at Giovanni. 'Ask him what he did to me and my family!' he howled. 'Ask him what he did to me!'

Bodyguards were posted outside Giovanni's door in hospital that night. They had not left his side since. Not long afterwards Marcello Fondacaro, an 'Ndrangheta informer, told Giovanni that the same Bellocco boss who had ordered Concetta be made to retract had also made a plan to kill Giovanni and his boss, Prestipino. 'The Belloccos thought Maria Concetta Cacciola's retraction would have ended the story,' said Giovanni. 'They were very angry when that didn't happen. Giuseppe Bellocco, in particular, was known as a very dangerous human being who held grudges and harboured great resentment.' According to Fondacaro, Bellocco planned to ambush Giovanni and Prestipino with gunmen and explosives as the two prosecutors drove to court. 'He knew I drove to Palmi twice a week during a trial I was dealing with,' said Giovanni. 'He knew the route, the colour of my armoured car and my escort car, and that Prestipino would have been following in his armoured car, with another escort car with him. He'd even asked permission from the Gallicos to carry out the attack.' The double assassination failed only because the trial in Palmi was unexpectedly adjourned. And while, to some, gunmen *and* explosives might have seemed like overkill, to the prosecutors it underlined how serious the 'Ndrangheta were about revenge. 'In Calabria they do it well or not at all,' said Giovanni.

It was time to get out. None of the anti-mafia prosecutors or their families could expect to live a normal life again. It was, in a way, their own life sentence. But Alessandra, for one, was finding inspiration from an unexpected source. 'Giuseppina knows what she did is another death sentence,' she said. 'Her betrayal has to be punished with death and it has to be her brother, the same blood, who kills her to restore the family honour. And one day, he will get out.' But Alessandra said it had been years since she had seen Giuseppina doubt herself. 'For Giuseppina,' she said, 'what she did was an act of love towards her children.' In the end, the contest between The Family and her own family had been no contest at all. 'She's fine,' said Alessandra. 'Actually, I think she's happy.'

From the moment 150 years earlier when a group of southern criminals met a band of revolutionary freemasons in jail and decided to veneer their thuggish criminality with myth and legend, the 'Ndrangheta had shown itself to be nothing if not adaptable. Calabria would always be the 'Ndrangheta's homeland. There were still plenty of *'ndrine* to pursue there and the trafficking, extortion, corruption and murder would continue. But as the prosecutors' Calabrian campaign against the 'Ndrangheta began to wind down, new surveillance evidence made clear that the centre of gravity for Italian organised crime was moving to the north of the country and even further afield. The change made sense. Italy was the only country in the world that even had a law of mafia association. Few other countries allowed such intrusive surveillance. Plenty of them made it far easier to legit-imise criminal wealth by buying assets like bonds, shares, property and businesses.

And if the 'Ndrangheta was moving, it was also changing shape. The Calabria prosecutors had made a point of mapping and destroy-ing the 'Ndrangheta's command structure. For the organisation, the intelligent response was to dismantle it. Prosecutors began reporting the emergence of a more informal, decentralised, diffuse group, a loose association, an ad-hoc gathering, even something as ephemeral as a state of mind. They likened its penetration of Italy's legitimate economy and, beyond it, Frankfurt, London and New York to liquid poured on a sponge.

And you couldn't squeeze the world. In their new positions, many of the prosecutors found their time in Calabria quickly began to feel like the golden years. Like the swordfish hunters of the Straits of Messina, the Calabrian prosecutors had harpooned a monster and forced it to the surface. But now the creature was disappearing back into the deep, vanishing into the folds of an international financial system that not only tolerated secrecy but, in the case of the $20 tril-lion offshore banking industry, actively depended on it. The prosecu-tors often felt like they were in a losing race against time. Hundreds of billions of 'Ndrangheta euros and dollars had been already success-fully laundered beyond reach or reproach. And to the prosecutors' frustration, in the world of frictionless global money movements, their fastidious objections were often viewed as pedantry. Franco Roberti, head of Italy's anti-mafia and anti-terrorism office, lamented the lack of cooperation his investigators received in London or New York or Hong Kong, let alone the centres of secret banking on para-dise islands around the world. Foreign governments 'don't want to believe that the problem of the 'Ndrangheta is their problem too', he said. 'They want to believe that their money doesn't stink.' Roberti was pessimistic about the chances of beating a global mafia in a world where politics was subordinate to business. 'Business dictates and politicians follow, and this has facilitated the absorption of mafia money and influence around the world,' he said. A world in which any idea of the common good had been replaced with greed and yawning inequality was one, said Roberti, whose gates were wide open to *mafiosi*. He called it the 'Snow White syndrome'. 'Nobody wants to look in the mirror,' he said.

That kind of thinking could lead a prosecutor down a dark path, as Alessandra knew. A world where financial and political scandal had become depressingly routine was one in which it was all too easy to conclude that what the prosecutors were really fighting was the night in human nature. The 'Ndrangheta wouldn't be able to corrupt business and politics unless businessmen and politicians already had the potential for it. Hadn't the serpent admirers of Milan understood centuries ago that enlightenment and darkness walked hand in hand? And if family itself was a form of corruption, as the mafia posited, then what chance did legality have in any country, let alone Italy? 'We can't fight the 'Ndrangheta just by putting people in jail,' said Alessandra. 'We need a cultural change. We need a change in people's minds.' The prosecutors had no way to assist that effort. Barricaded behind their steel doors and bullet-proof windows, all they could do was watch.

None of that would diminish what had been accomplished in Calabria. The 'Ndrangheta was reeling. However nimble they were, the clans could not adjust to betrayal. 'That's an unacceptable issue for them,' said Prestipino. 'It's unbearable. It threatens their entire existence.' The effect of the Calabrian campaign would be felt for generations. Prestipino's experience in Sicily had taught him that once a mafia's invincibility cracked, the floodgates opened. In Sicily, hundreds of *mafiosi* had come forward to testify. 'They never recovered,' he said.

In the hill villages and small towns of Calabria, the 'Ndrangheta was still ruthlessly punishing disloyalty. In February 2012, a thirty-year-old man called Fabrizio Pioli who was having an extramarital affair with a *mafioso*'s daughter was beaten to death with sticks outside Rosarno. In August 2013, Francesca Bellocco and Domenico Cacciola, whose affair had scandalised two of Rosarno's biggest crime families, disappeared. Such violent reprisals discouraged the flow of *pentiti*. But a steady stream was under way. By the end of 2015, the judiciary could count 164 *pentiti* and 29 witnesses who had testified against the 'Ndrangheta. That was hardly a cascade. But given that five years earlier even a single 'Ndrangheta *pentito* was almost unheard of, it felt significant.

Perhaps most remarkable was the number of 'Ndrangheta wives following the three women's example: fifteen, more than had ever testified in four decades of Cosa Nostra trials. Di Bella's youth court, in particular, had become a magnet for dissident 'Ndrangheta women. As sons – more than thirty by the end of 2016 – turned against their fathers, mothers chose their children over their husbands. 'It's a phenomenon we didn't predict,' said di Bella. 'Many women realise these measures are not punishing their children but protecting them. They come secretly and ask us to send their children far away.' One woman who wrote to di Bella in confidence in November 2015 was typical. Her husband had been convicted of murder. Her father, cousin and eleven-year-old nephew had all been killed. Her two teenage boys, she wrote, 'are rebellious and violent, hanging around with bad guys, and fascinated by the 'Ndrangheta and guns. My son Rosario thinks jail is an honour that will win him respect. Please send my children away. The thought tears me apart but it is the only solution. In my family, there is no one – no one – I can trust.'

This first act of rebellion by an 'Ndrangheta mother sometimes grew into something more. Di Bella said the youth courts could add another ten 'Ndrangheta women to the fifteen who had testified in the adult courts. As a result of his success, di Bella's programme was being rolled out across Italy. It helped that, at the same time, such global figures as Malala Yousafzai and Michelle Obama were making women's emancipation a worldwide issue. Di Bella found himself wondering whether Italy might have finally found its way to a mafia-free future. 'We're opening up these disagreements inside families that were previously thought to be impenetrable,' he said. 'We're a crack in the monolith, a light in the dark, a bright threat to the whole mafia family system.'

At times, the momentum was palpable. In June 2014, Pope Francis further splintered the mafia's consensus when he travelled to Calabria and, before a crowd of a hundred thousand, excommunicated all *mafiosi*, denouncing the 'Ndrangheta as an example of 'the adoration of evil and contempt for the common good'. Francis later followed his decree by condemning the Camorra in Naples and visiting *pentiti* at Paliano. The change felt seismic, grinned di Bella, and to the 'Ndrangheta more than anyone. 'They can feel the ground moving under their feet,' he said.

In their new offices in Milan and Rome, asked by their staff how it had been in the south, Alessandra and Giovanni would tell stories about Calabria.

Giovanni's favourite tale was about hope. He'd been listening to wiretaps of the Cacciolas one day, he said, when he heard them discussing a family called the Secolos, whom the Belloccos were gradually ruining through loan-sharking. It reminded him of a conversation he had had with Concetta. She had told him about the bind the Secolos were in and how the matriarch, Stefania Secolo, had asked Concetta if she could help them. Concetta had asked her father to intervene but he had dismissed her pleas. Giovanni wanted to know more. 'So I called Stefania Secolo in for a meeting,' he said. 'And in the days before she was due to come in, we also began listening to her phone. Her brothers and everyone else were saying to her: "Don't say anything! Don't honour the memory of someone who cannot come back to life! Don't be a hero! Heroes die!" But on 28 February 2012, she came to me and told me exactly what happened and with her evidence, we arrested the Belloccos and put them in jail.' Giovanni sighed. It was 'such a beautiful story', he said. 'Stefania Secolo spoke out because her friend Concetta had reminded her how a person should behave and how they could be free. Her friend had been killed for it. Yet Stefania still spoke.' From his five years in Calabria, 'that's the day that stays with me.' There was all the hope in the world in that one day, he said.

Alessandra was still in touch with Giuseppina Pesce and was happy to talk about her. But when people asked, she would often tell them the story of Giuseppina Multari. Just before Christmas in 2012, a few months after Giuseppina Pesce had resumed her cooperation and was preparing to testify against her family, a letter addressed to her arrived at the Palace of Justice in Reggio. The writer 'expressed her support for Giuseppina and urged her to believe in the institutions of the state and the people around her', said Alessandra. 'The letter read: "Go for it! Be brave!"' It was signed 'Giuseppina Multari, protected witness'.

'I was curious,' said Alessandra. 'Who was this woman who had sent this very special letter? She was in the witness programme and I'd never even heard of her.' Alessandra searched through the Palace of Justice archives, looking for records of a Multari. Eventually she found a letter Multari had written to the *carabinieri* in 2006 and some statements she had made in 2008. Alessandra read how Giuseppina Multari was Concetta's cousin by marriage. Her husband, Antonio Cacciola, was notorious in the *'ndrina* for dipping into his own drug supplies. He was also having an affair. One night in November 2005, Multari and Antonio had a fight, Antonio stormed out – and Giuseppina never saw him again. 'Officially it was a suicide but Giuseppina Multari was convinced his family had killed him,' said Alessandra. 'And after her husband's death, she was kept at home by his family like a slave. She could not go out. She could not drop off her children at school. She was only allowed to go to the cemetery.'

One night, the Cacciola men left the house to go to a wedding. Finally alone, Giuseppina fled. She walked to the coast. 'She was going to drown herself in the sea,' said Alessandra. 'But suddenly her phone went and it was her brother Angelo. She told him she was trying to kill herself. He came and found her.' By the time Angelo arrived, his sister was suffering from hypothermia. He drove her to hospital. When Angelo asked her why she was trying to commit suicide, she told him about the Cacciolas and the beatings and how she was living in a virtual prison. 'I am going to do something for you,' Angelo replied. 'I am going to help you.'

'The brother left,' said Alessandra. 'And *he* never came back.'

After six more months confined to her in-laws' home, Giuseppina managed to sneak a letter to the *carabinieri*. As a result, in 2008, she made several statements against the Cacciolas and was taken into witness protection. 'But no one ever acted on her evidence!' exclaimed Alessandra. 'I decided to go to see her. And when she saw me, she burst into tears. "I've been waiting six years for someone to come and talk to me," she said.'

Giuseppina described the Rosarno clans and the Cacciolas' empire in a series of statements that eventually ran to several hundred pages. A dozen 'Ndranghetisti were later convicted. But what was especially striking about the case, said Alessandra, was Giuseppina Multari's faith in herself. Even though the state had let her down, she had held on to her conviction and her courage. 'The best part?' said Alessandra. 'Some of the men who kept her in that house are now serving time for slavery.' It was, she added, a medieval conviction for medieval men.

It was Lea's story above all, however, which moved Italy. If Concetta represented tragedy, and Giuseppina Pesce embodied resilience, then Lea was both. Here was a woman born into the mafia who had tried all her life to escape it. Trapped even deeper by marriage, she discovered the strength to fight in her love for her daughter, before being let down by the state, and trapped by a husband pretending to fall in love with her again. It was an epic melodrama of such unbelievable twists and turns that people seemed to turn up at the commemorations of her life that were held across the country from 2013 just to check that what they had heard was true.

There was something else, though. After her death, a number of pictures of Lea and Denise found their way into the newspapers. There was Lea smiling through long dark hair, or sitting on a rock by the beach with Denise on her knee, or holding Denise aloft in a city piazza, or smoking a cigarette in sunglasses on the beach, or at the stove in Bergamo on the run with Denise. People began to feel they knew Lea. Before them was a whole life, from girlhood to marriage to motherhood, from love to fear, in the city and on the beach, in the north and the south. In time, Lea's story became one of the few ever to truly unite Italy. Posters of her face became a staple on walls across the country. There were documentaries and anti-mafia rallies, marches and newspaper profiles, plays and books and a television movie. Parks, bridges, piazzas and roads were named after her. Plaques were erected in Bergamo and Boiano and next to the warehouse outside Monza where she had died. In Milan, Lea's remains were buried in the Cimitero Monumentale beside the city's most illustrious citizens.[1] A monument was erected in Petilia depicting a ball splitting a rock in two. In his speech unveiling the statue, the mayor declared Petilia would be for ever after a beacon to 'women of courage' across Italy.

On 19 October 2013, nearly four years after her death, thousands of Italians gathered on a chilly morning in Milan to remember Lea in the city where, as an expectant mother, she had once hoped for a new life. Buses laid on to transport mourners from Pagliarelle and Petilia arrived ominously empty. Among the crowd bearing flowers and waving flags decorated with Lea's face, however, were hundreds of Calabrians who had made their own way. Enza Rando met one 'Ndrangheta wife who, following the service, walked immediately into a *carabinieri* station to make a statement against her family. 'She said: "Lea taught me to be brave,"' said Enza. '"Lea taught me to have courage."'

Alessandra, unable to attend such a public event, watched on television. Lea's coffin was carried through the streets around Sempione Park by pall bearers who included the mayors of Milan and Petilia and Don Luigi Ciotti, head of Libera. It was the size of the crowd that most caught Alessandra's attention. The roots of the 'Ndrangheta went back to 1861 and the unification of Italy. Everything that had followed since had sprung from that first refusal to accept an Italian nation state. As a result, Italy had never really come together. It had always been north and south, state and mafia, Piedmontese, Lombardian and Venetian against Campanian, Calabrian and Sicilian. And it was in those rifts that malevolence and murder had thrived. And yet here, on the streets of Milan, was all Italy together. This was what a modern, lawful, united nation looked like. Was it possible that in the funeral of a *mafioso*'s daughter there were glimpses of a nation finally made whole?

Lea's coffin was placed on a stand in front of the crowd. Over it hung a banner that read 'I hear, I see, I speak', a slogan which, alongside images of Lea, Giuseppina and Concetta, had become a fixture at anti-mafia rallies. Don Luigi then addressed a eulogy to Lea. She needn't worry, he told her. Denise now had a family of thousands to look after her. 'Your heart and your conscience will forever be wellsprings of freedom,' he said. 'You were a martyr to truth. Your spirit will never die.'

Don Luigi was followed by Denise.[2] She had been only a girl of seventeen when, a few streets away, her mother had disappeared into the night. Now she was a woman of twenty-one and a government witness who had sent her father and boyfriend to jail for murdering her mother. And finally she was able to say her goodbyes. The crowd stood in silence. Denise, close by but hidden from view on her bodyguards' insistence, spoke to the crowd through loudspeakers. 'Today is a very difficult day for me,' she began. After a long pause, in a gentle voice, she spoke to her mother. 'Thank you for all you did for me,' she said. 'Thank you for giving me a better life. Everything that happened, everything you did, I know now that you did it all for me and I will never stop thanking you for it.' Denise's voice was cracking. There was no revenge here, no honour and no justice. There was just Denise standing before Lea, telling her she had been a good mother. '*Ciao, Mama*,' she said.

Acknowledgements

An extraordinary selection of people tried to suppress the story of *The Good Mothers* and many of them did their best to frustrate the reporting and writing of this book. As with any investigation into the mafia, the 'Ndrangheta's violent enforcement of *omertà* ensured that many of its leading characters were unavailable. By the time I heard their story, two of the three Good Mothers, Lea Garofalo and Maria Concetta Cacciola, were dead, killed for their courage in standing up to the organisation; the third, Giuseppina Pesce, was unreachable in witness protection. Most *mafiosi* and those intimidated by them were also unwilling to speak. On those occasions when subjects did talk, their answers to my questions often contained warnings or veiled threats. That the book exists at all is due to the courage and determination of a rare few.

Foremost among those who stepped forward to be counted is my agent at Pew Literary, Patrick Walsh. Patrick was the first to spot the potential of this story and he remains the greatest champion for whom a writer could ask, somehow combining charm and warmth with sage advice and commercial precision. Patrick forms an unbeatable team with Luke Speed, my film agent at Curtis Brown, who immediately saw the promise of *The Good Mothers* and whose consequent effect on my professional life has been nothing less than transformational.

Arabella Pike at HarperCollins in London and David Highfill at HarperCollins in New York were both everything a writer wishes for in an editor: gracious in their welcome, generous in the time they allowed me to write, firm in their support against saboteurs, efficient and insightful in their editing – and providers of delicious lunches. Katherine Patrick at HarperCollins UK organised a publicity campaign that could have conquered worlds, Leo Nickolls created the fantastic cover and Iain Hunt ushered the final text to publication with the skill and collegial civility that has led to his universal acknowledgement as one of the best in the business. Tessa Ross and Juliette Howell at House Productions, who bought the film and television rights before there was even a proposal, let alone a book, have my everlasting gratitude for their brave and early support.

I first heard about the women of *The Good Mothers* on my first reporting trip to Italy (for a different story) when Laura Aprati, an Italian journalist whom I had asked to set up a couple of interviews, insisted that as part-payment I watch a one-woman play she had written with Enrico Fierro. The play, *O cu nui o cu iddi* (*With us or with them*), was being staged entirely in Italian to an audience of teenagers in a run-down, heavily mafia area on the outskirts of Rome. I picked up on the drama and the tragedy but little more. My confusion – and the audience's – was only heightened when Laura pushed me on stage to answer a few questions through an interpreter about my impression of the play, the mafia and the past, present and future of Italy.

Chastened by this exposure of my ignorance, I returned to my guesthouse knowing only the name of the woman on whose life the play was based: Maria Concetta Cacciola. Thus began the process of research and reporting that led me to her story, and those of Giuseppina Pesce, and Lea and Denise Garofalo. There was a lot to read. Though the Italian press initially missed the story of the Garofalos, it later made up for its inattention with blanket coverage of Carlo Cosco's trial. By then, Lea and Denise were becoming heroes to a generation of young Italian activists. The arrest of the powerful

Pesce clan, by contrast, was a big story from the start, especially when Giuseppina began testifying. As the press watched the unravelling of the Gioia Tauro 'Ndrangheta, Concetta's death also received significant coverage.

Still, many of the newspaper reports were frustratingly brief and incomplete. There are sound reasons for this: Italian journalists who report on the mafia in any depth are routinely forced to seek protection from the authorities. In addition, the 'Ndrangheta is a phenomenon whose scale and threat has only recently begun to be understood. Uncovering the detail of the criminal conspiracy that lies behind the story of *The Good Mothers* and exploring the history of the 'Ndrangheta required a painstaking two and a half years rummaging through the archives of the Italian judiciary, accumulating, translating and assessing tens of thousands of pages of court documents. These were then supplemented by lengthy and repeated interviews with the participants as well as historians and academics.

Laura was my guide throughout this process, along with Giuliana Clementi, the interpreter who first translated my ramblings that night at Laura's play. Laura's deep knowledge and resourcefulness left few stones unturned. Giuliana's pinpoint and nuanced translation in a world that the 'Ndrangheta would prefer to remain as murky as possible was essential to the accuracy of my understanding. I am forever grateful for their assistance. I also benefited immensely from the insight and generosity of Enrico Fierro, Laura's professional partner for many years and an encyclopedia of mafia knowledge; and from the generosity and expertise of Lucio Musilino, whose contacts in Calabria are unparalleled and who continues to report daily on the 'Ndrangheta in the face of numerous threats to his life. I also owe deep thanks to Teo Butturini, Marta Clinco and Francesco Creazzo for fixing and translating.

I should also acknowledge the generous assistance of Alessandra Cerreti, whose insight into the importance of women to the 'Ndrangheta and how feminism was the key to bringing down

Europe's most powerful mafia is the central theme of *The Good Mothers*. Alessandra allowed me to interview her for a total of eight hours over the course of a year. It was a personal and professional blow when our collaboration came to an end after Alessandra decided she wanted to write her own book, but it was a decision she was entitled to take and one I respect and understand – and my admiration for her and her work endures.

The openness of the Italian justice system, and its tradition of prosecutors presenting their entire case in official documents that contain transcripts of wiretaps and surveillance videos, as well as transcripts of interviews with key suspects and witnesses, is a treasure trove for any journalist, and it is those legal and evidential documents which form the backbone of this book. As well as Alessandra, I am indebted to numerous prosecutors in Calabria and across Italy for their assistance in providing the relevant documents and agreeing to lengthy interviews, particularly Franco Roberti, Michele Prestipino, Giovanni Musarò, Giuseppe Lombardo, Salvatore Dolce, Giuseppe Creazzo, Roberto di Bella, Federico Cafiero de Raho, Marcello Tatangelo and Gaetano Paci, and, despite a cold that had taken away his voice, the indomitable Nicola Gratteri. Renato Cortese took time out of his busy schedule to answer my questions. Raffaele Grassi, Reggio Calabria's steadfast police chief, was unfailingly solicitous on my visits to the city and granted me a rare and astonishing tour of the giant floor on the top of the police headquarters entirely given over to wiretapping, surveillance and bugging. Like many on the Gioia Tauro *piano*, I am also indebted to Antonino de Masi and Antonino Bartuccio, mayor of Rizziconi, who continue to speak out – to me and others – despite the repeated threats to their lives.

Among the lawyers who also assisted me, particular thanks are due to Annalisa Pisano, Lea Garofalo's only contact in the outside world for many years, who broke seven years of silence to speak tearfully and honestly to me in a quiet corner of a courthouse café in Catanzaro. Vincenza 'Enza' Rando, one of my first interviewees, dealt patiently with my frequently misjudged questions. Adriana Fiormonti, Giuseppina Pesce's lawyer, was charmingly instructive on her client and the workings of the 'Ndrangheta. Jules Munro at Simpsons solicitors in Sydney, Beth Silfin at HarperCollins and Nicola Landolfi in Rome all provided crucial legal advice.

I drew on a host of academic research in my investigation of the 'Ndrangheta. Among those who were especially helpful were Enzo Ciconte in Rome, Ernesto Savone in Milan, and John Dickie and Anna Sergi in London. Anyone interested in pursuing this subject could do worse than to peruse the considerable back catalogue belonging to these four experts.

I also relied on a small army of readers to proof and offer suggestions, all of which were invaluable. My deep thanks to Max Askew, Colin Perry, and members of southern England's best book club: Venetia Ellvers, Serena Freeland, Cleodie Gladstone, Wiz Hok, Susie Honey, Cheryl Myers, Millie Powell, Louisa Robertson, Amanda Sinclair, Sally Turvill and Anna Worthington. Deep thanks as ever to Tess, who read every draft, endured countless discussions and offered limitless incisive advice. None of it works without you, Tess.

To the many lawyers and various others on several continents who tried to frustrate this book – and whose tactics bore a marked resemblance to those employed by the 'Ndrangheta – I hope you can still enjoy it. A number of you made the argument that this was not my book to write, because I was neither Italian nor a woman. As someone who has worked as a foreign correspondent for more than two decades, I know the pitfalls of the profession only too well. The outsider is hindered by ignorance, language and expense. A very fair question is often: who are you to tell this tale? My own view is that these obstacles are formidable but not insurmountable; that distance can sometimes lend perspective; and that empathy, imagining yourself in the shoes of another, is the duty of any writer and the basis of any good writing. If the story of *The Good Mothers* tells us anything, it is that to define human capacity by the accident of gender or skin colour, religion or nationality, is folly. The entire world gained because a small group of southern Italian women sought a different destiny from the one others had marked out for them. It is their example, above all else, that has been my guide in these pages.

Notes

The story of *The Good Mothers* relies heavily on official court documents released during the trials of those charged with the murders of Lea Garofalo and Maria Concetta Cacciola, and the cases that followed Giuseppina Pesce's revelations. The Italian justice system is an invaluable tool for the reporter trying to reconstruct a story after the fact. At each stage of the trial process, the prosecutor will release, in printed form, all the evidence he or she intends to rely on in court, including all transcripts of tapped phone conversations and other intercepted communications. These documents are detailed and comprehensive: each set of trial documents for Giuseppina Pesce ran to more than 1,000 pages, and more than 2,000 in the latter stages of the process. They also carry an unimpeachable legal privilege, as do the trial transcripts. It's hard to imagine a legal system where more trouble is taken to ensure that justice is seen to be done.

For each of the three Good Mothers, as well as for other cases that feature in their story, my method was to digest the official documentation, then follow it up with supplementary interviews with the protagonists. Italy's anti-mafia prosecutors were unfailingly accommodating and most direct quotations from prosecutors in the text are from those interviews, though I have marked the source where it might be unclear or where that is not the case. (A full list of those prosecutors who assisted me, along with my thanks, can be found in the acknowledgements.) *Mafiosi*, 'Ndranghetisti and their legal representatives tended to be less forthcoming: such are the restrictions of *omertà*. I also interviewed a number of experts – academics, law enforcement officers, judges, lawyers, politicians, officials. Again, any quotations that appear in the text should be assumed to be sourced to my interviews unless I have indicated otherwise. Finally, as part of my research, I read thousands of articles in the Italian and international press, as well as a slew of books and academic articles, and I have indicated in the text where I have relied on them for points of information.

I

1. This chapter is based on official transcriptions of Denise Cosco's testimony in court on 20 September and 13 October 2011, judicial documents from the murder trial that followed, and transcripts of her interviews with the *carabinieri* on 25 November 2009 and 5 March 2010. I also conducted several supplementary interviews, notably with Denise's lawyer, Vincenza Rando, Lea's lawyer, Annalisa Pisano, and prosecutors Alessandra Cerreti, Giuseppe Creazzo and Salvatore Dolce.

II

1. Interview with the author, Pagliarelle, May 2016.
2. Estimates of the 'Ndrangheta's earnings vary wildly. Partly this is because the 'Ndrangheta is such a secretive organisation, partly because it is laterally structured, giving no one boss much knowledge of the 'Ndrangheta's finances beyond his own *'ndrina*. Some variation is also accounted for by Italian researchers' habit of focusing only on revenues from inside Italy. Finally, some of the more spectacular figures seem to be explained by researchers, journalists and prosecutors wishing to draw attention to the group.

Transcrime, a respected criminal research unit run by Professor Ernesto Savone, who I interviewed at his offices at the Catholic University in Milan, estimates the 'Ndrangheta's annual earnings at $3.49 billion. In a paper published in *Global Crime* in 2014 ('Mythical numbers and the proceeds of organized crime: Estimating the mafia proceeds in Italy'), Transcrime also estimated 'Ndrangheta annual earnings to be in the range of $2.5 billion to $4 billion.

Most other estimates of the 'Ndrangheta's earnings are far higher, in the $40–$80 billion range. In December 2008, for instance, the US Consul General to Naples, Patrick Truhn, returned from a fact-finding tour to Calabria to file a report which began with the arresting opening statement: 'If it were not part of Italy, Calabria would be a failed state. The 'Ndrangheta organized crime syndicate controls vast portions of its territory and economy and accounts for at least three percent of Italy's GDP (probably much more) through drug trafficking, extortion and usury' (Wikileaks released the cable: www.wikileaks.org/plusd/cables/08NAPLES96_a.html).

The figure of $100 billion comes from anti-mafia prosecutor Giuseppe Lombardo, who is based in Reggio Calabria and has studied the 'Ndrangheta's money, domestic and international, for a decade. Lombardo is not an individual given to exaggeration and there are few people in the world who know about the 'Ndrangheta's money. It is his figure that I have used here as an upper limit.

Why the variation in figures? And why use Lombardo's figure, which is one of the highest? Savone was keen to puncture what he considered to be the wilder estimates of mafia wealth, a laudable aim in an area prone to hyperbole. Still, anecdotal evidence such as the value of the European cocaine trade (4.5–7 billion euros a year at wholesale prices, or 22 billion euros a year at street prices), the embezzlement and defrauding of billons of euros in European Union funds and the uncovering of mafia money-laundering networks processing tens of billions of euros a year suggests Transcrime's figures are low. Possibly this is because, in its admirable effort to nail the facts, Transcrime focused only on documented domestic seizures and Italian police evidence of criminal revenues, plus academic and media reports. In other words, it concentrated only on the known and local and took no account of the unknown or foreign. It's worth noting that in a separate 2013 study, Transcrime itself estimated that 80 per cent of the 'Ndrangheta's money is earned overseas. Lombardo, on the other hand, took a global view and has information on the 'Ndrangheta not available to academic researchers. His figures also accord much more closely with other international estimates of the value of global organised crime.

3. Milka Kahn and Anne Véron, *Women of Honour* (London: Hurst, 2017), p. 77.

4. Although Italian law recognised the imperative of defending honour until 1981, allowing the defence of reputation as mitigation for murder. See Pierfilippo Saviotti, 'Le donne contro la 'ndrangheta, Pavia incontra il procuratore Cerreti', *Stampo Antimafioso*, 16 November 2013: www.stampoantimafioso. it/2013/11/16/pavia-procuratore-cerreti/#sthash.zns0zKkt.dpuf

5. Michele Inserra, 'Quaderni del Sud, Locri la giornata della memoria Al cimitero di Rosarno per le donne "sparite"', *Il Quotidiano del Sud*, 17 March 2017: www.quotidianodelsud. it/calabria/societa-cultura/2017/03/17/quaderni-sud-locri-giornata-memoria-cimitero-rosarno-donne

6. Netflix, *Amanda Knox*, 2016: www.
   netflix.com/title/80081155

III

1. This section is based primarily on several interviews with Alessandra Cerreti conducted between July 2015 and May 2016, as well as supplementary research.
2. *Profile: Bernardo Provenzano*, BBC, 11 April 2006: news.bbc.co.uk/1/hi/world/europe/4899512.stm
3. *La Repubblica*, 'Imprenditore arrestato per frode all'erario E' accusato di aver sottratto un miliardo', 9 February 2007: www.repubblica.it/2007/02/sezioni/cronaca/arresto-cetti-serbelloni/arresto-cetti-serbelloni/arresto-cetti-serbelloni.html; *La Repubblica*, 'Islam, nell'aula del tribunale è polemica fra giudice e imputato sul copricapo', 26 February 2009: www.milano.repubblica.it/dettaglio/islam-nellaula-del-tribunale-e-polemica-fra-giudice-e-imputato-sul-copricapo/1596678
4. Emanuela Zuccalà, 'La 'ndrangheta esiste, che fatica dimostrarlo ogni volta', *Io Donna*, 9 October 2012: www.iodonna.it/personaggi/interviste/2012/alessandra-cerreti-pubblico-ministero-mafia-calabria-40999238466.shtml

IV

1. This chapter is based on official transcriptions of Denise Cosco's testimony and of her interviews with the *carabinieri* on 25 November 2009 and 5 March 2010, as well as supplementary interviews with Denise's lawyer Vincenza Rando, Lea's lawyer Annalisa Pisano, and prosecutors Alessandra Cerreti, Giuseppe Creazzo and Salvatore Dolce.

V

1. John Dickie, professor of Italian Studies at University College, London, is a rare example of an outsider in a field – mafia history – dominated by Italians. His studies of *mafiosi*, *Cosa Nostra*, *Mafia Brotherhoods* and *Mafia Republic*, draw on earlier work by Italian scholars but also Dickie's original research. Alessandra read works by many mafia scholars, most of them Italian. But it was Dickie's research that revealed to her the 'Ndrangheta's early attachment to prostitution. It is a measure of Dickie's stature that Alessandra later struck up a correspondence with him. In this passage, I quote from Dickie's work as well as from a supplementary interview in London in June 2016.
2. John Dickie, *Mafia Brotherhoods* (London: Sceptre, 2011), pp. 171–4.
3. See for example the founding myths of the Chinese triads, the Japanese yakuza or the South African prison gangs, the 26s, 27s and 28s.
4. León Arsenal and Hipólito Sanchiz, *Una Historia de las Sociedades Secretas Españolas* (Planeta, 2006), pp. 326–35.
5. Dickie, *Mafia Brotherhoods*, p. 5.
6. Antonio Zagari, *Ammazzare Stanca* (Periferia, 1992, reprinted by Aliberti 2008).
7. Interview with the author, Rome, May 2016.

VI

1. This section is largely sourced from repeated interviews with Alessandra Cerreti, Giovanni Musarò and Michele Prestipino between July 2015 and November 2016.

2. Rachel Donadio, 'Corruption Is Seen as a Drain on Italy's South', *New York Times*, 7 October 2012: http://www.nytimes.com/2012/10/08/world/europe/in-italy-calabria-is-drained-by-corruption.html

3. Antonino de Masi interviewed by the author at his offices in Gioia Tauro, June 2016.

4. Alex Perry, 'Cocaine Highway', *Newsweek Insights*, 17 November 2014: www.amazon.co.uk/Cocaine-Highway-lines-habit-terror-ebook/dp/B00PSI1M42/ref=sr_1_1?ie=UTF8&qid=1481295939&sr=8-1&keywords=cocaine+highway

5. Steve Sherer, 'A Very Special Flower Arrangement', Reuters, 11 April 2016: www.reuters.com/investigates/special-report/italy-mafia-flowers/

6. The best description of the 'Ndrangheta's structure and the evidence gathered for it can be found in the judicial documents supporting the case that eventually resulted from these inquiries, codenamed Operazione Crimine. Copies can be found at the following web addresses: www.casadellalegalita.info/doc/sentenza-GUP-CRIMINE.pdf (939 pages) and www.casadellalegalita.info/doc/Decreto-Fermo-CRIMINE.pdf (2,681 pages). These documents also document the election of Domenico Oppedisano and give further detail on the *carabinieri*'s surveillance methods.

7. For an account of the summit, see this interview with the centre's manager Paderno Dugnano: www.youtube.com/watch?v=xGsOuUHH0WA

8. Stephan Faris, 'Italy Braces for a New Mafia War', *TIME*, 14 October 2010: content.time.com/time/world/article/0,8599,2025423,00.html; AKI, 'Italy: Police uncover mafia drug ring in Milan convent', 12 May 2010 (a reprint of the story, containing details of the government crackdown, can be found on a chat thread of the Gangsters Inc. blog at: z14.invisionfree.com/GangstersInc/index.php?showtopic=1605&st=720); Nick Squires, 'Italy claims finally defeating the mafia', *Daily Telegraph*, 9 January 2010: www.telegraph.co.uk/news/worldnews/europe/italy/6957240/Italy-claims-finally-defeating-the-mafia.html

VII

1. Much has been written about Lea Garofalo's death. In this account, I have stuck to the official transcriptions of her testimony in 1996, July 2002 and April 2008; Denise Cosco's statements on 25 November 2009 and 5 March 2010, and her testimony in court on 20 September and 13 October 2011; and judicial documents from the murder trial that followed. I also conducted supplementary interviews with Vincenza Rando, Alessandra Cerreti, Marisa Garofalo and Salvatore Dolce in 2015 and 2016.

2. Kahn and Véron, *Women of Honour*, p. 107.

VIII

1. The source material for most of this chapter is the same as for Chapter 7.
2. I have supplemented quotes from my own interview with Enza Rando with some from this court report: Emanuela Zuccalà, 'L'ultimo sms di Lea Garofalo: torno a Milano per ricominciare', *Corriere della Sera*, 14 November 2012: www.27esimaora. corriere.it/articolo/ lultimo-sms-di-lea-garofalo-allavvocatotorno-a-milano-mi-rifaro-una-vita/

IX

1. *La Repubblica*, 'Reggio Calabria, bomba al tribunale alto potenziale, danni, nessun ferito', 3 January 2010: www.repubblica.it/2010/01/sezioni/ cronaca/reggio-bomba/reggio-bomba/reggio-bomba.html; Nick Pisa, 'The moped Mafia: CCTV catches bomb delivery by Italian mobster on scooter driven by his moll', *Daily Mail*, 8 January 2010: www.dailymail.co.uk/news/ article-1241682/The-moped-Mafia-CCTV-catches-bomb-delivery-Italian-mobster-scooter-driven-moll. html
2. 'Rosarno, polizia: 'Ndrangheta dietro a scontri. Via 1.100 immigrati', Reuters, 11 January 2010: it.reuters.com/article/topNews/ idITMIE60A0AB20100111?sp=true
3. Reports of the discovery of the car can be found on this Gangsters Inc. chat thread: www.z14.invisionfree. com/GangstersInc/index. php?showtopic=1605&st=720
4. The passages on the early life and friendship in Rosarno of Maria Concetta Cacciola and Giuseppina

Pesce are based on official court documents, dated 13 July 2013, released by the Italian prosecutor, Giuseppe Creazzo, who oversaw the case relating to Cacciola's death, as well as transcripts of Giuseppina's testimony to those proceedings, dated 7 February 2013. Supplementary material is available in official documents relating to the subsequent trial of lawyers representing the Cacciola family, dated 30 July 2014, and a custody hearing for Concetta's father, Michele Cacciola, dated 4 February 2012.

X

1. This chapter is based on official transcriptions of Denise Cosco's statements on 25 November 2009 and 5 March 2010, and of her testimony in court on 20 September and 13 October 2011; on judicial documents from the murder trial that followed; and on statements made to police and in court by Carmine Venturino in 2012 and 2013.

XI

1. 'Operazione "All Inside", colpo al clan Pesce di Rosarno', CN24TV: www.cn24tv.it/news/30318/ operazione-all-inside-colpo-al-clan-pesce-di-rosarno-30-arresti.html
2. Caterina Scaffidi Domianello, 'Donne contro la 'ndrangheta', Narcomafie, July/August 2013: www. liberanet.org/narcomafie/2013_07. pdf
3. Julian Gavaghan, 'Italian mob boss arrested after 17 years on the run is cheered by crowd as police lead him

to jail', *Daily Mail*, 27 April 2010:
http://www.dailymail.co.uk/news/
article-1269304/Italian-mobster-
arrested-17-years-run-cheered-
crowd-police-lead-jail.html

4. Tom Kington, 'Italian police arrest
300 in raids on Calabrian mafia',
Guardian, 13 July 2010: www.
theguardian.com/world/2010/jul/13/
calabria-mafia-arrests-italy; Stephan
Faris, 'Italy vs. the mafia: Beheading
the 'Ndrangheta', *TIME*, 13 July
2010: content.time.com/time/world/
article/0,8599,2003598,00.html

5. Interview with the author, July 2015,
Milan.

6. Interview with the author, July 2015,
Modena.

7. Interview with the author, July 2015,
Milan.

8. Ibid.

XII

1. Stephan Faris, 'Italy Braces for a
New Mafia War', *TIME*, 14 October
2010: content.time.com/time/world/
article/0,8599,2025423,00.html

2. Author interview with Alessandra
Cerreti, May 2016, Milan.

3. Clare Longrigg, 'Women Breaking
the Mafia's Rules', Mafiology, 14
October 2013: mafiologytest.
wordpress.com/tag/
alessandra-cerreti/

4. Ibid.

5. Cerreti spoke about her
conversation with Giuseppina in
several fora, such as in Rome in
March 2014: *Experts commend
mafia-linked woman's help in crime
fight*, Xinhua, 15 March 2014: china.
org.cn/world/Off_the_Wire/2014-
03/15/content_31793448.htm. She
also gave several accounts during

more than seven hours of author
interviews with Cerreti in July 2015,
and February and May 2016. This
quotation is a compilation of
Cerreti's public remarks and her
quotations in interview.

6. Clare Longrigg, 'Women Breaking
the Mafia's Rules', Mafiology, 14
October 2013: mafiologytest.
wordpress.com/tag/
alessandra-cerreti/

7. Interview with the author, July 2015,
Milan.

8. Ibid.

9. Ibid.

10. Interview with the author, February
2015, Rome.

11. Interview with the author, July 2015,
Milan.

12. Interview with the author, July 2015,
Rome.

13. Giuseppina Pesce's statement to
prosecutors, sourced from official
transcripts of her testimony included
in several subsequent trial
documents.

XIII

1. This chapter is based on numerous
trial documents relating to the Lea
Garofalo case. In the earlier stages of
the investigation, the *carabinieri*
made some false allegations and
were mistaken over some factual
details which were corrected as their
inquiries proceeded at later stages of
the investigation and the trial.

2. Interview with Enza Rando,
Modena, July 2015. See also Michele
Brambilla, 'The Tragedy and
Courage of a Mobster's Daughter', *La
Stampa in English*, 17 April 2014:
www.lastampa.it/2014/04/17/esteri/
lastampa-in-english/the-tragedy-and-

courage-of-a-mobsters-daughter-lrpU6aQB445if2MPCiJM9I/pagina.html

XIV

1. This section is based on trial documents relating to Operation All Inside, the prosecution of the Pesce clan, and statements made by Giuseppina Pesce both to Alessandra Cerreti and during the subsequent trial.
2. Clare Longrigg, 'Women Breaking the Mafia's Rules', Mafiology, 14 October 2013: mafiologytest.wordpress.com/tag/alessandra-cerreti/
3. *Calabria Ora*'s website has since closed. I am grateful to the veteran journalist Franco Abruzzo, whose website is an invaluable archive on a diverse range of matters, including the *Calabria Ora* controversy: www.francoabruzzo.it/public/docs/palmi-articolicommenti-9fb13.rtf

XV

1. This chapter is based on official records of statements made by Maria Concetta Cacciola to Alessandra Cerreti and Giovanni Musarò on 25 May and 28 June 2011; trial documents relating to the prosecution of Michele Cacciola, Giuseppe Cacciola, Anna Lazzaro, Gregorio Cacciola and Vittorio Pisani; and supplementary interviews with Giuseppe Creazzo, Giovanni Musarò and Alessandra Cerreti. I'm also grateful to Laura Aprati and Enrico Fierro for a transcript of their one-woman play about Concetta, *O cu nui o cu iddi*,

which is also closely based on the official evidence.
2. Caterina Scaffidi Domianello, 'Donne contro la 'ndrangheta', Narcomafie, July/August 2013: www.liberanet.org/narcomafie/2013_07.pdf
3. Interview with the author, May 2016, Milan.
4. Interview with the author, May 2016, Rome.
5. Clare Longrigg, 'Mafia witness "forced to drink acid"', Mafiology, 2 February 2014: mafiologytest.wordpress.com/tag/alessandra-cerreti/
6. Interview with the author, May 2016, Rome.

XVI

1. This section is based on the author's interview with Alessandra Cerreti in May 2016 in Milan.
2. Interview with the author, May 2016, Milan.
3. Caterina Scaffidi Domianello, 'Donne contro la 'ndrangheta', Narcomafie, July/August 2013: www.liberanet.org/narcomafie/2013_07.pdf
4. Various reports of the correspondence between Giuseppina Pesce and her family can be found online. The most complete is Caterina Scaffidi Domianello's account in 'Donne contro la 'ndrangheta', Narcomafie, July/August 2013: www.liberanet.org/narcomafie/2013_07.pdf. Others that proved useful include two reports on strill.it: www.strill.it/citta/2011/10/la-famiglia-scrive-a-giuseppina-pesce-le-lettere-ricevute-in-carcere/; and www.strill.it/

citta/2011/09/le-lettere-di-giuseppina-pesce-collaboro-per-dare-un-futuro-ai-miei-figli/. Excerpts were also included in the judicial documents accompanying the trials that followed Operations All Inside and All Clean. Finally, Alessandra Cerreti read some of the letters to the author in interview and at other times summarised their contents.

XVII

1. This chapter is based on evidence and transcripts presented in official judicial documents relating to the trial of Michele Cacciola, Anna Lazzaro and Giuseppe Cacciola, and the subsequent trial of the two lawyers, Vittorio Pisani and Gregorio Cacciola. This material is supplemented by the author's interviews with Alessandra Cerreti, Giovanni Musarò and Giuseppe Creazzo, as well as reference to the play *O cu nui o cu iddi* by Laura Aprati and Enrico Fierro.
2. Dario Crippa, 'Sciolse la mamma nell'acido, nessuna pietà per mio padre', *Il Giorno*, 4 July 2011: www.ilgiorno.it/milano/cronaca/2011/07/04/537205-sciolse_mamma.shtml
3. Santo Della Volpe, 'Le Donne e La Lotta di Liberazione dale Mafie', Libera, 2012: www.libera.it/flex/cm/pages/ServeBLOB.php/L/IT/IDPagina/6462
4. The eleven-minute recording of Concetta's 'retraction' is on the StopNdrangheta website: http://www.stopndrangheta.it/stopndr/art.aspx?id=1419,La+ritrattazione+estorta+alla+Cacciola

5. Clare Longrigg, 'Mafia witness "forced to drink acid"', Mafiology, 2 February 2014: mafiologytest.wordpress.com/tag/alessandra-cerreti/

XVIII

1. This chapter is based on evidence and transcripts presented in official judicial documents relating to the trial of Michele Cacciola, Anna Lazzaro and Giuseppe Cacciola, and the subsequent trial of the two lawyers, Vittorio Pisani and Gregorio Cacciola. This material is supplemented by the author's interviews with Alessandra Cerreti, Giovanni Musarò and Giuseppe Creazzo.
2. Interview with the author, May 2016, Milan.
3. Interview with the author, May 2016, Rome.
4. 'Orsola Fallara in condizioni disperate al Riuniti di Reggio dopo un tentativo di suicidio', 16 December 2010: www.cn24tv.it/news/16616/orsola-fallara-in-condizioni-disperate-al-riuniti-di-reggio-dopo-un-tentativo-di-suicidio.html
5. Carlo Macri, 'Il suicidio della testimone anti clan', *Il Corriere*, 23 August 2011: www.corriere.it/cronache/11_agosto_23/il-suicidio-della-testimone-anti-clan-carlo-macri_7e7fbc74-cd49-11e0-8914-d32bd7027ea8.shtml
6. The full letter can be found here: www.sdisonorate.it/wordpress/wp-content/uploads/2014/03/Le-testimoni-di-giustizia-calabresi.pdf
7. Ibid. *Calabria Ora*'s front page can be seen a few pages further on.

XIX

1. This chapter is based on official transcriptions of Denise Cosco's statements on 25 November 2009 and 5 March 2010, and of her testimony in court on 20 September and 13 October 2011, as well as judicial documents from the murder trial that followed.
2. Milka Kahn and Anne Véron, *Women of Honour*, Hurst, 2017, p. 118.
3. Marika Demaria, *La Scelta di Lea* (Milan: Melampo Publisher, 2013), p. 26. I am indebted to Ms Demaria, the only reporter to stay in court throughout the nine months of the trial, whose persistence allowed for a complete, public account to be given.

XX

1. This section is based on trial documents relating to Operation All Inside, the prosecution of the Pesce clan, and statements made by Giuseppina Pesce to Alessandra Cerreti and during the subsequent trial.
2. Much of the Pesce correspondence is also reprinted in full in Caterina Scaffidi Domianello's invaluable articles in 'Donne contro la 'ndrangheta', Narcomafie, July/August 2013: www.liberanet.org/narcomafie/2013_07.pdf. Excerpts from Giuseppina's letter of 23 August 2011 are also reprinted here: www.strill.it/citta/2011/09/le-lettere-di-giuseppina-pesce-collaboro-per-dare-un-futuro-ai-miei-figli/
3. Caterina Scaffidi Domianello, 'Donne contro la 'ndrangheta', Narcomafie, July/August 2013: www.liberanet.org/narcomafie/2013_07.pdf
4. Gaeta Piero, 'Condannati a 20 anni Vincenzo e Ciccio Pesce', *Gazetta del Sud*, 21 September 2011: http://www.calabrianotizie.it/condannati-anni-vincenzo-ciccio-pesce-sentenza-esemplare-del-gup-roberto-carrelli-palombi-che-ieri-sera-condannato-undici-imputati-ordinato-maxi-risarcimento/
5. Paul Toscano, 'Giuseppina Pesce si è pentita di nuovo', *Gazetta del Sud*, 22 September 2011: www.calabrianotizie.it/giuseppina-pesce-pentita-nuovo-dopo-avere-interrotto-collaborazione-con-magistrati-della-dda-reggina-figlia-del-boss-salvatore-ripreso-riferire-vicend-e-della-cosca-figli/
6. Ibid.
7. 'Giuseppina Pesce domani al processo di Palmi', CN24TV, 22 September 2011: www.cn24tv.it/news/32497/ndrangheta-giuseppina-pesce-domani-al-processo-di-palmi.html; 'Clan pesce, Palaia scrive alla moglie pentita: "stai rovinando te stessa ed i tuoi figli", CN24TV, 23 November 2011: www.cn24tv.it/news/32639/clan-pesce-palaia-scrive-alla-moglie-pentita-stai-rovinando-te-stessa-ed-i-tuoi-figli.html
8. 'Operazione "All clean 2": I dettagli', CN24TV, 13 October 2011: www.cn24tv.it/news/33781/operazione-all-clean-2-i-dettagli.html
9. 'Processo al clan Pesce, la testimone di giustizia sarà sentita da un luogo segreto', CN24TV, 21 October 2011: www.cn24tv.it/news/34338/

processo-al-clan-pesce-la-testimone-di-giustizia-sara-sentita-da-un-luogo-segreto.html

10. Nick Pisa, 'Judge hands 1,000-year prison sentence to 110 Mafia mobsters in massive show trial', *Daily Mail*, 22 November 2011: www.dailymail.co.uk/news/article-2063932/Judge-hands-1-000-year-prison-sentence-110-Mafia-mobsters-massive-trial.html

11. Author interview with Alessandra Cerreti. Also see the account in Francesca Chirico, 'Rosarno, donne e 'ndrangheta: il processo del contrappasso', Stop'Ndrangheta, 25 November 2011: www.stopndrangheta.it/stopndr/art.aspx?id=1215,Rosarno%2c+donne+e+%27ndrangheta%3a+il+processo+del+contrappasso

XXI

1. This section is based on two interviews with Roberto di Bella at his offices in Reggio Calabria in July 2015 and May 2016, as well as a visit to the hostel housing 'Ndrangheta children in Messina and interviews with the staff there.

2. Riccardo Francesco Cordì, 'Voglio una Vita Normale', *Corriere della Sera*, 8 May 2014: www.corriere.it/cronache/14_maggio_08/voglio-vita-normale-6f0f1dc2-d672-11e3-b1c6-d3130b63f531.shtml

XXII

1. Translation from the United Nations Office of Drugs and Crime, *Review of implementation of the United Nations Convention against Corruption*, Italy, p. 4: www.unodc.org/documents/treaties/UNCAC/WorkingGroups/ImplementationReviewGroup/26-27November2013/V1387842e.pdf

2. *Il Quotidiano della Calabria*'s front page for 10 February 2012 can be seen here: www.stopndrangheta.it/file/stopndrangheta_1381.pdf. The page includes the start of Matteo Cosenza's editorial, as well as stories on Maria Concetta Cacciola, Giuseppina Pesce and Lea Garofalo, perhaps the first time that the three women and their stories had been reported collectively. The full editorial is here: 19luglio1992.com/index.php?option=com_content&view=article&catid=2%3Aeditoriali&id=5213%3Ail-simbolo-dell8-marzo-tre-donne-coraggiose&Itemid=33

3. For example, see Giuseppe Baldessaro, 'Lea, Concetta, Giuseppina è l'8 marzo della Calabria', *La Repubblica*, 2 March 2012: www.repubblica.it/cronaca/2012/03/02/news/donne_ndrangheta_8_marzo-30721686/

4. Ilaria Calabro, 'Dagli studenti una lettera alla Pesce, "nel tuo riscatto è possibile il riscatto di tutti"', strettoweb.com, 8 March 2012: www.strettoweb.com/2012/03/reggio-8-marzo-dagli-studenti-una-lettera-alla-pesce-nel-tuo-riscatto-e-possibile-il-riscatto-di-tutti/25999/#07DWLhJEL6JRX3w0.99

5. Matteo Cosenza, 'Vicini a Denise che ha scelto la verità e la giustizia', *Il Quotidiano*, 8 March 2012: www.stopndrangheta.it/file/stopndrangheta_1485.pdf

XXIII

1. This section is based on official transcripts of the court proceedings held in Palmi, 21–26 May 2012.

XXIV

1. Marika Demaria, 'Processo Lea Garofalo, riprendono le udienze', Narcomafie.it, 2 December 2012: www.acmos.net/processo-lea-garofalo-riprendono-le-udienze

2. 'Sei ergastoli per l'omicidio di Lea Garofalo', *Il Fatto Quotidiano*, 30 March 2012: www.ilfattoquotidiano.it/2012/03/30/milano-ergastoli-lomicidio-garofalo-testimone-sciolta-nellacido/201316/. See also Tom Kington, 'Italian mobster condemned by daughter's evidence', *The Observer*, 1 April 2012: www.theguardian.com/world/2012/apr/01/italian-mobster-jailed-by-daughters-evidence

3. Simona Ravizza, Cesare Giuzzi e Redazione Milano online, 'Viale Montello 6, sgomberato dopo 40 anni il "fortino delle cosche"', 21 June 2012, *Corriere della Sera*: www.milano.corriere.it/milano/notizie/cronaca/12_giugno_21/viale-montello-fortino-cosche-sgombero-polizia-cosco-lea-garofalo-201694845491.shtml. *Corriere della Sera* also has pictures of No. 6 Viale Montello as it was when Carlo ruled it and how it might be renovated here: Elisabetta Andreis, 'Una "corte" moderna nell'ex fortino della mafia', 29 August 2016: www.milano.corriere.it/notizie/cronaca/16_agosto_29/viale-montello-fortino-mafia-stabile-abbandonato-progetto-demolizione-41cb3f10-6d58-11e6-baa8-f780dada92e5.shtml

4. Michele Brambilla, 'The Tragedy and Courage of a Mobster's Daughter', *La Stampa in English*, 17 April 2014: www.lastampa.it/2014/04/17/esteri/lastampa-in-english/the-tragedy-and-courage-of-a-mobsters-daughter-lrpU6aQB445if2MPCiJM9I/pagina.html

5. This account of Carmine Venturino's confession is based on official court documents. There are also numerous press reports of Carmine Venturino's letter. See for instance Sandro De Riccardis, 'Il verbale dell'orrore sulla pentita Garofalo: "Bruciai il suo corpo finché rimase cenere"', *La Repubblica*, 20 March 2013: www.milano.repubblica.it/cronaca/2013/03/20/news/il_verbale_dell_orrore_sulla_pentita_garofalo_bruciai_il_suo_corpo_finch_rimase_cenere-54945861/?ref=search; Alessandra Coppola and Cesare Giuzzi, 'Uccisi Lea Garofalo, il coraggio di Denise mi ha spinto a collaborare', *Corriere della Sera*, 4 December 2012: www.senzatarga.wordpress.com/2012/12/04/lea/; Demaria, *La Scelta di Lea*.

6. This section relies chiefly on official records provided by prosecutor Marcello Tatangelo of his interrogation of Carmine Venturino on 3 and 11 October 2012, as well as later transcripts of Carmine's questioning by Tatangelo in court. Once again, I am also indebted to Marika Demaria of Narcomafie, who doggedly followed the case and published intermittent reports as well as her book, *La Scelta di Lea*.

Also useful were various other press reports, as indicated.

XXV

1. 'All Inside, il dispositivo della sentenza (I grado)', Narcomafie, 3 May 2013: www.stopndrangheta.it/stopndr/art.aspx?id=1709,All+Inside%2c+il+dispositivo+della+sentenza+(I+grado)
2. When the final sentences were delivered four years later, some were slightly altered but the impact remained the same: ''Ndrangheta, diventano definitive le condanne inflitte al clan Pesce di Rosarno', *Zoom 24*, 29 March 2017: http://www.zoom24.it/2017/03/29/ndrangheta-pesce-condanne-rosarno-45842/
3. Giuseppe Baldessarro, ''Ndrangheta: nessuno demolisce la casa del boss, accetta solo l'imprenditore sotto scorta', *La Repubblica*, September 2014: www.repubblica.it/cronaca/2014/09/16/news/calabria_ndrangheta_boss-95872877/
4. Barbara Conforti, *Mafia, la trahison des femmes*, Canal+, 2 March 2014.
5. 'Omicidio Lea Garofalo, in appello confermati 4 ergastoli', *Il Fatto Quotidiano*, 29 May 2013: www.ilfattoquotidiano.it/2013/05/29/omicidio-lea-garofalo-in-appello-confermati-4-ergastoli-assolto/610120/
6. Vincenzo Ruggiero, '17 arresti a Crotone e in altre 4 regioni. Decisive le dichiarazioni di Lea Garofalo', CN24TV, 29 October 2013: www.cn24tv.it/news/77515/omicidi-di-ndrangheta-17-arresti-a-crotone-e-in-altre-4-regioni-decisive-le-dichiarazioni-di-lea-garofalo.html

XXVI

1. Kahn and Véron, *Women of Honour*, p. 127.
2. There are several videos of Lea's funeral online which include Denise's short speech. See www.youtube.com/watch?v=4oR9kFYFVcs or www.youtube.com/watch?v=I9jxIMRQlT8

Illustration Credits

Lea Garofalo. The picture is undated but seems to capture Lea in her early twenties, just after she became a mother. The image became iconic. *(http://www.wikimafia.it)*

Lea, on the left, and Denise captured by CCTV in Milan in their last minutes together on the evening of 24 November 2009. *(Milan Carabinieri)*

Alessandra Cerreti, pictured in her office in Reggio Calabria. *(FILIPPO MONTEFORTE/AFP/Getty Images)*

Reggio Calabria, as seen from the hills to the south-east of the city, looking north-west across the Straits to Messina. *(Anna Quaglia/ Alamy Stock Photo)*

San Luca. For decades, the 'Ndrangheta have convened an annual meeting on 2 September in this Aspromonte hill village, using a religious festival as cover. *(ROPI/Alamy Stock Photo)*

Carlo Cosco in a police mugshot taken after his arrest in February 2010. *(Lanese /Epa/REX/Shutterstock)*

Giuseppina Pesce the day after her arrest in April 2010. *(ANSA)*

Domenico Oppedisano being driven through the streets after his arrest in Rosarno in July 2010. *(Franco Cufari/Epa/REX/ Shutterstock)*

Giuseppina Pesce in her mugshot after her arrest. *(ANSA)*

Maria Concetta Cacciola. Confined to the family home for weeks at a time, only one other picture of her has ever surfaced. *(ANSA)*

The gate of the warehouse in San Fruttuoso, Monza, where Lea's remains were discovered in October 2012, three years after her death. *(Fabrizio Radaelli/Epa/REX/Shutterstock)*

Breaking a lifetime of *omertà*, Carlo speaks in court on 9 April 2013. *(Corriere TV)*

Giuseppina's mother Angela Ferraro and sister Marina Pesce. *(ANSA)*

Concetta's mother Anna Rosalba Lazzaro and father Michele Cacciola. *(ANSA)*

Lea's funeral on 19 October 2013. Thousands from all over Italy turned out for a woman who, four years after her death, united the nation against the mafia under the slogan 'I see, I feel, I speak'. *(Marco Aprile/NurPhoto/Corbis via Getty Images)*

Index

Addiopizzo movement 33
Alcuri, Francesco 116
Alfano, Angelino 135
Anti-Mafia and Anti Terrorism
  Directorate, Milan 29
Anti-Mafia Directorate, Calabria 178
Aprilia 147, 165, 167
Ascoli Piceno 88

Barbaros clan 72–3
Bella, Roberto di 205, 233; arranges for
  Giuseppina's and Concetta's children to
  be removed from their grandparents
  215–16; character and description 213;
  experience of child offenders 212–15;
  proposes deprogramming of
  'Ndrangheta children 218–19; success
  of his ideas 219, 220–1, 272–3;
  understands mafia family dynamics
  216–18; wishes to change the system
  215
Bellocco clan 57–8, 107, 109, 139, 158,
  162, 211, 265–6, 273–4
Bellocco, Francesca 272
Bellocco, Gregorio 158
Bellocco, Umberto 158
Benedict XVI, Pope 107
Bergamo 4, 82, 83, 90, 93, 128, 276
Berlusconi, Silvio 244

Blanca, Paolo 29, 30, 35–6, 54, 243, 267
Boiano 94, 95, 96, 276
Bolzano 162, 180, 186–7
Bonarrigo, Giuseppa 153, 209, 239, 259,
  260
Borsellino, Paolo 30, 31, 32, 33, 71, 82,
  136, 228
Buccafusca, Tita 197

cacciatori 43
Cacciola, Antonio 274
Cacciola clan 109–10, 117, 198–9, 204–5,
  222–30
Cacciola, Domenico 272
Cacciola, Giuseppe 111, 155, 157, 264–5,
  266
Cacciola, Gregorio 184, 187, 265
Cacciola, Maria Concetta: accused of
  having an affair 155; asks to be
  re-admitted into witness protection
  188–90; character and description 110;
  children removed from their
  grandparents 215–16; death of 116,
  190–1, 195–9, 222–4; effect of her
  escape on her family 162–4; effect of
  media support for her bravery 224–7,
  229, 230–1; enters witness protection
  158, 159–62, 171; explores the world
  through the internet 117–18; flees to

Cacciola, Maria Concetta (*cont ...*)
  Genoa 116; friendship with Giuseppina
  109–12; Giuseppina's evidence in trial
  concerning 264–5; interviewed by the
  carabinieri 156–9, 161–2; leaves letters
  for her family 159–60; male treatment
  of 111–12, 117, 155, 156, 157; marriage
  and children 111–12; online
  relationships 118, 155, 156–7; partial
  closure in her case 264–6; secretly
  records statement at Cacciola family
  lawyer's office 185–8, 204; succombs to
  pressure from her family 180–5; tries to
  help Stefania 273–4
Cacciola, Michele 155, 163–4, 180, 181,
  183, 190, 196, 224, 265, 266
Cacucci, Maira 202
Calabria Ora 149–52, 173, 199, 200, 208
Camorra 46, 50, 68, 71, 135, 273
Campobasso 94, 96, 97, 120, 121, 122,
  244, 249, 262
carabinieri: accused of disgraceful
  conduct by Cacciola family 198–9;
  acquire further evidence against Carlo
  121–2; arrest Carlo for attack on Lea
  120; arrest Concetta's parents 224;
  cacciatori squad 43; help to recapture/
  rescue Giuseppina 166–8; interview
  Concetta 156–9; interview Denise 37–8,
  125; investigate death of Concetta
  196–8; keep an eye on Venturino
  119–20; keep mafia under surveillance
  43–5, 57–8, 70, 71–3, 78, 79, 119, 166,
  228; large-scale arrests of 'Ndrangheta
  128–32; listen-in to Cacciola family
  conversations 180–5; move in on the
  Pesce empire 128–9; reunite Giuseppina
  and her children 144; unable to rescue
  Concetta from her family 188–90
Carcagnosso 49, 51
Carli, Carlo 156–7
Caselli, Gian Carlo 33
Catanzaro city 84, 123
Catanzaro jail 82–3
Ceraudo, Francesco 37

Ceraudo, Thomas 78, 79
Cerreti, Alessandra: accused of taking
  advantage of Concetta's mental state
  198; arrival in Reggio Calabria 16,
  35–6; at trials of 'Ndrangheta 208–11,
  227, 230; attitude towards deception
  and facts 27–8, 29–30; becomes
  involved in Concetta's case 157–9, 161,
  162–3, 164, 189, 190, 222–4; believes
  she can change Giuseppina's mind
  152–4, 165; birth, childhood and
  education 24, 27, 28–9; character and
  description 21, 30–1; cold-blooded
  detachment of 132, 133–4; comment on
  'Ndrangheta's bigotry 23; continues to
  arrest members of the Pesce clan 146,
  148; gives Elisea a teddy bear 235–6;
  investigations against west coast
  'Ndrangheta 131; joins the Anti-Mafia
  and Anti-Terrorism Directorate 29–31,
  35–6; as lead anti-mafia prosecutor
  59–60; leads Giuseppina through her
  testimony 238–43; as liability to
  judiciary 152; listens to Giuseppina's
  evidence 136–41; marriage 29; media
  attacks on 149–52; meets Giuseppina
  and confirms her continued
  collaboration 172–3; moves Giuseppina
  to Paliano prison 233–4; organises
  re-capture/rescue of Giuseppina 165–8;
  prepares Giuseppina to give evidence at
  trial 236–7; reaction to death of
  Concetta 195–6; reads Giuseppina's
  correspondence 168–71; realises
  importance of sentiment, empathy,
  emotion 225–7; realises importance of
  women to 'Ndrangheta 108–9; receives
  a gift from Giuseppina 237–8; receives
  letter from Giuseppina 205–8;
  reflections on Calabria 18, 19; reflects
  on destruction of the Pesces and
  'Ndrangheta 261; relationship with
  Giuseppina 237–8, 242–3, 269, 274;
  researches the 'Ndrangheta 45–58;
  resumes collaboration with Giuseppina

234–6; tells story of Giuseppina Multari 274–5; theory concerning the undoing of the 'Ndrangheta 57–8, 86, 108–9, 148; understanding of patriarchy and female emancipation 21–2

Cersosimo, Nadia 234, 243

Ciconte, Enzo 52

Ciollaro, Maria Laura 210

Ciotti, Don Luigi 93, 246, 277

Colle degli Ulivi 160–2

Comberiati, Antonio 78–80, 85, 122

Comberiati, Gina 78, 79

Condello, Pasquale 44–5

Conforti, Anna 264

Constantino, Domenico 118, 129, 170, 207, 239–40

Coppola, Francis Ford 28

Cordi, Riccardo 219, 220–1

Corleone family 28

Corleone (place) 33

Cortese, Renato 35, 267

Cortese, Salvatore 82–3, 201

Cosa Nostra 27, 31–4, 35, 46, 48, 65, 68, 82, 135, 136

Cosco, Andrea 8, 10, 13, 37, 38, 39

Cosco, Carlo: accession and elevation of Cosco family 78–80; arrested for attacking Lea 120; Carmine's evidence against 247–58; celebrates his daughter's birthday without her 41; character and description 5, 7, 76; confesses his part in Lea's murder 261–4; destruction of his empire 247; evidence against 121–2; insinuates himself back into Lea and Denise's life 4–5, 6–8, 96–7, 99–101; involved in murder of Comberiati 80; Lea's statements against 38, 41, 74, 81, 84–6; marries Lea 76–7; orders the death of his daughter 126–7; presumed involvement in Lea's disappearance and death 8–14; professes his love for Lea and Denise 262–3; standing within 'Ndrangheta 246–7; state indictment against 132–3, 142–3; takes Denise to

Pagliarelle 38–40, 119; trial and sentence 179, 200–3, 244–7, 261–4; under constant police surveillance 44; vendetta against Lea 81–4, 89–90, 97–9; violence and imprisonment 4, 23

Cosco, Denise: binge eats to relieve stress 119; birth of 77; Carlo orders her death 126–7; defiantly chooses freedom and her own life 178–9; escapes to Libera safe house near Turin 125–6; family background 3–4; gives eulogy at her mother's funeral 277–8; gives evidence at trial of her father 202, 244, 246; has affair with Venturino 123–4; interviewed by the carabinieri 37–8, 125; learns to fit in with her family and not mourn 40–2; listens to Carmine's confession concerning the death of her mother 257; looked after by Venturino 119–20; open letter written to 231–2, 245; publicly declares loyalty to the family 125; re-enters witness protection 178; realises that her mother has been killed 11–14; spends time with her father 5, 6, 7–8, 96, 98–101, 250, 262; stays with her aunt, uncle and cousins 8–11; taken to Pagliarelle by her father 38–40; visits her father in prison 81, 82, 123, 142; in witness protection with her mother 82–4, 88–95

Cosco, Domenico 8, 10, 37, 96

Cosco, Giuseppe 8, 10, 11, 14, 37, 78, 80, 81, 179, 200, 201, 245, 250, 264

Cosco, Piera 96, 97

Cosco, Renata 8, 9, 10, 13, 37

Cosco, Vito 9, 10–11, 37, 78, 84, 89, 123, 125, 179, 200, 201, 202, 245, 249, 250, 264

Cosenza, Matteo 224–7, 231–2, 245

Cosenza (place) 186

Costantino, Domenico 129, 165, 261

Create, Antonella 210

Creazzo, Giuseppe 117, 118, 161, 180, 265

Crotone 46, 125, 143, 248, 264

Cucino a Modo Mio, New York 16
Curcio, Rosario 38–9, 90, 121, 179, 200,
    245, 249, 250, 252, 253–6, 264

Dickie, John 48, 52, 56, 288; *Mafia
    Brotherhood* 48
Dolce, Salvatore 84–6, 91–2, 109, 265
drugs (cocaine, heroin) 7, 9, 16, 34–5,
    65–7
Duisberg massacre (2007) 55, 70

Elisa 39
Epifanio, Concettina 210
Esposito, Salvatore 188–9

Fabriano 93
Falcone, Giovanni 30, 31, 32, 33, 71, 82,
    136, 228
Fallara, Orsola 197
Fata Morgana 25, 26
Ferraro, Angela 148, 169, 173–5, 209, 211,
    241, 259
Ferraro, Angelo 116
Ferraro clan 209
Ferraro, Rosa 209, 239
Ferraro, Sara 174, 175
Figliuzzi, Alfonso 111, 155, 156, 160, 215,
    224
Figliuzzi, Rosalba 'Rosi' 112, 155, 184–5,
    190
Figliuzzi, Salvatore 111–12, 117, 156, 159,
    169, 196, 215
Figliuzzi, Tania 112, 155, 180, 184
Floreale, Massimiliano 252, 254
Florence 90, 167
Fondacaro, Marcello 268
Francesco (mafia boy) 219
Francis, Pope 273

Gallico clan 267–8
Gallico, Domenico 268
Galluci, Teresa 116
Garduña 50
Garibaldi, Giuseppe 18, 20, 25
Garofalo, Antonio 15, 74–5

Garofalo, Floriano 15, 75, 76–7, 78, 79, 80,
    81, 83–4, 85, 89, 122
Garofalo, Francesco 202
Garofalo, Genevieve 90
Garofalo, Gennaro 90
Garofalo, Giulio 15, 75
Garofalo, Lea: arrests in connection with
    her death 142–3; assassination attempt
    97–9, 121; attempted reconciliation
    with Carlo 4–5, 6–8, 96–7, 99–101;
    Carlo's confession concerning her
    murder 261–4; Carlo's *vendetta* against
    81–4, 89–90, 97–9; Carmine's evidence
    concerning her murder 247–58;
    character and description 5, 8, 15, 75,
    85, 92, 93, 94; court case in Florence
    101; disappearance and death 8–14, 21,
    38–9, 74, 134, 196, 201, 245; effect of
    media support for her bravery 224–7,
    229, 230–1; family background 3–4,
    74–6; funeral of 264, 276–8; her story as
    inspirational 275–6; marriage and
    childbirth 76–7; name never spoken 15;
    press coverage 22; reaction to murder
    of Comberiati 78–80; state
    abandonment of 133; supposedly in
    Australia 200, 202–3, 245; testifies
    against Carlo and the 'Ndrangheta 38,
    41, 74, 80, 83, 84–6, 87; testimony
    concerning attack on 121–2; vigils held
    for 179; in witness protection with
    Denise 4, 82–4, 88–95, 96
Garofalo, Mario 75, 89
Garofalo, Marisa 13, 15, 38, 41–2, 75–6,
    82, 96, 119, 125–6, 249
Garofalo-Mirabelli *faida* 89
Gazetta del Sud 149, 199
Gennari, Giuseppe 142–3
Genoa 162, 180, 187, 209
Gentile, Emanuela 162, 183
Getty III, John Paul 60–1, 228
Getty Snr, John Paul 61
Gioia Tauro 34–5, 47, 59, 60–5, 70, 72–3,
    107, 114, 128, 157
The Godfather (book and film) 28, 50, 228

Goodfellas (film) 50
Grasso, Piero 33
Grata, Mother 82
Grisolia, Filippo 203
Guardian di Finanza 44
Guarnotta, Leonardo 32

Homer, *Odyssey* 26

Ietto, Angelo 147, 209
Il Quotidiano della Calabria 224–7, 230, 231–2, 245
Impastato, Giuseppe 82
Improta, Pasquale 156–7, 161, 181, 183–4, 188
Interdonato, Enrico 219, 221
International Women's Day 227
Introini, Anna 244, 245
Italy 17–20, 46

Kercher, Meredith 22
Knox, Amanda 22

la mattanza 28–9, 34, 62, 65
Lazio 166, 243
Lazzaro, Anna Rosalba 156, 159–60, 163, 180, 181–3, 184–5, 189, 196–7, 199, 224, 265, 266
Legato, Dominica 115–16
Lello, Giuseppe di 32
Libera group 33–4, 93, 125, 246
Locri 219, 220
Lombardo, Giuseppe 67–70
Lucca 165–6, 167, 207
Lucia, Dr Fortunato 191
lupara bianca 15, 123

Macri, Palmiro 158
Madia, Giuseppe 147, 150, 151, 172, 173, 208
Maffei, Valeria 172
mafia: all-out war of assassination 28–9; anti-mafia protests 33–4; children and family dynamics 212–21; large-scale arrests of 128–32; law against 32; and

lupara bianca 15; murder of prosecutors 31–2; southern battle against 31; spread of 46–50; state campaign against 70–3, 106; success of anti-mafia prosecutors 32–3; treatment of women 240; under surveillance by all police forces 43–5, 78, 106, 166, 228; *see also* Camorra; Cosa Nostra; 'Ndrangheta
Manconi, Luigi 107
Mancuso, Pantaleone 197
Maroni, Roberto 132
Masi, Antonino de 64
Massimo (friend of Carlo's) 6–7
Mastrosso 49, 50, 51
Maxi trial 32
Messina: anti-mafia protests 33–4; description 24, 26; historical background 25; and the mafia 27–9; myth and legend 26–7; plague, earthquakes and war 25
Messina, Salvatore 158
Mezzogiorno 18, 20
Mignini, Giuliano 22
Milan 3, 5, 16, 29, 44, 71, 97, 125, 128, 179, 200–3, 205, 264, 271; Bar Barbara, Piazza Baiamonti 9, 37; Cimitero Monumentale 276–7; Cuarto Oggiaro 78, 79, 85; Green Dragon restaurant 38, 254, 256; Hotel Losanna 6; No. 6 Viale Montello 9, 10–11, 38, 39, 76, 77–82, 85, 89, 122, 201, 248, 254; Piazza Baiamonti 77, 78; San Vittore prison 4, 81, 136, 138, 244; Sempione Park 252, 253, 277; Via San Vittore 252–4
Milan University 29
Mirabelli clan 75
Modena 93
Monza 90, 253, 255, 276
Mount Etna 24, 35
Multari, Giuseppina 117, 274–5
Musarò, Giovanni 189; accused by Concetta's family of taking advantage of her 198; attempts on his life 267–9; believes Pesce clan destroyed 269–70; convinced Concetta's family behind her

Musarò, Giovanni (*cont ...*)
killing 222; dismisses Lazzaro's interview out of hand 196–7; involved in thirty separate investigations 131; as junior to Alessandra 59; listens to Concetta's evidence 157–9, 161–2; reaction to death of Concetta 195–6; tells the story of Stefania 273–4

Naples 16, 20, 40, 46, 48, 50, 156, 157, 273
Napolitano, Giorgio 94–5, 106, 107–8
'Ndrangheta 6, 9, 15; accidents, death and suicide 115–17, 196, 197, 272; acts of rebellion by the women 272–3; blood, family and tradition 20, 55–8, 108–9, 287; bomb attacks 105–7; centre of gravity moved to the north 269–70; changes in command structure 270; children and family dynamics 212–21; clan rivalry 109–10; compared to Islamist militants 21; Concetta's information concerning 156–9, 161–2; continued threat to anti-mafia prosecutors 267–9; destruction of base in Viale Montello 247; destruction of its homeland 62–5; destruction of organisation in Calabria 267, 271–3; force Giuseppina to withdraw her cooperation 145–8; Giuseppina's evidence against 136–41, 178; global drug empire 16–17, 34–5, 56, 62, 65–7, 77, 78; global power 69–70, 230, 270–1; ignorance concerning 17–18, 23; increased sophistication of members 131–2; kidnapping and ransom money 60–1; language used by 53–4; large-scale arrests and trials 128–32, 179, 200–3, 208–11, 226, 227–8, 230, 244–7, 259, 261–4; Lea testifies against 38, 41, 74, 80, 84–6; loss of image and invincibility 228–9; modern rise of 60–5; money-laundering and international finance 67–9; as near perfect criminal organisation 22; origins, myths and development 16,
45–53, 228; press campaign against 224–7; press support for 149–52, 173, 199, 200, 208; prosecutor attitude towards 132–4; racism of 107; reaction to women's treachery 161–4, 196, 197, 204–5; reassertion of 200, 204–5; relationship with the church 54–5; resumes pressure on Giuseppina and her family 169–77; revenues 17, 22, 286–7; rituals 51–3; secret summit with other mafia leaders 135; signs of weakness in 205; state crackdown on 35, 70–3, 106–8; structure and organisation 70–3, 109, 230, 289; threats against anti-mafia prosecutors 130–1; treatment of women 20–1, 56, 110–11, 112, 117, 169, 239–40; under constant surveillance by police 43–5, 57–8, 70–3, 78, 106, 115, 153, 162–3, 269–70; uses Viale Montello as mafia base 77–82; and *vendetta* 75, 81–4; violent bigotry of 23; women's influence and position 57–8, 108, 110; you leave, you die attitude 74

Obama, Michelle 272
Operation All Clean (2011) 149, 210
Operation All Inside (2010) 128–9, 131, 149, 208, 210
Operation All Inside II (2010) 146, 210
Operation Crimine 210
Operation Infinity (2010) 131
Operation Shame (2011) 224
Oppedisano, Domenico 72–3, 131, 132, 227, 230
Osso 49, 50, 51

Pagliarelle 13, 15, 40–2, 45, 46, 74, 82, 83–4, 90, 96, 119, 201, 249, 264, 276
Palaia, Angela (Giuseppina's aunt) 144–5, 146, 147, 169, 175, 176–7, 209
Palaia, Angela (Giuseppina's daughter) 111, 130, 138, 144–5, 146, 165–6, 171, 174, 175, 176, 177, 206, 209, 233, 235, 242

Palaia clan 209

Palaia, Elisea 130, 138, 144, 165, 171, 174, 175, 209, 233, 235–6

Palaia, Gaetano (Giuseppina's father-in-law) 175, 206, 209

Palaia, Gaetano (Giuseppina's son) 130, 138, 144, 165, 175, 206, 209, 233, 235

Palaia, Gianluca 146, 147, 171, 209

Palaia, Giovanni 209

Palaia, Rocco 111, 112, 114, 129, 130, 169, 170–1, 175–6, 206, 208, 209, 210, 239, 259

Palermo 31, 33, 82, 136

Paliano prison, Rome 233–4, 235, 243, 265, 273

Palmi 47, 60, 117, 136, 209, 236, 261, 264, 265, 267

Pangallo, Nidola 150–1

Peci, Giovanni 90

Pelles clan 72–3

Persurich, Marshal Christian 37–8

Perugia 22, 90

Pesce, Annunziata 116

Pesce, Antonino 116–17, 128, 209, 259

Pesce clan: Bellocos as main rival 107, 109–10, 139, 158; bugged by *carabinieri* 115; destruction of 259–61, 269–70; firepower of 114; Giuseppina's evidence against 136–41, 147, 209–11, 238–40, 259; investigations, arrests and trial 128–9, 146, 226, 259; as number one target 73; put pressure on Giuseppina 146–8; respect, shame and death 114, 115–17, 139–40; rise of 109; weapons managed by Rocco Palaia 111

Pesce, Francesco 'Ciccio' 114, 129, 139, 153, 208, 239, 240–1, 259

Pesce, Giuseppe 260

Pesce, Giuseppina: agrees to collaborate again 172–3; arrested by *carabinieri* 129–30; believed to be in mortal danger 152–4; believed to be weak and disturbed 150–2; calmly gives evidence in court 238–42; character and description 110; children removed from their grandparents 215–16; clandestine affair with Costantino 118, 129, 170; continues to be pressured by her family and the 'Ndrangheta 169–71, 173–7; correspondence monitored by Alessandra 169–71; deaths of family members 116–17; effect of media support for her bravery 224–7, 229, 230–1; fears for her children 130; friendship with Concetta 109–12; gives evidence against the 'Ndrangheta 136–41, 147; gives evidence at trial of her family 209–11, 238–40, 259; gives present to Alessandra 237–8; learns the family business 113–15; little sympathy for 132, 134; male treatment of 112–13; marriage and children 111, 112; prepares for trial against her family 236–7; pressured into ending her collaboration with the authorities 145–8; recaptured/rescued by the *carabinieri* 165–8; receives loving letter from her daughter 177; relationship with Alessandra 237–8, 242–3, 274; resumes collaboration with Alessandra 234–6; reunited with her children 138, 144; sends letter of explanation to Alessandra 205–8; suicide attempts 130, 132; taken to Paliano prison 233–4; uses teddy bear to encourage changes in her children 235–6; withdraws her allegations against the 'Ndrangheta 149–52, 196; in witness protection 144–8, 154

Pesce, Marina 148, 169, 173, 174, 175, 209, 211, 241, 259, 260

Pesce, Salvatore 112–13, 115, 130, 152, 239, 241–2, 259

Pesce, Vicenzo 129, 208

Petilia Policastro 15, 75, 79, 84, 99, 264, 276

picciotti 48–9, 54, 107, 114, 129

Pignatone, Giuseppe 33, 35, 59, 70, 108, 131, 132, 135, 149, 189, 205, 214, 230, 267

Pioli, Fabrizio 271–2
Piromalli clan 63–4
Pisani, Vittorio 187, 265, 266
Pisano, Annalisa 87–9, 92–4, 123, 258
Plati 72
Polistena 190–1
Prestipino, Michele 33, 35, 59, 70, 108, 115–16, 129, 139–40, 168, 172, 189, 214, 237, 243, 267, 268, 269
Provenzano, Bernardo 28, 33
Puzo, Mario 28
Pythagoras 46

Radio Olimpia 129
Rando, Vincenza 'Enza' 75, 76, 81, 82, 93, 101, 125, 178, 245, 246, 264, 276
Rebibbia prison, Rome 234–5, 236, 237, 238–40
Reggio Calabria 188–9, 212, 214, 230; as bandit country 36; bomb attacks 105–8; earthquakes and war 25; electronic espionage in 44–5; historical background 25; large-scale arrests in 131; Mattia Preti girls' high school letter 230–1; myths and legends 26; power and organisation of 'Ndrangheta in 70–3; state fightback in 108; surveillance in 70–3, 166; trials in 227, 266
Reggio Emilia 39, 181, 187
Riacce Bronzes 25
Riina, Salvatore 28, 136
Roberti, Franco 270–1
Rome 60, 93, 97
Rosarno 59, 60, 62, 70, 72–3, 107, 110–11, 116, 128, 128–9, 139, 144, 149, 155, 158, 163, 165, 175, 178, 209, 211, 260–1, 265, 266, 272
Rozzano massacre (2003) 89

Sabatino, Massimo 120, 121–2, 132, 136, 179, 201–2, 244, 245, 249, 250, 262, 263, 264
Sabatino, Rosi 121
Saffioti, Gaetano 261

San Ferdinando 158
San Frutuoso, Monza 253, 254–6, 257
San Luca 54, 55
Sansonetti, Piero 208
Scolo clan 273
Secolo, Rita Stefania 162
Secolo, Stefania 273–4
Second World War 25, 27, 216
Sicily 16, 24–9, 46–7, 48, 50, 233
Snow White syndrome 271
Sorrentino, Salvatore 121–2, 201–2
Steinberg, Daniel Sussman 261
Straits of Messina 24–5, 26, 30, 35, 106

Tatangelo, Marcello 201, 247, 248, 257, 264
Tegano, Giovanni 131
Toscano, Silvano 78, 79
Turin 125, 178

United Nations Convention on the Rights of the Child 216

Venturino, Carmine 263; arrested for death of Lea 143; awkward attitude towards Denise 38, 39; evidence concerning murder of Lea 247–58; falls in love with Denise 123–4, 143, 178–9, 257; family background 248; as friend of Carlo's 6–7; gives Lea some hash 6, 38; ordered to kill Denise 126–7; ordered to look after Denise 119–20; trial and sentence 179, 200, 201, 202, 245, 264
Vibo Marina 165
Viterbo prison, Rome 268

witness protection 88–96, 133, 158, 159–62, 171, 178, 188–90

Yousafzai, Malala 272

Zagari, Antonio, *Tired of Killing: Autobiography of a Repentant 'Ndranghetista* 51–2